GW01157294

2 Dads
food for family and friends

Blair Tonkin & Paul Bullpitt

First published in 2014 by New Holland Publishers Pty Ltd
London • Sydney • Auckland

The Chandlery Unit 114 50 Westminster Bridge Road London SE1 7QY United Kingdom
1/66 Gibbes Street Chatswood NSW 2067 Australia
218 Lake Road Northcote Auckland New Zealand

www.newhollandpublishers.com

Copyright © 2014 New Holland Publishers Pty Ltd
Copyright © 2014 in text: Blair Tonkin and Paul Bullpitt
Copyright © 2014 in images: Mandi Cook except coastal photos Darren French

All rights reserved. No part of this publication may be reproduced, stored in a retrieval system or transmitted, in any form or by any means, electronic, mechanical, photocopying, recording or otherwise, without the prior written permission of the publishers and copyright holders.

A record of this book is held at the British Library and the National Library of Australia.

ISBN 9781742576022

Managing director: Fiona Schultz
Project editor: Jodi De Vantier
Designer: Caryanne Cleevely
Food photography: Mindi Cook
Food stylist: Lyndel Miller
Coastal photography: Darren French
Production director: Olga Dementiev
Printer: Toppan Leefung Printing Ltd

10 9 8 7 6 5 4 3 2 1

Keep up with New Holland Publishers on Facebook
www.facebook.com/NewHollandPublishers

2 Dads
food for family and friends

Blair Tonkin & Paul Bullpitt

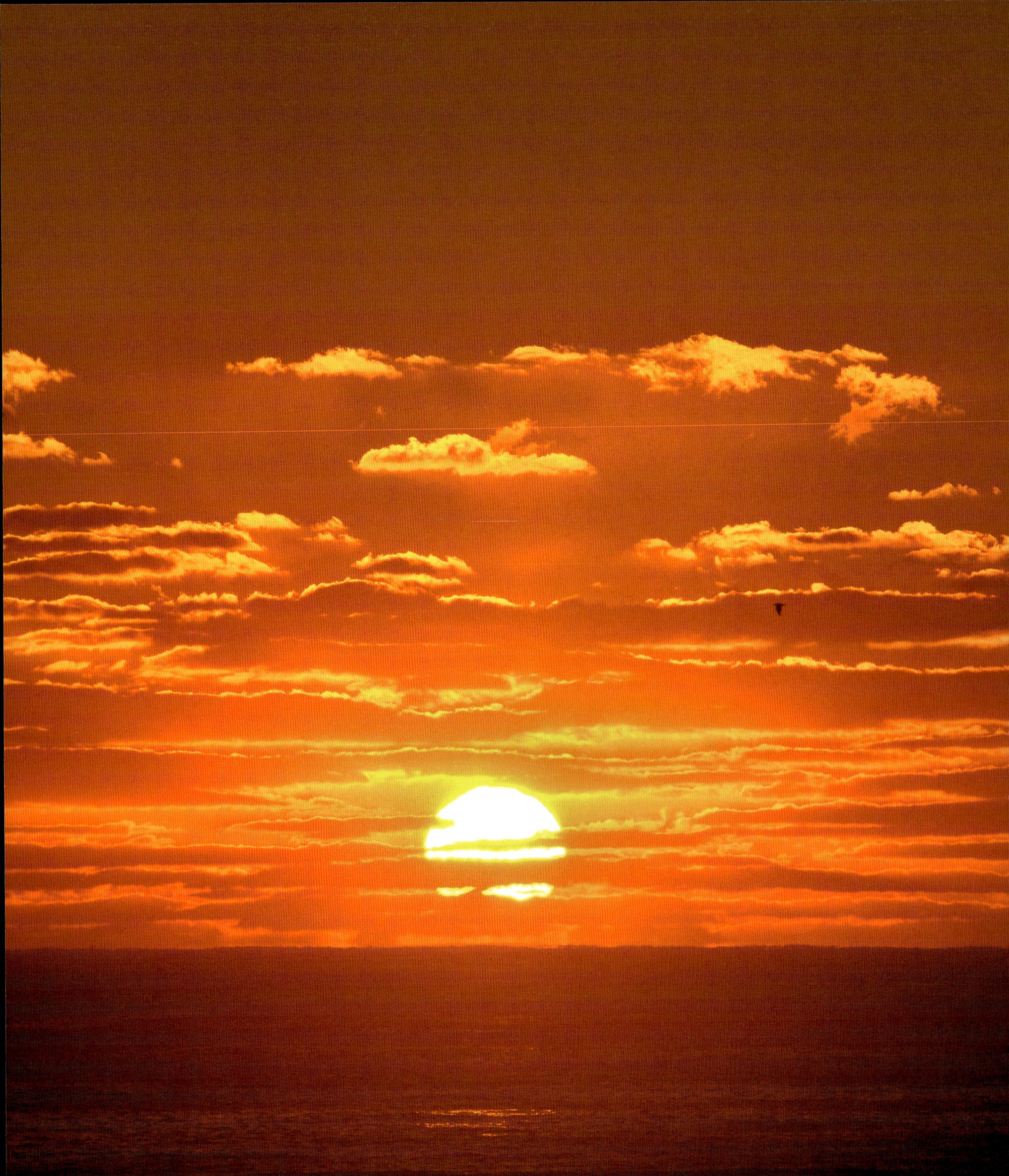

Foreword

I feel privileged to have met these two boys through the television show *My Kitchen Rules*. At the beginning, they didn't think of themselves as cooks but they wanted to give it a go. They worked amazingly hard and advanced far enough to prove a point.

Paul and Blair believe in living a well-balanced life and in being life-long learners. As dads and teachers, healthy food choices are a part of that education. I think the fact that Paul and Blair have decided to write a cookbook together is a fabulous idea. Paul and Blair found a new passion and they have decided to share it with the world. They are a great inspiration to every man and dad; these boys cook simple, healthy but *delicious* meals.

Guys, I wish you all the best and don't forget to live your own motto: cook, create and inspire.

Bon appétit!

Manu Feildel

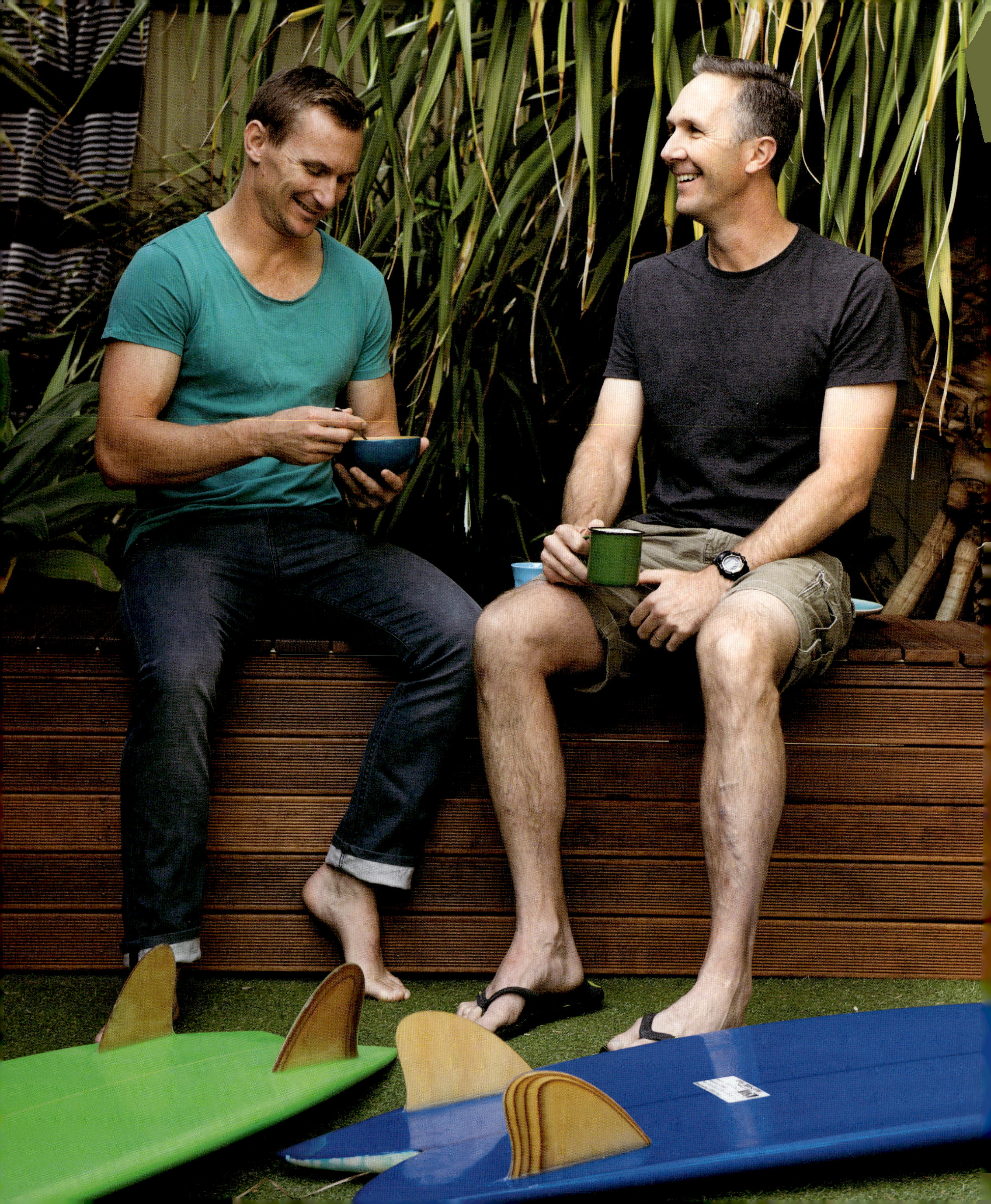

Contents

Introduction	9
What's for Breakfast?	13
Midday to Midnight	35
The BBQ	103
Treats	125
Dining In	149
Menu 1: Mediterranean	150
Menu 2: Asian	158
Menu 3: Asian 2	166
Menu 4: Mexican	174
Menu 5: Greek	182
Index	192

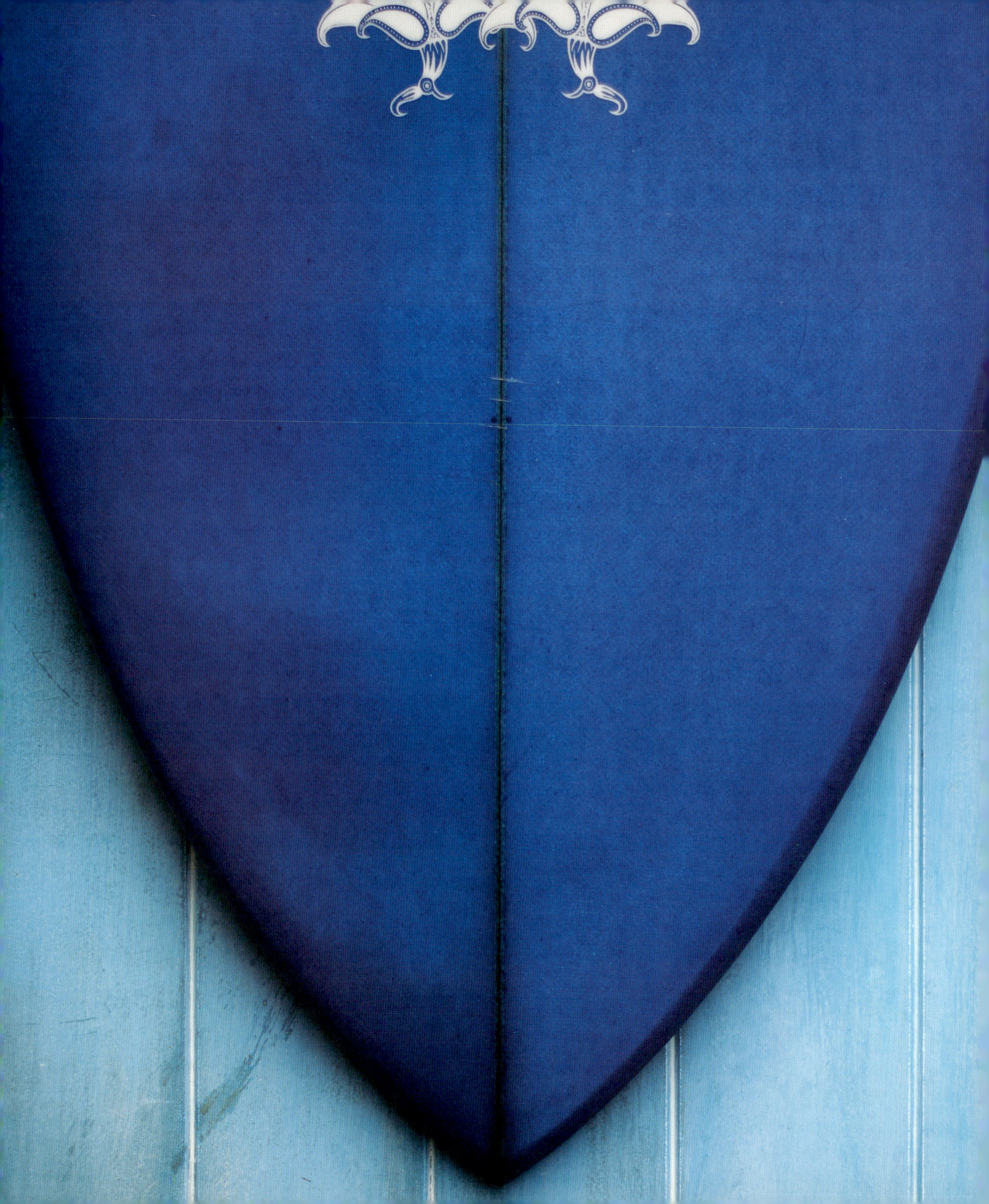

Introduction

We have been described as 'two average Aussie blokes, but above average cooks'. For us, this is a badge we can wear with pride. Our love of cooking stems from our love of food and more importantly, our love of eating. The pleasure of cooking, for us, is about producing meals that are nutritious and delicious, are made from beautiful and simple ingredients, then sharing them with family and friends. For us, cooking, like life, is about balance. Most of the meals we prepare are healthy and wholesome. However, we realise the need to treat ourselves occasionally.

Paul

My inspiration lies with my mum, Annie. Together we spend most of our time talking about and planning meals. I love nothing better than digging around in mum's pantry and any one of the many freezers she has, and getting out some beautiful produce to cook. When I left home, I took with me a handwritten book of all my best-loved recipes, and so began my love of cooking.

I have spent many years traveling, and these travels have heavily influenced my cooking style and taste. I distinctly remember tasting a chicken curry on my first trip to Bali and thinking to myself, 'I need to learn how to cook this'—that was the start of me cooking dishes from scratch. I've always enjoyed spicy food and will always be drawn to a mix of Asian and Mediterranean foods.

Above all else, I like to know what I'm eating and where that food has come from. I think too many people rely on convenience foods, and in my job as a teacher I see so many parents and kids with poor eating habits. You really are what you eat. My passion for food is in its preparation, the tasting and the social and health benefits it brings to our lives. Most evenings you will find me cooking in our family kitchen for my wife and son. The food I create ranges from simple dishes to those that are a little more intricate. The one ingredient that is always present is love.

I hope people get some joy from the recipes in our book and that the dishes you choose to make bring family and friends together. Enjoy!

Blair

I am the first to admit that I am a late bloomer in the kitchen. Like most blokes, the barbecue was the sole focus of my culinary skills and I was content cooking up a mean sausage or steak. The kick-start I needed to get into the kitchen and become more creative with my cooking came when I became friends with Paul. I couldn't help feeling inspired (and a little envious) when my family ate dinner at his home and his culinary knowledge and passion for food were displayed on the dining room table. And so began our now-famous Tuesday night cook-offs in which we'd take turns to provide a delicious feed for each other and friends. Loving a good challenge and being highly competitive, my quest for better food knowledge and techniques began. I believe that a good and happy life will be attained by surrounding yourself with supportive people. The effect on my life, of this friendship, has been positively influential.

Leading a healthy and active lifestyle is important to me. I strive to influence everyone I know and meet about the benefits of such a lifestyle. Being a physical education teacher and personal fitness trainer, I have the opportunity to develop and strengthen a love for being physically active for a diverse range of people in our society. Providing and maintaining healthy and strong bodies is a major passion of mine and now I have acquired the food knowledge to complement this.

I have enjoyed my culinary journey to date, particularly the discovery of many diverse taste combinations. The options are endless. My kitchen is the heart and soul of my home and I love having an entertaining area that is centred around my kitchen. Cooking for family and friends brings me immense pleasure, and I have found that I love to create food and entertain at the same time. Being a dad, I endeavour to show my son that healthy and delicious food can be simple to produce. Is there anything better than creating meals with your kids? I think not! This is one dad who has enjoyed stepping outside of his comfort zone, and looks forward to future culinary experiences both in and out of the kitchen.

I hope you enjoy the book. Happy cooking.

As a result of our *My Kitchen Rules* experience, we have met hundreds of people. A common question we are asked is 'what did you learn from being on the show?'. The answer is simple—LOTS! We had to broaden our scope of cooking, including tastes, techniques and the range of produce we used. How did we do this? For two teachers, we had to complete a role reversal and become the students. We soaked up information and learned a lot from self-study, as well as from the other contestants and the judges, Pete Evans and Manu Feildel. However, this alone will not get you anywhere in a competition like *My Kitchen Rules*. We had to turn this new-found knowledge into practical recipes and that is exactly what we did. Above all, we learnt that flavour balance and texture are paramount in producing a great dish. Every spare moment was spent in the kitchen of our make-shift home apartment cooking, tasting, adjusting, cooking again and tasting some more. The area of expertise in which we were most lacking was desserts. We both enjoy a healthy lifestyle and desserts are a rarity at home. You won't be surprised to know that we both noticed extra kilograms creeping on the scales during our dessert trials and triumphs.

Being fathers, we understand the importance of providing children with nutritious meals. However, these meals don't need to be time-consuming to make and boring to eat. So, what's our secret for getting nutritious foods into the kids? The answer is simple, you have to outsmart them and be sneaky! We had a school challenge on the show in which we had to provide food for 150 primary school children. The brief was to make the meals 'nutritious and delicious'. We chose to produce a twist on the classic fish and chips. Instead of deep-fried chips, we created vegetable fritters cut into wedges. The vegetables where finely grated into the batter mix and the kids where none the wiser. Needless to say, all the serves that day 'walked out the door'.

Another misconception that we have about kids is that they don't have the palate for spices. The golden rules for kids and spices is moderation. We both enjoy cooking and eating Asian-influenced meals and regularly serve spiced food to our own children. In the beginning, we reduced the amount of spices used and then slowly increased them. This goes for chillies as well. Try it, you will be surprised.

Disasters do and will happen in the kitchen. We have both had our fair share of trials and tribulations in the including misreading and miscalculating ingredients. The result might be an awkward silence around the dinner table with everyone being far too polite to say anything. We hope your family and friends are just as polite.

I (Blair) have a story to share on cooking and children. The first meal I cooked after coming home from *My Kitchen Rules* was eye fillet steak on sweet potato mash, with blanched asparagus and a mushroom sauce. The meal was plated up with a restaurant quality feel and I was feeling pretty proud of my dinner-time masterpiece. That night my son entered the kitchen and asked his standard question of 'Dad, what's for dinner?' After seeing my 'masterpiece' he rolled his eyes and left the kitchen with a sigh of 'Oh, really Dad, steak?'. Let me just say that he was very lucky not to get vegemite on toast that night.

This book came about after our *My Kitchen Rules* experience. Our journey from dads cooking in our home kitchens to contestants on the reality TV show has fueled our food passion and enhanced our technical skills immensely. We now want to inspire parents and kids alike to cook simple and healthy food. Whether it is breakfast for the kids, a dinner party for friends or food for that special occasion, we hope our recipes can bring people together. We will show you that with a little organisation and by limiting the amount of produce on the plate, you can produce 'restaurant-quality dishes that are cooked to perfection'. Sorry, had to get some classic *My Kitchen Rules* lines in here somewhere. It is our goal to inspire families to engage with healthier choices using our recipes. This would indeed make us happy men.

Cook, create and inspire!

Paul and Blair

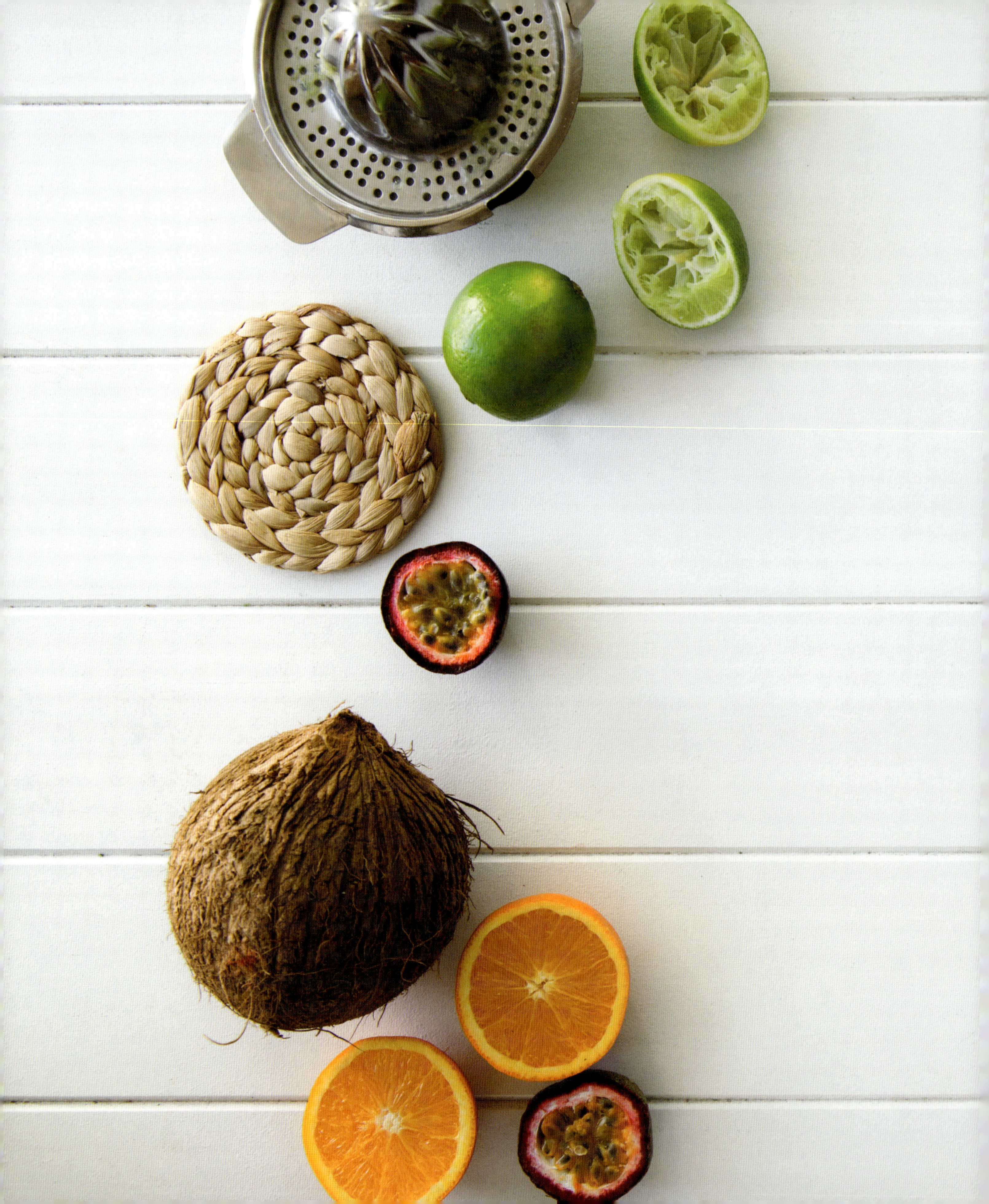

It is a well-known fact that breakfast is the most important meal of the day. As teachers, we are constantly aware of the fact that plenty of kids either skip breakfast or begin the day with bad food choices. Sadly this is probably the same in the adult world too. You can't run your car on empty and neither will your car thank you for supplying it with the wrong type of fuel. So, why do it to yourself and your kids? Having a good breakfast is such a simple step and the health benefits are numerous and long term. Whether you're after a quick bite before your hectic morning routine or are enjoying a leisurely Sunday morning, we know these delicious meals have you covered.

What's for Breakfast?

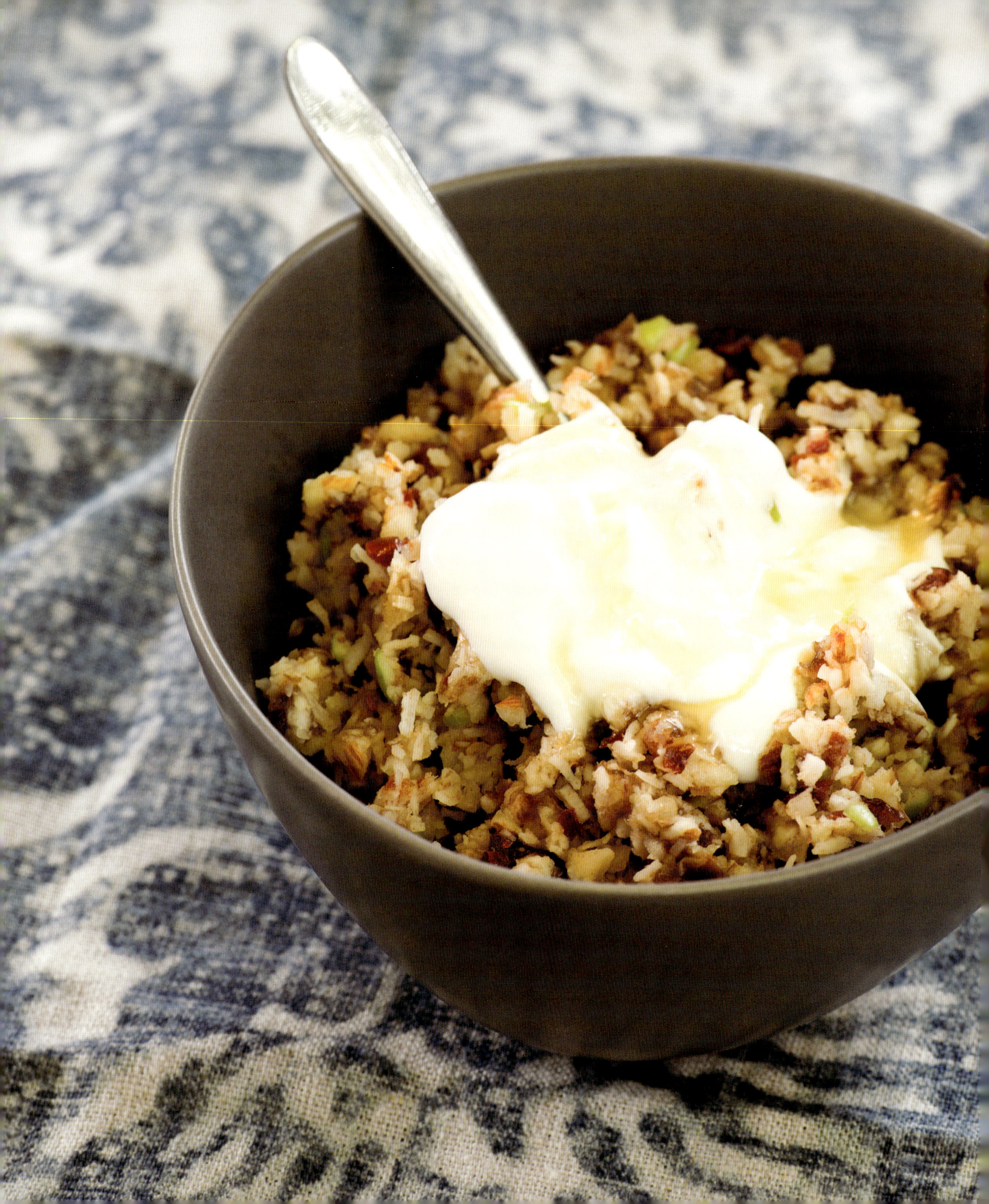

The Kickstarter

This is a nutritious and light breakfast that will start your day off on the right foot. It can be used as a topper on muesli or eaten by itself with a dollop of natural yogurt and a swirl of honey. It's simple to make, so get into it.

Ingredients

- 80 g/2½ oz dessicated (dry unsweetened, shredded) coconut
- 40 g/1½ oz almonds
- 40 g/1½ oz walnuts
- 40 g/1½ oz Medjool dates, pitted
- 4 tablespoons dried cranberries
- 2 green apple, cored and quartered
- juice of ½ a lemon (optional)
- 125 ml/4 fl oz natural (plain) yogurt
- 1 tablespoon honey

Method

1. Place all the ingredients, except the yogurt and honey, in a food processor and pulse until the desired consistency is reached. We like it chunky.
2. Mix the yogurt and honey together in a small bowl.
3. Serve a portion in a bowl with a spoonful of honeyed yogurt.

Tip
This will store in a sealed container in the refrigerator for up to 2 days if lemon juice is used.

Nasi Goreng

There is one dish that screams Bali and that is nasi goreng. We always make it our first meal when we go there no matter what time of day it is. The classic combo of fried rice topped with an egg and liberally coated with sambal asli (chilli sauce) is just heaven.

Ingredients

- 3 tablespoons oil
- 100 g/3½ oz chicken, finely chopped
- 200 g/7 oz cooked jasmine rice
- 3 shallots, chopped
- 5 garlic cloves, finely chopped
- ¼ leek, finely chopped
- 1 large red chilli, seeded and chopped
- 175 g/6 oz cabbage, chopped
- 1 tablespoon tomato paste
- ½ teaspoon rice wine vinegar
- 2 teaspoons kecap manis (sweet soy sauce)
- ½ teaspoon fish sauce
- salt and pepper, to taste
- 4 eggs
- 1 tablespoon fried shallots, to garnish
- kaffir lime leaves, shredded, to garnish
- chilli sauce, to serve

Method

1. Heat 2 tablespoons of the oil in a wok over a medium flame. Fry the chicken until nearly cooked through. Add the cooked rice, shallots, garlic, leek, chilli, cabbage, tomato paste, rice wine vinegar, kecap manis and fish sauce and cook until the vegetables are wilted. Season with salt and pepper.
2. Fry the eggs in the remaining oil in a separate pan, until cooked to your liking.
3. Pack a serving of nasi goreng in a small bowl or ramekin. Invert in the centre of a plate. Top with the fried egg and garnish with fried shallots, shredded kaffir lime leaves and as much chilli sauce as you can handle.

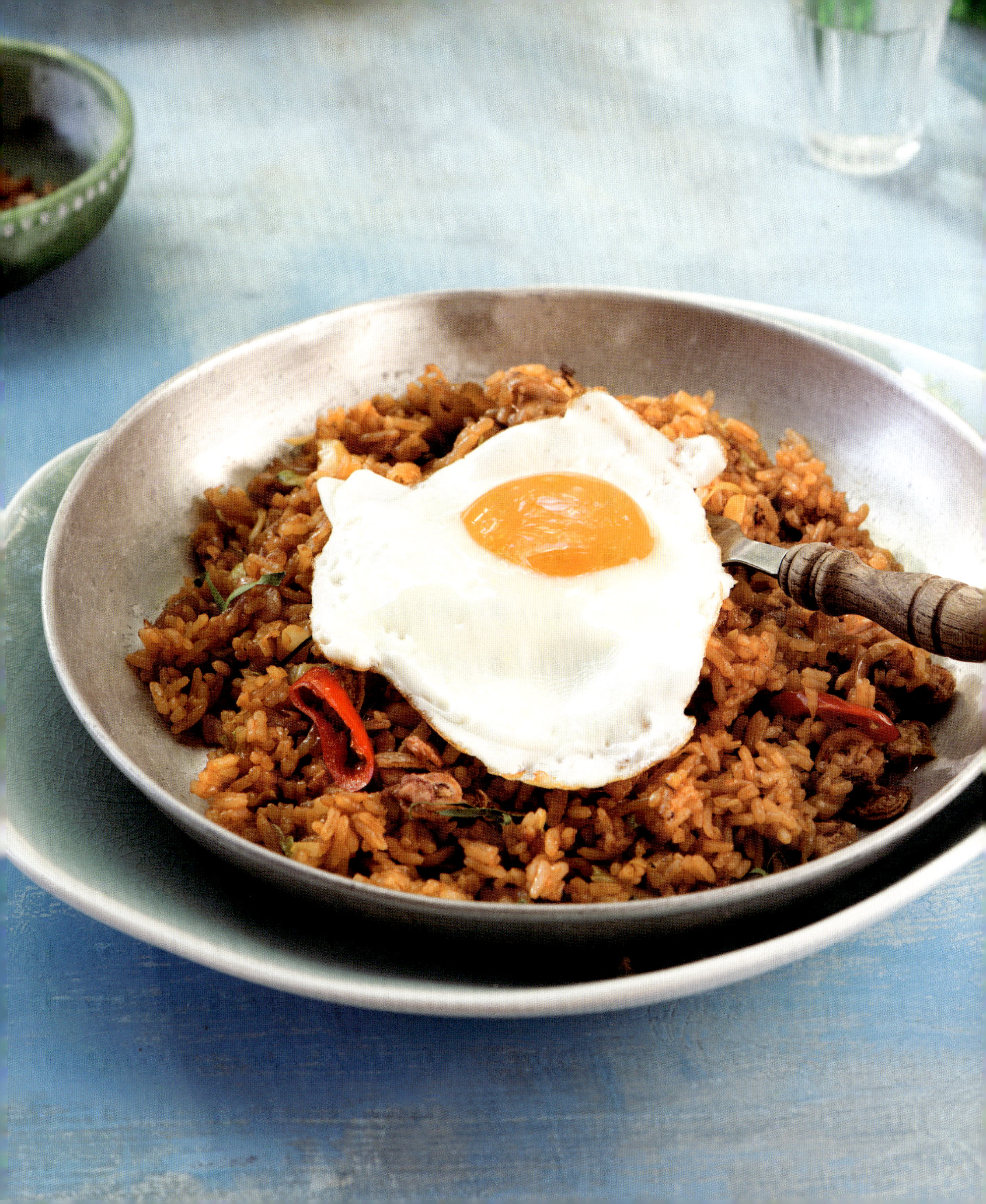

Baked Beans, Chorizo and Eggs

Eggs are a natural choice for breakfast. So too are baked beans. The Spanish way of serving eggs with baked beans and chorizo is one of the best ways of combining these ingredients. The taste of the chorizo and the smoky taste of the beans topped with a baked egg are just magnificent. If you want to add a little more spice to this recipe, add some chilli.

Ingredients

- 2 tablespoons olive oil
- 1 chorizo sausage, sliced
- 1 small onion, chopped
- 2 garlic cloves, crushed
- 1 tablespoon red wine vinegar
- 1 teaspoon smoked paprika
- 1 teaspoon brown sugar
- 200 g/7 oz can chopped tomatoes
- 400 g/14 oz can cannellini beans
- salt and pepper, to taste
- 4 large eggs
- ½ bunch flat-leaf parsley, chopped, to garnish

Method

1. Preheat the oven to 180°C/350°F/Gas mark 4.
2. Preheat a frying pan over a medium flame and add the oil. Cook the chorizo until it's almost crispy, then remove and set aside.
3. In the same frying pan, fry the onion and garlic with the red wine vinegar until the onion softens. Add the paprika, sugar and tomatoes and allow to simmer for 5 minutes.
4. Add the beans and the cooked chorizo and mix through, then season to taste with salt and pepper.
5. Add the bean mixture to 4 ovenproof ramekins. Make a well in the centre of each and crack an egg into it. Bake for about 8–10 minutes, or until the egg is cooked to your liking.
6. Scatter with the chopped parsley just before serving.

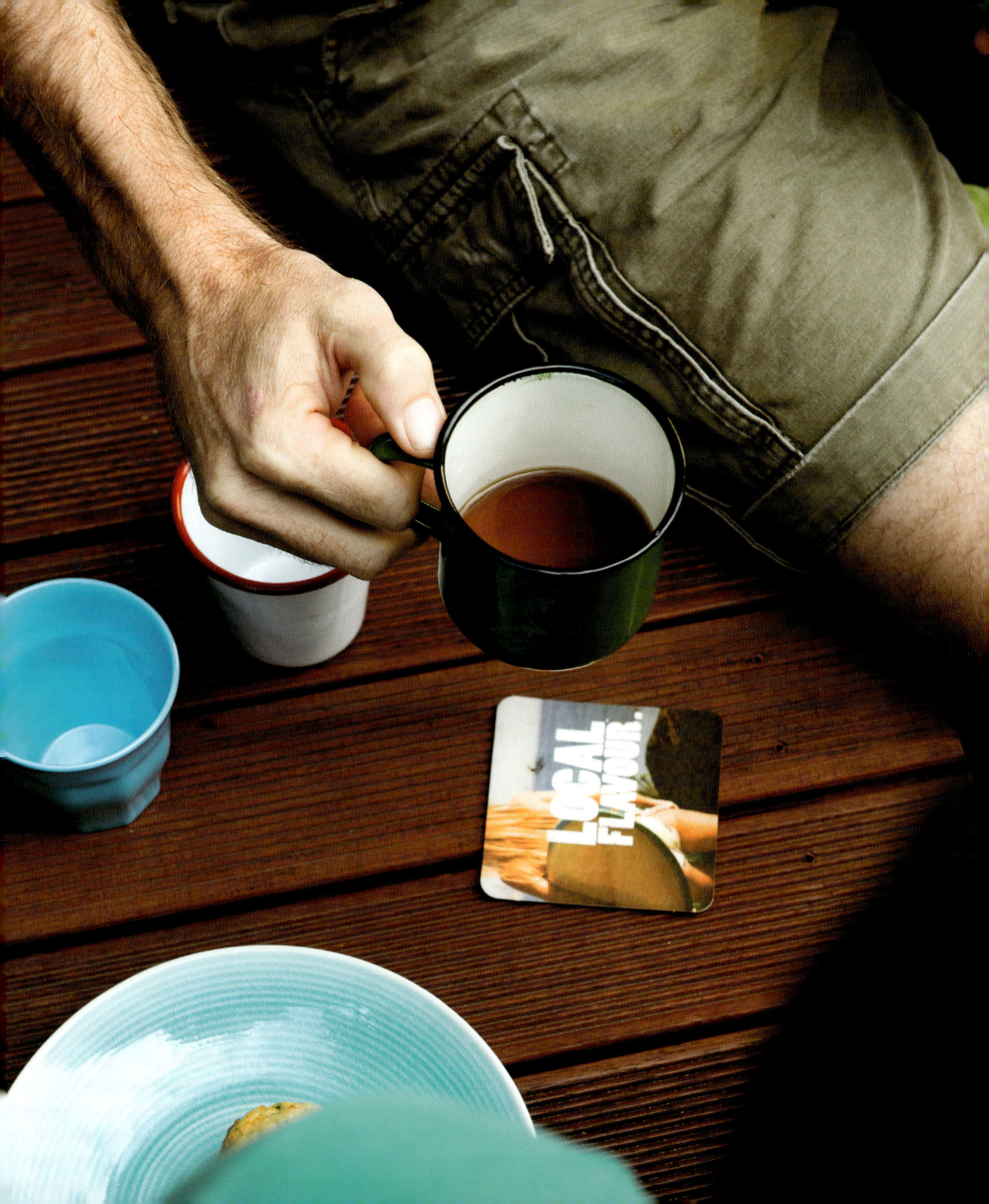
LOCAL
FLAVOUR.

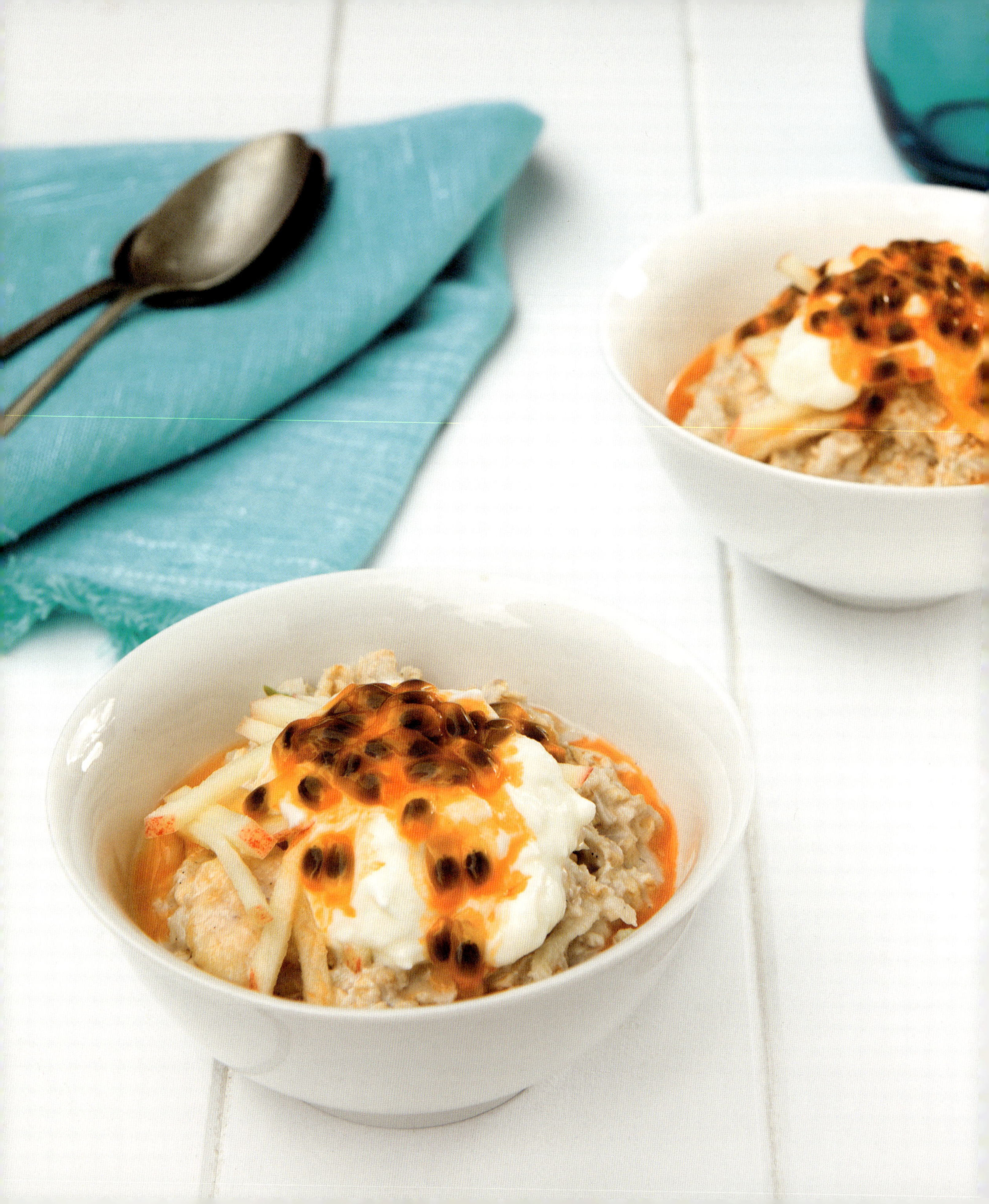

Bircher Muesli

Check out any funky café and we guarantee that you will see bircher muesli on the menu. Oats are nutritious, low in calories, high in fibre and linked with many health benefits. Bircher muesli is just plain tasty and a great start for any active day. It does require you to be organised the night before. Make the effort, you'll be glad you did.

Ingredients
- 150–200 g/5–7 oz rolled oats
- 300 ml/10½ fl oz milk
- 200 ml/7 fl oz apple juice, low sugar preferably
- 2 small bananas, chopped
- 2 green apples, grated
- zest and juice of ½ lemon
- 2 tablespoons honey
- ¼ teaspoon vanilla paste
- 1 pink lady or any red apple
- 150 g/5 oz natural (plain) yogurt
- pulp of 2 passionfruit

Method
1. To make the bircher muesli, combine all the ingredients, except for the red apple, yogurt and passionfruit, in a bowl and leave to soak, covered, overnight.
2. Slice the red apple into thin matchsticks. To serve, spoon the muesli mix into a serving bowl. Add a couple of spoonfuls of yogurt, some apple matchsticks and some passionfruit pulp.

Tips
You can replace the oats with cooked quinoa for variety. Now you're really hip and happening.

You can change the apple and passionfruit to any selection of berries if you wish. It will still taste beautiful.

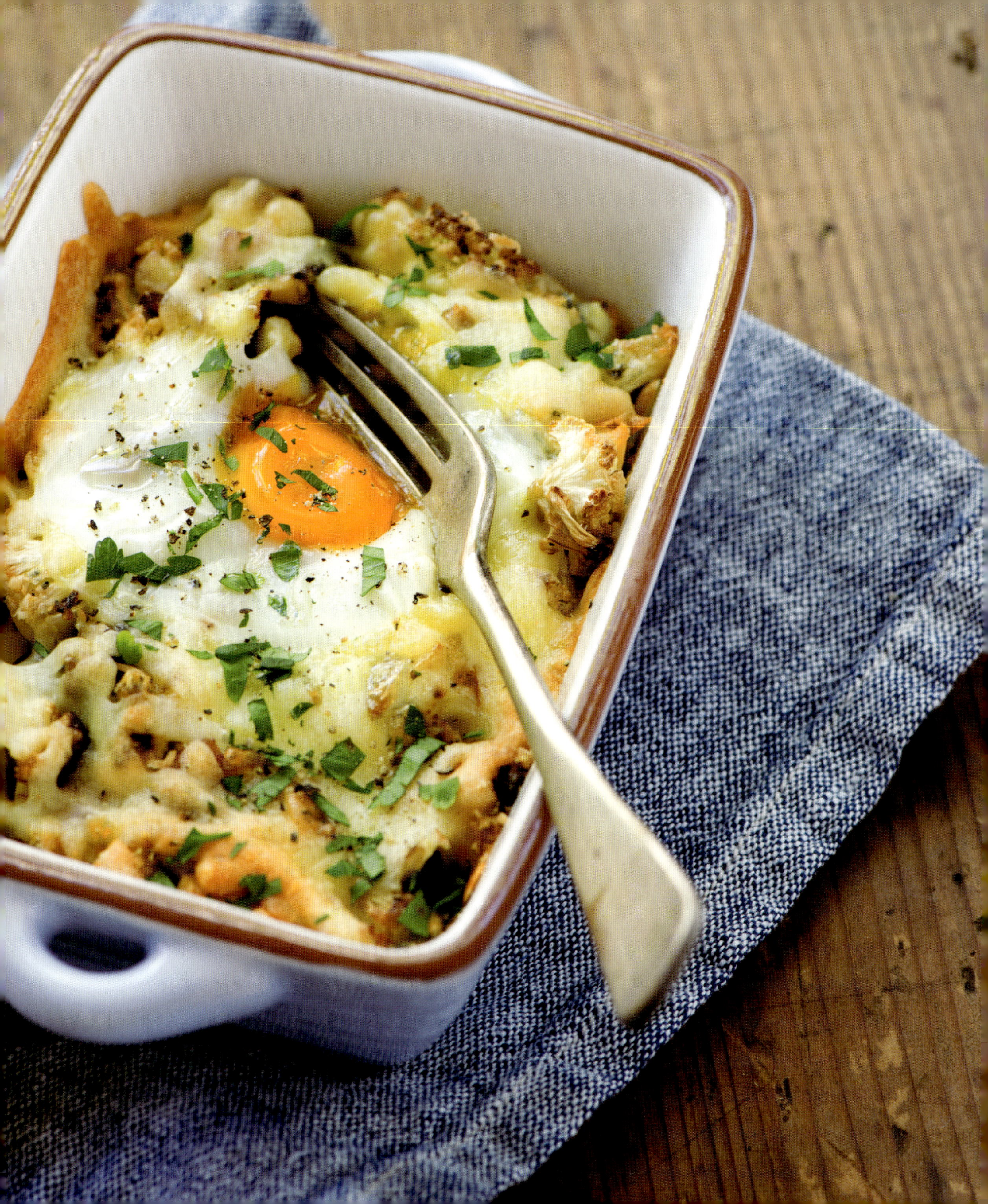

Baked Eggs with Cauliflower and Gorgonzola

This may sound like a strange dish to have for breakfast. Cheesy cauliflower is a baked favourite at our houses. Add in some bacon, mushrooms and Gorgonzola cheese with an egg and it's hard not to fall in love with this. If the taste of the Gorgonzola is too intense, change it to a mix of Cheddar and Parmesan cheese. Once you've had this you are sure to love it.

Ingredients

- 1 tablespoon olive oil
- 4 rashers (strips) of bacon, rind removed, and flesh diced
- 400 g/14 oz cauliflower, cut into small florets
- 100 g/3½ oz button (white) mushrooms, sliced
- 50 g/1¾ oz Gorgonzola cheese, crumbled
- 20 g/⅔ oz Parmesan cheese, grated (shredded)
- 4 large eggs

Method

1. Preheat the oven to 180°C/350°F/Gas mark 4.
2. Place a frying pan over medium heat and add the oil when hot. Add the diced bacon and cook for about 2 minutes, or until crispy. Add the cauliflower and fry for about 5 minutes, or until the cauliflower softens, then add the mushroom and fry for another 2 minutes.
3. Remove the pan from the heat and add the cheeses. Stir to combine
4. Transfer the mixture to 4 ovenproof dishes. Make a small well in the centre of each and crack an egg into each well.
5. Bake in the oven for about 8 minutes, or until the eggs are cooked to your liking.

French Toast 2 Ways

This has to be one of the most simple, yet tasty breakfast treats. This dish is easy to cook and also versatile. The French toast tastes good with a multitude of toppings from bacon to fruit, all with the addition of some maple syrup. Mix it up depending on how healthy you want to be. We've given you two options here, but berries and yogurt work just as well.

Ingredients

6 large eggs
2 tablespoons icing (confectioners') sugar
2 teaspoons butter
6–8 thick slices of bread

Bacon and Maple Syrup

250 g/9 oz middle cut bacon, rind removed
3 tablespoons maple syrup or honey

Caramelised Peaches

40 g/1½ oz butter
4–5 ripe peaches, sliced and pit removed
2 tablespoons brown sugar
icing (confectioners') sugar, to dust

Method

1. To make the French toast, whisk the eggs and icing sugar in a shallow bowl until smooth.
2. Preheat a frying pan over medium heat and then add the butter to melt.
3. Soak the bread in the egg and sugar mixture for a few seconds on both sides. Fry each side of the bread until golden.
4. To make the bacon and maple syrup French toast, in another pan, fry the bacon over a medium heat until crispy. Serve the French toast with a few pieces of bacon and drizzle over the maple syrup.
5. To make the caramelised peaches French toast, melt the butter in a frying pan over medium heat until foaming. Add the peaches, cook and turn after about 4 minutes, or until golden brown. Add the sugar and cook, stirring, until the mixture thickens. Be careful not to overcook the peaches as they will fall apart. Add slices of caramelised peaches to the French toast and dust with icing sugar, to serve.

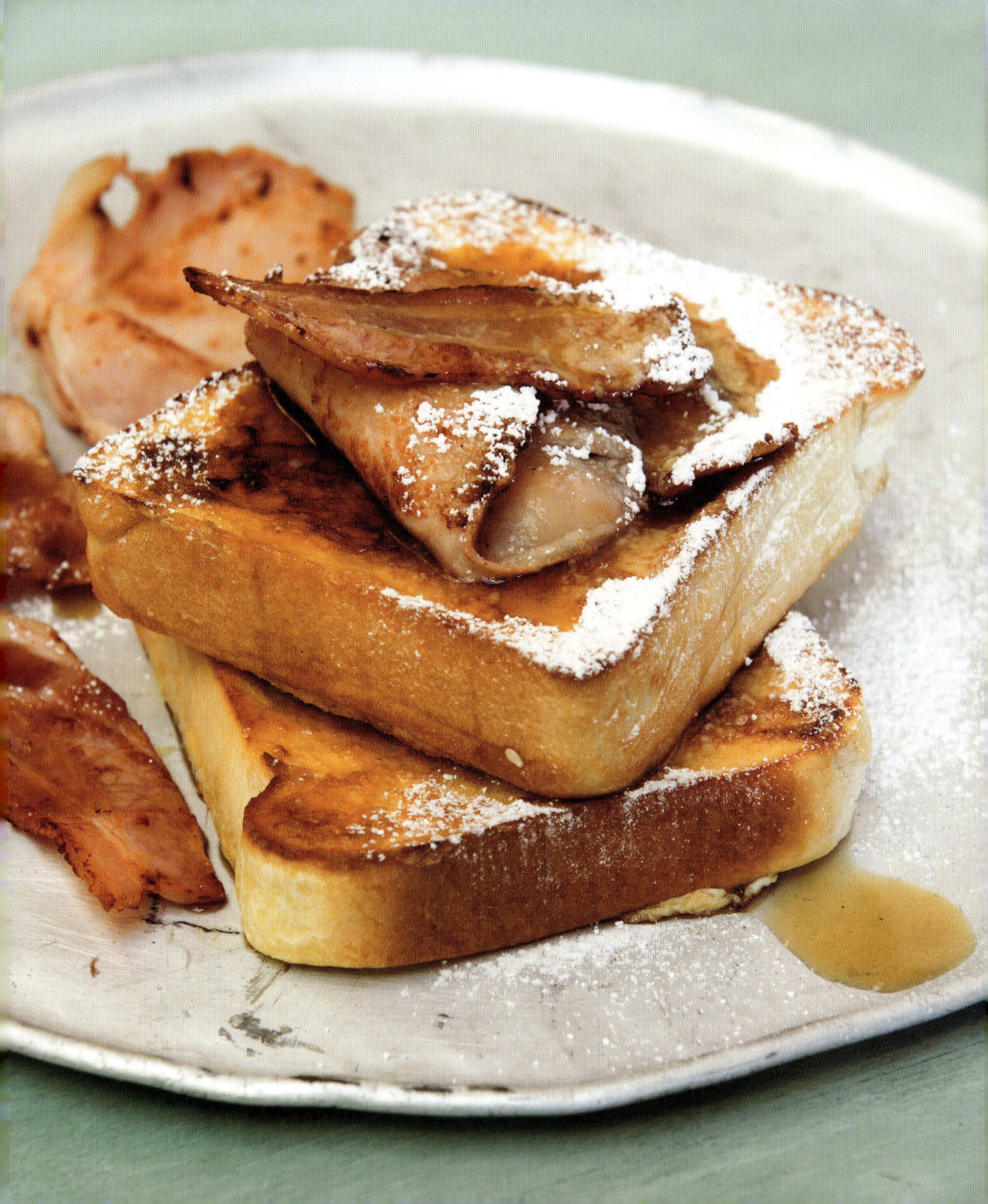

Baked Tomatoes with Pesto and Bacon Dust

We love this meal due to its simplicity and freshness of taste. It can be eaten by itself as a light breakfast or served as a side dish with classic bacon and eggs. The tastes just bounce around in your mouth.

Ingredients

5 rashers (strips) bacon
12 vine-ripened or Roma tomatoes, halved
2 tablespoons balsamic vinegar
salt and pepper, to taste
100 g/3½ oz feta cheese
sourdough loaf, sliced thinly and toasted

Pesto

1 cup parsley, chopped
1 cup basil, chopped
45 g/1½ oz Parmesan cheese, grated (shredded)
30 g/1 oz pine nuts, toasted
1 garlic glove, crushed
125 ml/4 fl oz olive oil

Method

1. Preheat the oven to 180°C/350°F/Gas mark 4.
2. Line a baking tray and place a wire rack on top. Place the bacon on a wire rack and bake for 10 minutes, or until the bacon is very crisp. Remove from the oven and allow to cool. When cooled, pulse in a food processor until the bacon is a fine crumb.
3. For the pesto, process all the ingredients, except for the oil, in a food processor until combined. Pulse the processor while adding oil gradually until it is all combined. Season to taste.
4. Brush the tops of the tomatoes with balsamic vinegar, season with salt and pepper and place on a lined baking tray. Bake for 10–15 minutes, or until tender.
5. To serve, place 3 tomatoes on each plate and drizzle with balsamic vinegar. Place a teaspoon of pesto on each tomato and sprinkle with feta and bacon dust. Garnish with some chopped parsley. Serve with a slice of toasted sourdough.

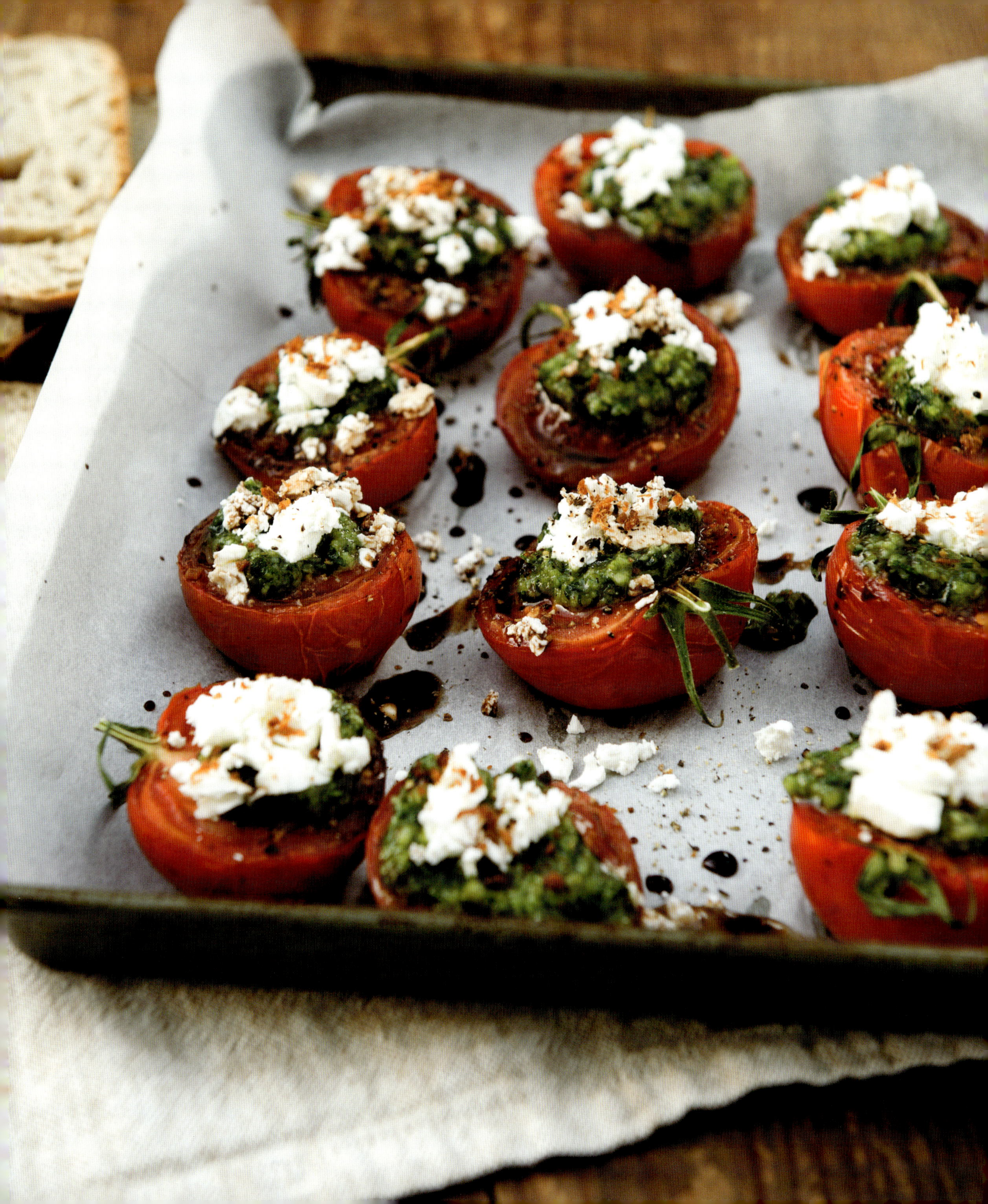

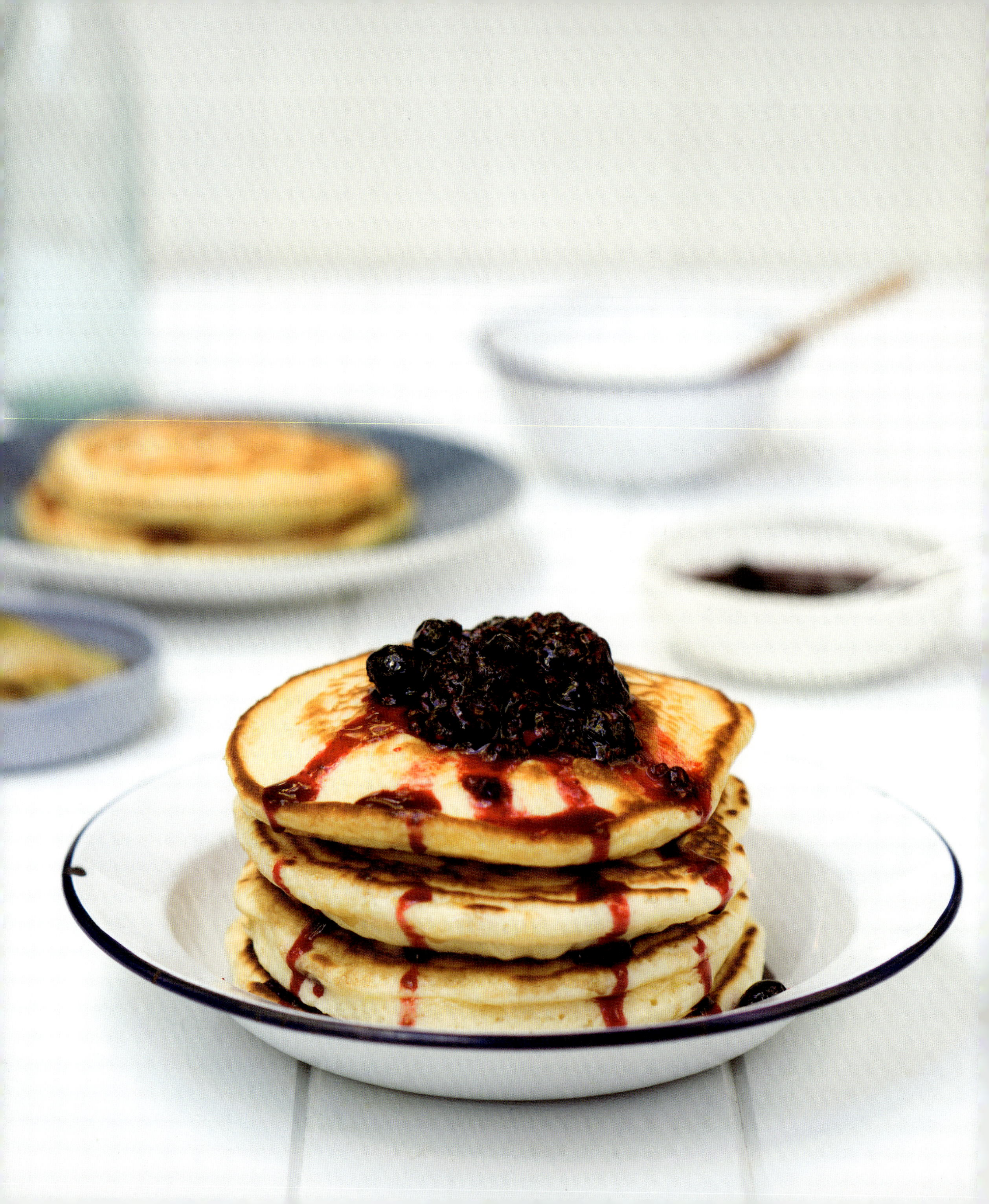

Ingredients

MAPLE SYRUP
225 g/8 oz self-raising (self-rising) flour
60 ml/2 fl oz maple syrup
2 eggs
250 ml/8 fl oz milk
butter, for frying

BUTTERMILK CLASSIC
8 fl oz/250 ml milk
juice of 1 lemon
225 g/8 oz self-raising (self-rising)
60 g/2 oz sugar
2 eggs
butter, for frying

Method
Maple

1. Preheat the frying pan over a medium heat.
2. Place the flour, maple syrup and eggs into a bowl and whisk to beat. Slowly whisk in the milk until you have a thick and slightly runny consistency.
3. Melt a small slice of butter in the frying pan and use a small ladle to pour in some pancake batter. When bubbles appear on most of the batter, flip the pancake and fry for another 1 minute. Remove from the pan and set aside on a plate covered with kitchen towel.
4. Repeat to make more pancakes until the batter is used up.

Buttermilk Classic

1. Preheat the frying pan over a medium heat.
2. Whisk the milk and lemon juice together in a bowl then allow to stand for about 5 minutes. This will make buttermilk
3. Combine the rest of the ingredients in a separate bowl. Slowly whisk in the buttermilk until you have a thick and slightly runny consistency.
4. Melt a small slice of butter in the frying pan and use a small ladle to pour in some pancake batter. When bubbles appear on most of the batter, flip the pancake and fry for another 1 minute. Remove from the pan and set aside on a plate covered with kitchen towel.
5. Repeat to make more pancakes until the batter is used up.

Pancakes

A weekend ritual at both our households is pancakes for breakfast. Over the years we have experimented with the basic pancake mix to give a bit of variety. It's one meal where there are guaranteed to be no leftovers. Here are four simple but yummy pancake recipes that you and the kids will absolutely love.

Pancakes cont.

Ingredients

Citrus
225 g/8 oz self-raising (self-rising) flour
60 g/2 oz sugar
2 eggs
zest and juice of 2 oranges
175 ml/6 fl oz milk
butter, for frying

Health Kick
90 g/3 oz rolled oats
250 ml/8 fl oz apple juice
115 g/4 fl oz self-raising (self-rising) flour
115 g/4 oz almond meal (ground almonds)
2 teaspoons baking powder
2 eggs
250 ml/8 fl oz milk
butter, for frying

Citrus
1. Preheat the frying pan over a medium heat.
2. Place all the ingredients, except for the milk, into a bowl. Slowly whisk in the milk until you have a thick and slightly runny consistency.
3. Melt a small slice of butter in your frying pan and use a large kitchen spoon to pour in some pancake batter. When bubbles appear on most of the batter, flip the pancake and cook for another 1 minute. Remove from the pan and set aside on a plate covered with kitchen towel.
4. Repeat until the remaining batter is used up.

Health Kick
1. The night before, mix the oats and apple juice together in a bowl and place in a sealed container in the refrigerator overnight.
2. The following morning, preheat the frying pan over a medium flame.
3. Meanwhile, place all the ingredients, except for the milk, into a bowl and beat together. Slowly whisk in the milk until you have a thick and slightly runny consistency.
4. Melt a small slice of butter in the frying pan and use a ladle to pour in some pancake batter. When bubbles appear on most of the batter, flip the pancake and fry for 1 more minute. Remove from the pan and set aside on a plate covered with kitchen towel.
5. Repeat to use up the remaining batter.

Pancake Toppers

Everyone loves a dash of maple syrup or honey on their pancakes, especially the sweet toothed–it's a match made in heaven. Here are some toppers that are different from the normal. The kids will be impressed for sure.

Mixed Berry Syrup

60 g/2 oz caster (superfine) sugar
60 ml/2 fl oz water
150 g/6 oz frozen berries, including raspberries, blueberries and blackberries
juice of ½ lemon

1. Pour the sugar and water into a small pan and place over low heat until the sugar dissolves.
2. Add the frozen berries and lemon juice, then increase the heat until the syrup begins to boil. Reduce the heat and simmer for about 5 minutes.
3. Remove from the heat and allow to cool before serving.

Cinnamon Apples

100 g/3½ oz caster (superfine) sugar
60 ml/2 fl oz water
1 teaspoon ground cinnamon
2 Granny Smith apples, cored, halved and thinly sliced

1. Put the sugar, water and cinnamon in a small pan and place over low heat until the sugar dissolves.
2. Add the apple slices, then increase the heat to a simmer for 5 minutes, or until the apple begin to soften. Remove from the heat and allow to cool before serving.

Honeyed Yogurt

1 tablespoon honey
125 ml/4 fl oz natural (plain) yogurt
cinnamon, to taste

1. Mix the honey and yogurt together in a small bowl. Add a pinch of ground cinnamon for variety.

The Breakfast Burrito

This is our take on the legendary Breakfast Burrito served at our favourite cafe. We challenge you to find a meal that fills the tummy better after a morning surf or walk. Not only is it filling, but flavoursome too.

Ingredients

1 tablespoon oil
1 red onion, diced
2 garlic gloves, finely chopped
6 shortcut bacon rashers (strips), roughly diced
200 g/7 oz can four bean mix, drained and rinsed
1 large red chilli, seeded and thinly sliced (optional)
2 tablespoons tomato purée or 12 cherry tomatoes, quartered
¼ cup loosely packed flat-leaf parsley
salt and pepper, to taste
sour cream, to serve
avocado, sliced, to serve
8 wholemeal (whole wheat) burrito wraps

Scrambled Egg

4 eggs
2 tablespoons single (light) cream
salt and pepper, to taste
100 g/3½ oz Cheddar or Parmesan, grated (shredded)

Method

1. To make the scrambled eggs, whisk together the eggs, cream and seasoning in a small bowl. Pour the mixture into a small non-stick pan and heat over a low flame. Occasionally stir with a large spoon to prevent the egg mixture from sticking to the sides.
2. When the egg mixture starts to form small lumps, add the cheese and stir until it melts through. Remove from the heat when the mixture has a small amount of liquid in the base of the pan. Continue to stir occasionally as the residual heat from the pan will cook the rest of the egg mixture.
3. Heat the oil in a frying pan over medium flame. Add the onion, garlic and bacon and fry until the bacon is crispy.
4. Add the beans, chilli, tomato purée and 2 tablespoons of water and cook until the beans soften slightly. Remove from the heat, add the parsley, season to taste and mix through.
5. To serve, spread sour cream and sliced avocado on the burrito. Add some bean mixture and scrambled eggs. Fold your burrito and enjoy.

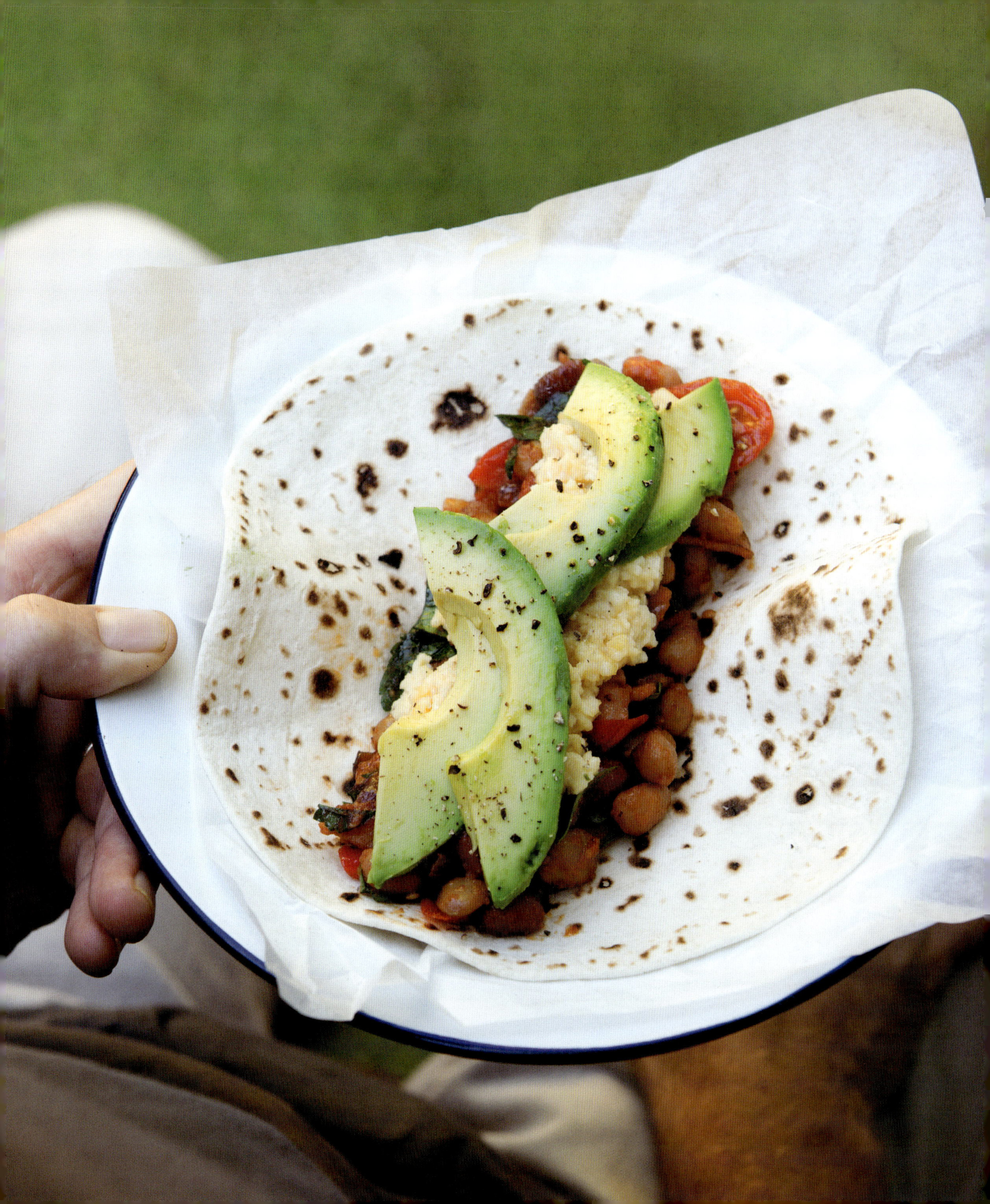

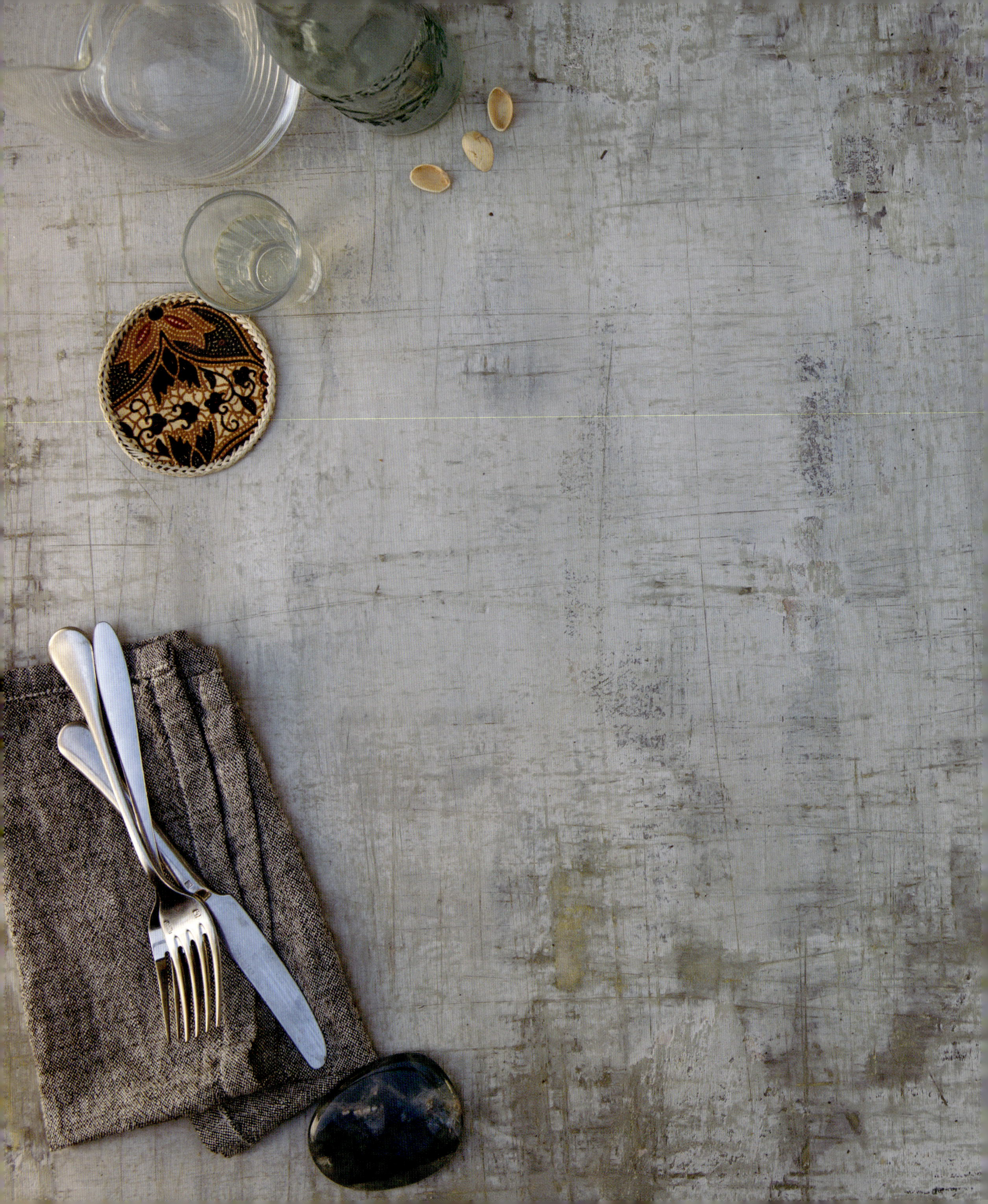

During the early drafting stages of this cookbook we envisioned having typical lunch and dinner chapters. However, it become apparent very quickly that classifying some of our meals was going to cause us headaches. So, how does any good man deal with a difficult decision? That's right, we simply don't make it. This chapter is the result. Here we've simply put together some of our best recipes and it's up to you to decide when to eat them. Another crisis averted for mankind.

Midday to Midnight

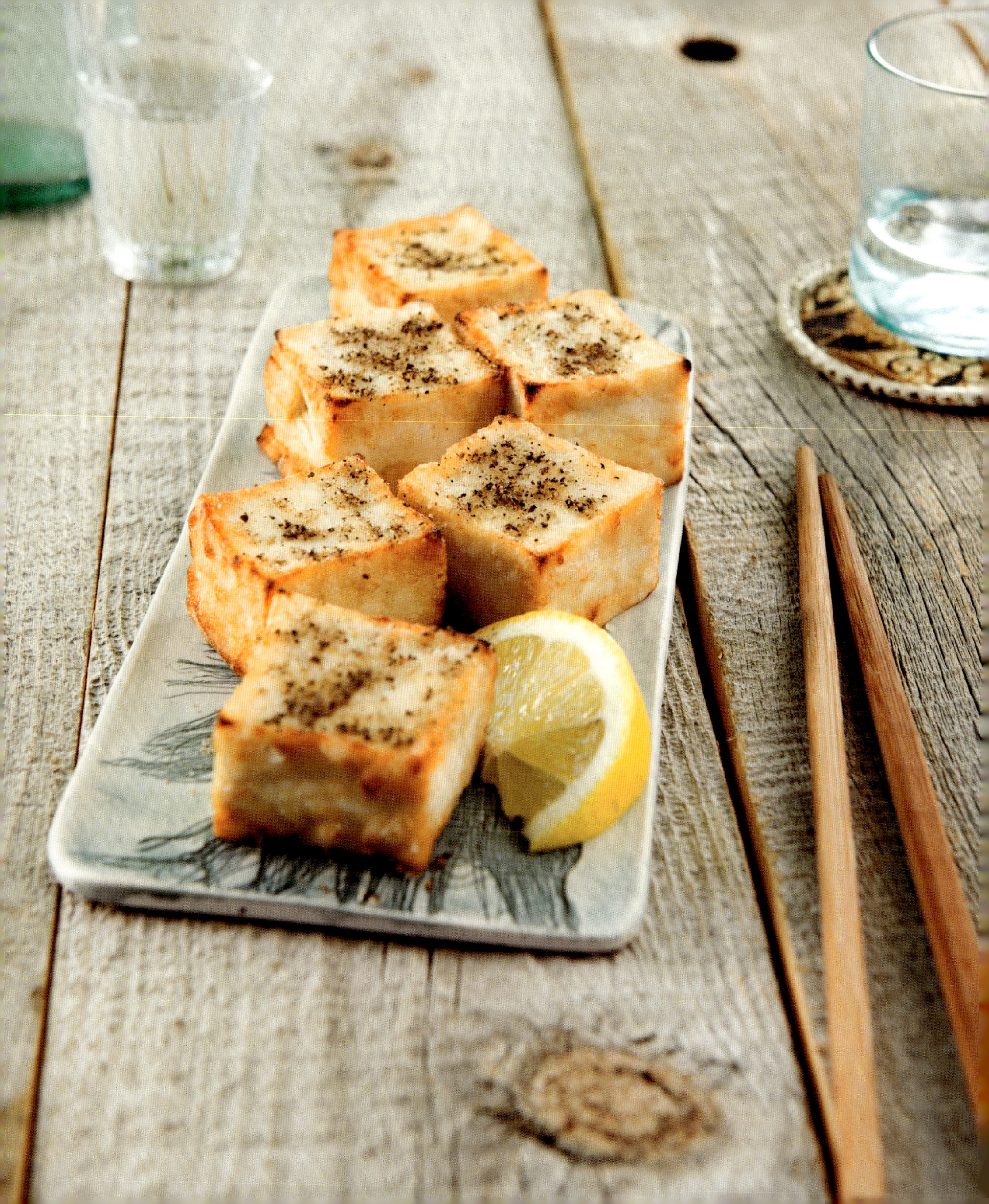

Sichuan Salt and Pepper Tofu

If you are one of those people that think tofu is only for vegetarians or hippies, think again. Once you taste this dish you will be converted. This dish uses firm tofu, and it is always a good idea to put the tofu on paper towel to drain any excess moisture from it before cooking. We have shallow-fried the tofu, but this dish works equally well in a deep fryer. This is a great appetiser and can be made more substantial when served with an Asian salad.

Ingredients
- 600 g/1 lb 5 oz firm tofu
- 1 tablespoon Sichuan peppercorns
- 2 teaspoons white pepper
- 2 tablespoons sea salt or flakes
- 250 ml/8 fl oz vegetable oil, for shallow frying
- 70 g/2½ oz cornflour (corn starch)
- salt and pepper, to taste
- lemon wedges, to serve

Method
1. Cut the tofu into 3–4 cm/1¼–1¾ in cubes and place on paper towel. Arrange another paper towel on top and leave for about 15–20 minutes to drain any excess moisture.
2. Put the Sichuan peppercorns, white pepper and salt in a dry frying pan and cook over a high heat until the peppercorns start to smoke and pop. Remove from the pan and allow to cool before grinding to a powder in a spice grinder or using a mortar and pestle.
3. Heat the oil in a wok over a high heat. Place the cornflour in a bowl and roll each piece of tofu in it to coat evenly.
4. Shallow-fry tofu a couple of pieces at a time, rolling them over to give each side a beautiful golden tone. Remove the pieces and drain on paper towels.
5. Liberally sprinkle with the salt and pepper mixture and serve with a lemon wedge.

Coconut and Shrimp Soup

We don't make a lot of soups, but this one is hard to turn down. The Asian-inspired flavours make this a great starter to an Asian banquet or a beautiful meal for two—up to you!

Ingredients

750 ml/24 fl oz coconut milk
12 large shrimp (prawns), shelled and veined
3 teaspoons galangal, minced
1 teaspoon ginger, minced
2 red bird's eye chillies, sliced
2 coriander (cilantro) roots, finely cut
5 red shallots, sliced lengthwise
2 kaffir lime leaves
1 lemongrass stalk, finely chopped
zest of 1 lime
750 ml/24 fl oz fish stock
75 ml/2½ fl oz fish sauce
50 ml/1¾ fl oz lime juice
salt and pepper, to taste
4 kaffir lime leaves, shredded, to garnish
2 red bird's eye chillies, finely sliced, to garnish
2 tablespoons coriander (cilantro) leaves, to garnish
2 shallots, sliced and fried

Method

1. Bring the coconut milk to the boil for a few minutes in a large pan. When boiling, add the shrimp for 2 minutes, or until cooked, then remove with a slotted spoon.
2. Add the galangal, ginger, chillies, coriander, shallots, lime leaves, lemongrass stalk and lime zest. Reduce the heat and simmer for 5 minutes.
3. Stir in the stock and fish sauce and simmer for another 15 minutes.
4. Pour the soup through a fine sieve, discarding the solids. Add the lime juice. Taste and adjust the seasoning, if required.
5. To serve, divide the shredded lime leaves, chillies, and coriander leaves among the bowls and ladle on the hot soup. Arrange the shrimp in the centre of the soup and scatter with fried shallots.

Tip
Scampi can be used to replace shrimp with the same delicious results.

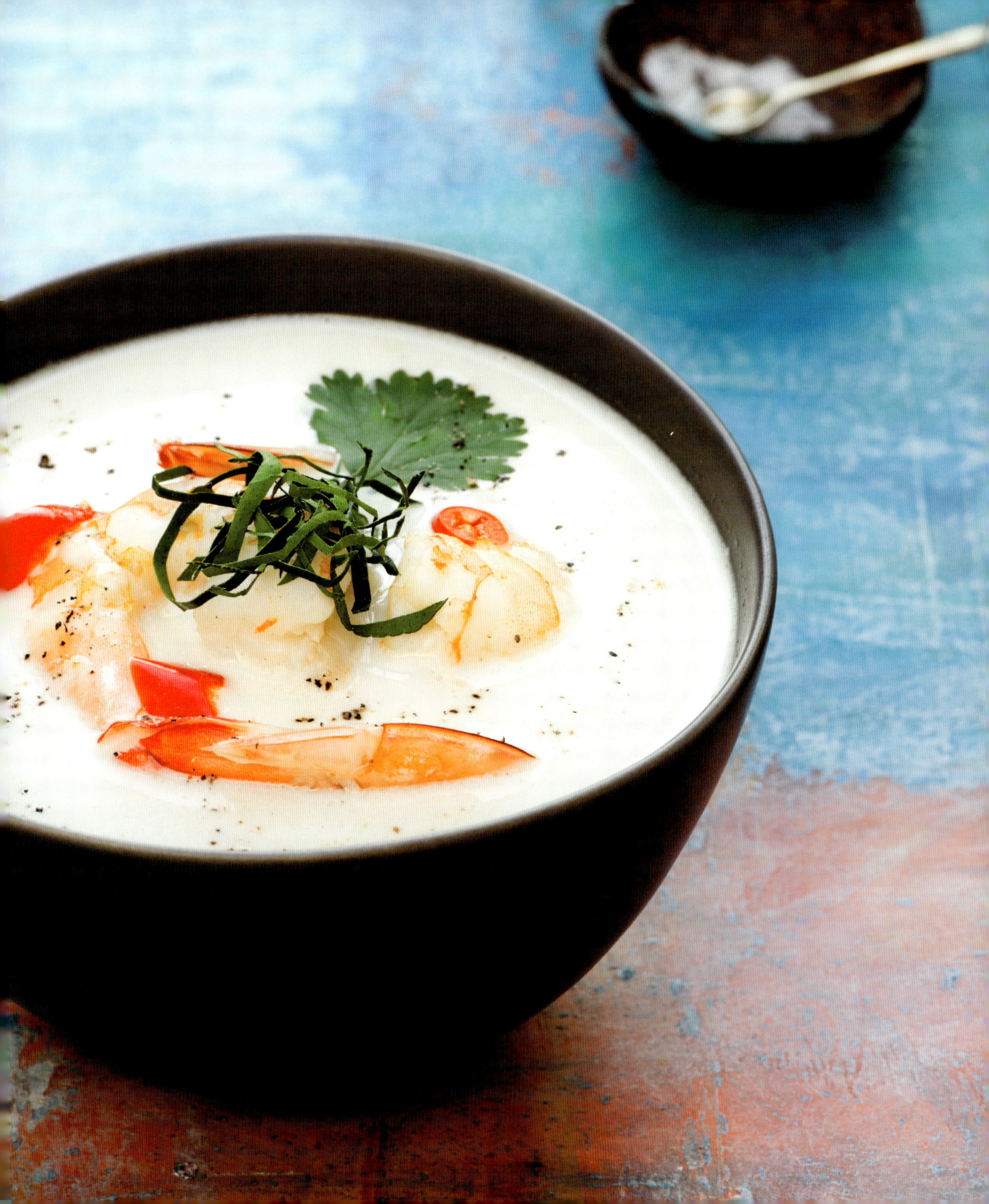

Annie's Zucchini Slice

This is Paul's mum's dish and a favourite family recipe. No doubt there are similar recipes out there, but I've always loved mum's. Even to this day when we have a roast chook for Sunday lunch, the zucchini slice comes out and I still find it hard to have just one piece.

Ingredients
- 1 large onion, ½ grated (shredded), ½ diced
- 375 g/13 oz zucchini (courgette), grated (shredded)
- 115 g/4 oz self-raising (self-rising) flour, sifted
- 1 cup tasty cheese, grated (shredded)
- 5 eggs, beaten
- salt and pepper, to taste
- 25 g/¾ oz Parmesan cheese, grated (shredded), to sprinkle

Method
1. Preheat the oven to 180°C/350°C/Gas mark 4. Grease and line the base of a 16 x 26 cm/6½ x 10 in slice tin (pan).
2. In a pre-heated frying pan set over a medium heat, heat the olive fry the grated onion until it softens.
3. In a large bowl, tip the zucchini, grated onion, sifted flour, oil, cheese and beaten eggs. Season with salt and pepper, then sprinkle Parmesan cheese onto the mix. Stir to combine thoroughly. Pour the mixture into the prepared tin and bake for 30–40 minutes, or until cooked through.
4. To serve, cut the zucchini slice to the desired size.

Tips
You could bake the mixture in muffin trays. Simply decrease the cooking time. Large muffins take about 20 minutes. This slice is great for kids, big and small to take for a packed lunch.

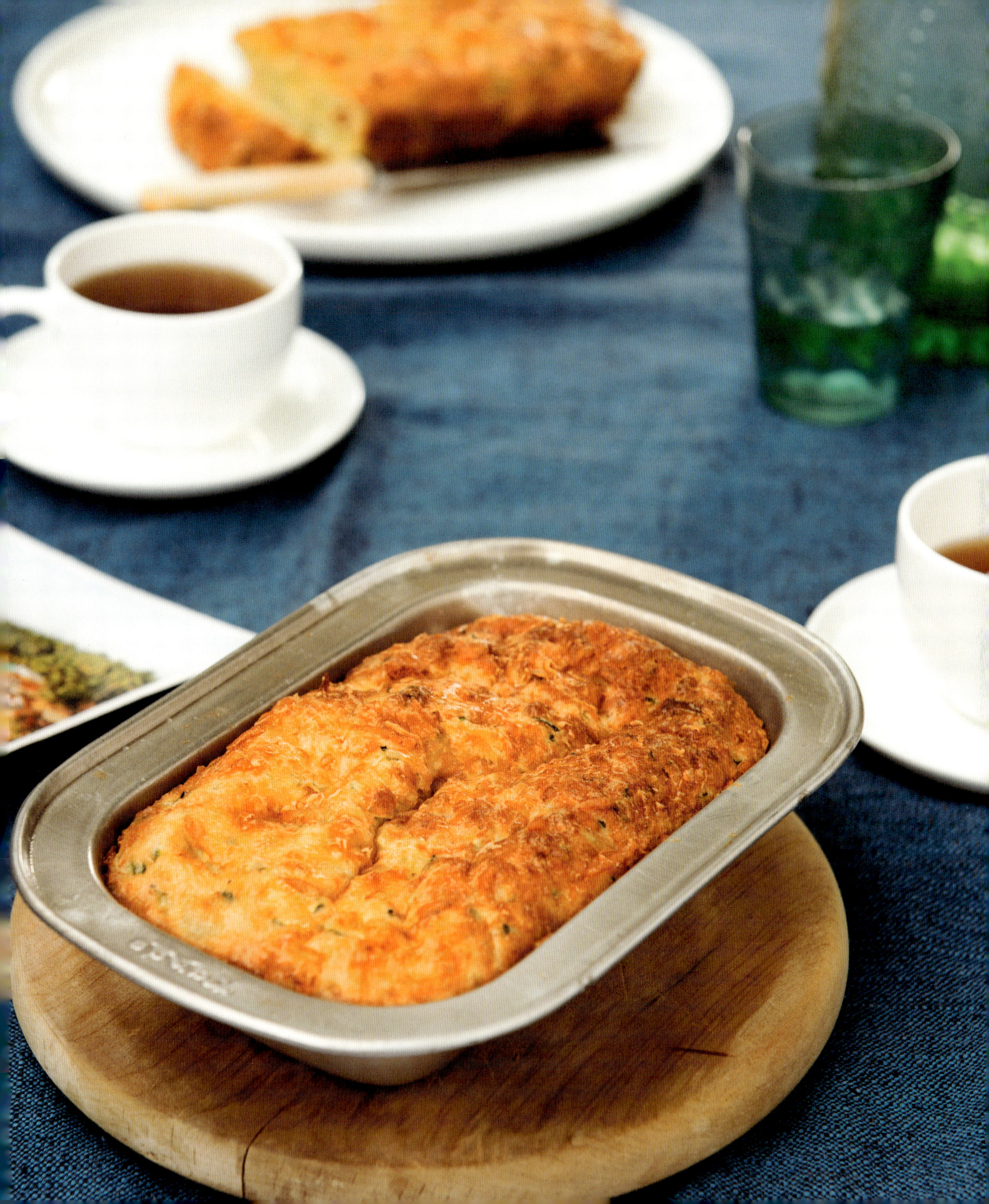

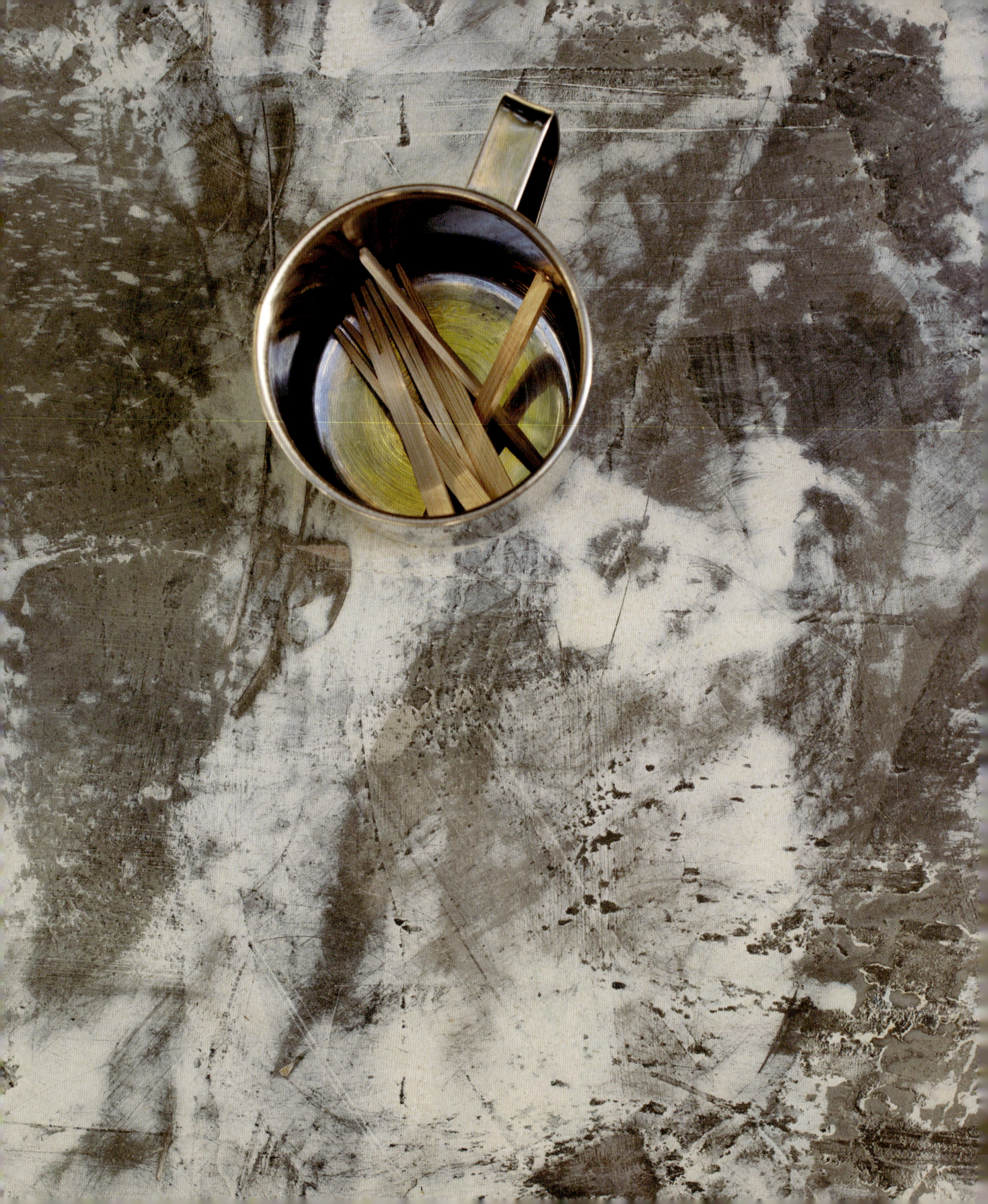

Pork Belly with Caramelised Apple

As soon as you mention pork belly people picture crackling in their mind's eye and their mouths start to water. This easy dish will certainly have them doing that and more. The pairing of pork and apple is a classic one. This dish can easily be served as a starter or a main.

Ingredients

- 2 tablespoons salt
- 1 teaspoon ground cumin
- 1 teaspoon ground star anise
- 1 teaspoon ground fennel
- 1.5 kg/3 lb 5 oz boned pork belly
- 12 shallots, peeled
- 12 garlic cloves
- 6 Granny Smith apples
- 20 g/²⁄₃ oz butter
- 80 g/2½ oz brown sugar
- 1 cinnamon quill
- 4 cloves
- 60 ml/2 fl oz cider vinegar
- 80 g/2½ oz sultanas (golden raisins)
- lemon wedges, to serve

Method

1. Preheat the oven to 180°C/350°F/Gas mark 4.
2. Mix the salt and ground spices together and rub the mixture into the pork. Arrange the pork, skin side down, in a heavy roasting pan. Roast for approximately 1½ hours, then turn the pork skin-side up and add the shallots and garlic. Increase the oven temperature to 220°C/420°F/Gas mark 7. Roast for another 30 minutes, or until the skin is crisp. Set aside to rest in a warm place.
3. Peel and core the whole apples, and slice off the top and base. Melt the butter in a frying pan over medium heat. Add the brown sugar and fry the apples until light and golden. Add the cinnamon and cloves. Cook until the sugar melts. Add the vinegar and sultanas and cook for 5 minutes.
4. Thickly slice the pork and serve with the apples, shallots, garlic and lemon cheeks.

Beef Rendang and Spicy Eggplant

Beef rendang is a dish we fell in love with many times over in Bali. There are many regional versions of this dish across Asia. This version, unlike others, is not a dry curry, but rather has a beautiful sauce that can be mopped up with some turmeric rice. If you like the dry version simply reduce the sauce during the cooking process. The blend of aromatics in this dish means you can also reduce the level of chilli heat without affecting the taste. Having said that we love this one hot! Up to you.

Ingredients

3 tablespoons olive oil

1 kg/2¼ lb chuck steak, cut into 4 cm/1¾ in pieces

500 ml/16 fl oz coconut milk

1 lemongrass, white stalk only, bruised

1 cinnamon quill

2 kaffir lime leaves, shredded, plus extra to serve

100 g/3½ oz desiccated (dry, unsweetened, shredded) coconut

Paste

2 medium brown onions, peeled and roughly chopped

2 garlic cloves, peeled and chopped

1 tablespoon ground coriander

Method

1. Place all the paste ingredients in a food processor and blend to a smooth paste.
2. Heat 2 tablespoons of the oil in frying pan set over medium heat and fry the paste until fragrant. Add the chuck steak and cook on a medium heat for 2–3 minutes, turning the meat until it is sealed on all sides. Add the coconut milk, bruised lemongrass, cinnamon and kaffir lime leaves and reduce the heat to a simmer. Cook, uncovered, for 90 minutes, stirring occasionally, until reduced and the beef is tender.
3. Toast the desiccated coconut in a dry frying pan until golden brown. Pulse in a food processor or spice grinder until grainy in texture and add to the rendang.

1 tablespoon ground cumin
¾ tablespoon ground fennel
3 large red chillies, seeded and chopped
2 lemongrass, white stalks only, sliced finely
3 cm/1¼ in ginger root, sliced finely
1 tablespoon tamarind paste
1½ tablespoons palm sugar
1 teaspoon salt
2 kaffir lime leaves
1 tablespoon water

Spicy Eggplant
1 large eggplant (aubergine), cut into 2 cm/¾ in cubes
1 tablespoon tamarind purée
2 tablespoons kecap manis (sweet soy sauce)
3 tablespoons water
juice of 1 lemon
½ teaspoon dried chilli flakes
½ teaspoon salt
1 tomato, chopped
2 kaffir lime leaves, stems removed, rolled and thinly sliced
3 shallots, sliced

4. Meanwhile, to make the spicy eggplant, place all the ingredients, except for the shallots, into a medium bowl and mix well. Cover and marinate for at least 10 minutes.
5. Heat the remaining tablespoon of oil in a frying pan over a medium heat. Add the shallots and fry until golden brown. Add the eggplant mixture and cook, stirring occasionally, for 8 minutes, or until the eggplant softens.
6. Serve the rendang with spicy eggplant and a side serving of your choice of rice. Garnish with shredded kaffir lime leaves.

Poached Chicken with a Cranberry and Pistachio Quinoa Salad

Quinoa has certainly become the fashionable food for those wanting a healthy meal, so we figured we had better get on board. This dish combines quinoa with the healthy method of poaching to give you a dish that is both good for you and very tasty. Poaching a chicken breast is very versatile and the method makes it very hard to end up with dry chicken.

Ingredients

1 litre/1¾ pints chicken stock
1 teaspoon whole peppercorns
1 lemon, sliced
1 large chilli, sliced
4 sprigs lemon thyme
2 chicken breasts

Quinoa Salad
175 g/6 oz quinoa
80 g/2½ oz pistachio nuts, shelled
100 g/3½ oz dried cranberries
3 tablespoons flat-leaf parsley, chopped
3 tablespoons coriander (cilantro) leaves, chopped

Dressing
3 tablespoons orange juice
3 tablespoons lemon juice
1 teaspoon Dijon mustard
½ teaspoon sweet paprika
salt and pepper, to taste

Method

1. Place the stock, peppercorns, sliced lemon, chilli and lemon thyme in a deep frying pan and bring to the boil. Add the chicken and cook for 3 minutes. Remove the pan from the heat and cover with a lid. Leave it to stand for about 10 minutes. Larger chicken breasts make take a few more minutes to cook through. When cooked, the chicken remove from the pan and reserve the cooking liquid.
2. Rinse the quinoa thoroughly, then soak it for 15 minutes in a bowl of water. Drain and tip the quinoa into a pan with enough water to cover the quinoa. Bring to the boil, then cover and simmer for about 15 minutes, or until the water is absorbed. Remove from the heat and let stand for 5 minutes.
3. Placed the cooled quinoa, nuts, cranberries, parsley and coriander in a large bowl and stir to combine.
4. Mix together all the dressing ingredients and whisk lightly to combine in a bowl.
5. Slice the chicken and add to the salad. To serve add the dressing to the salad and season with salt and pepper.

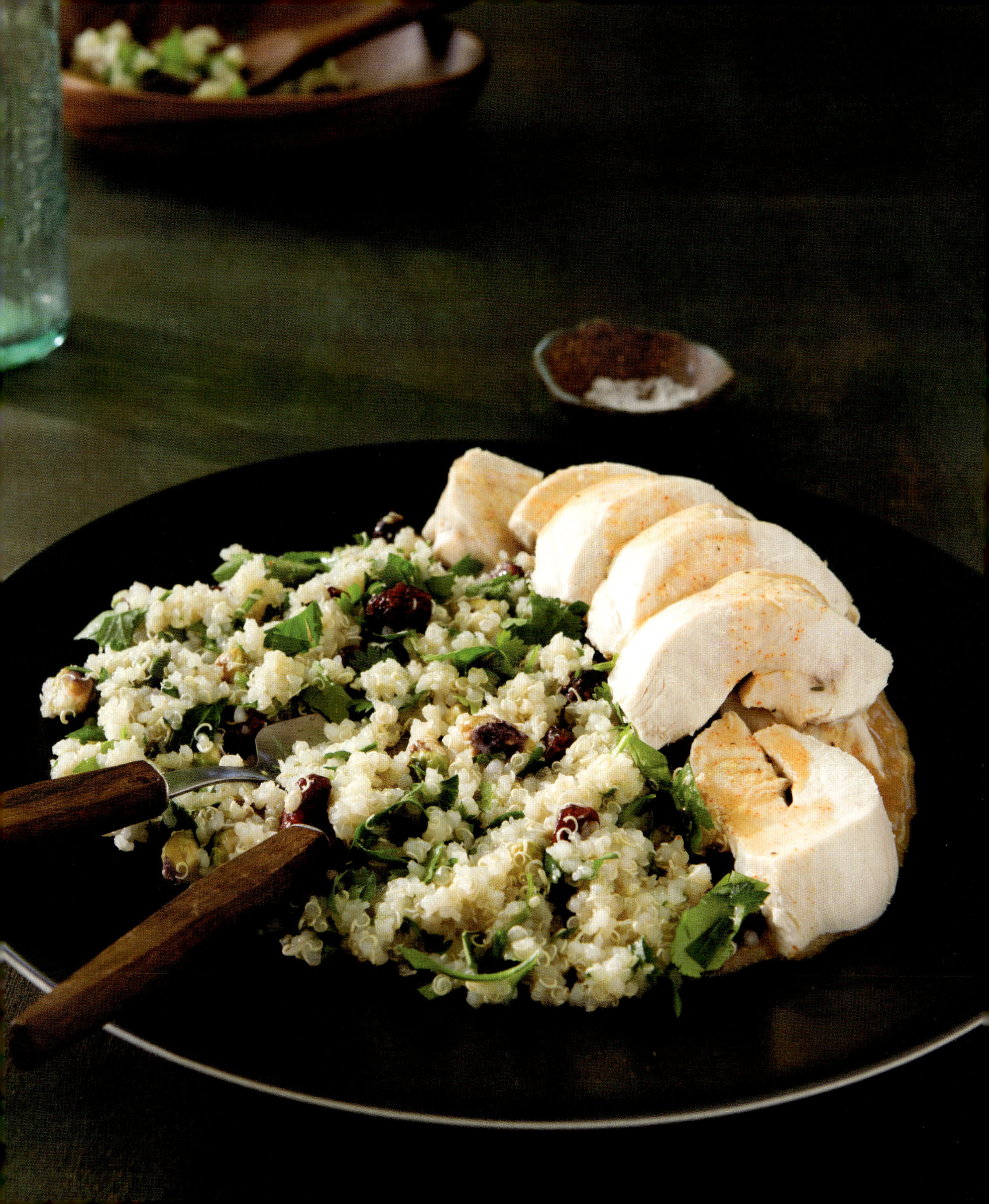

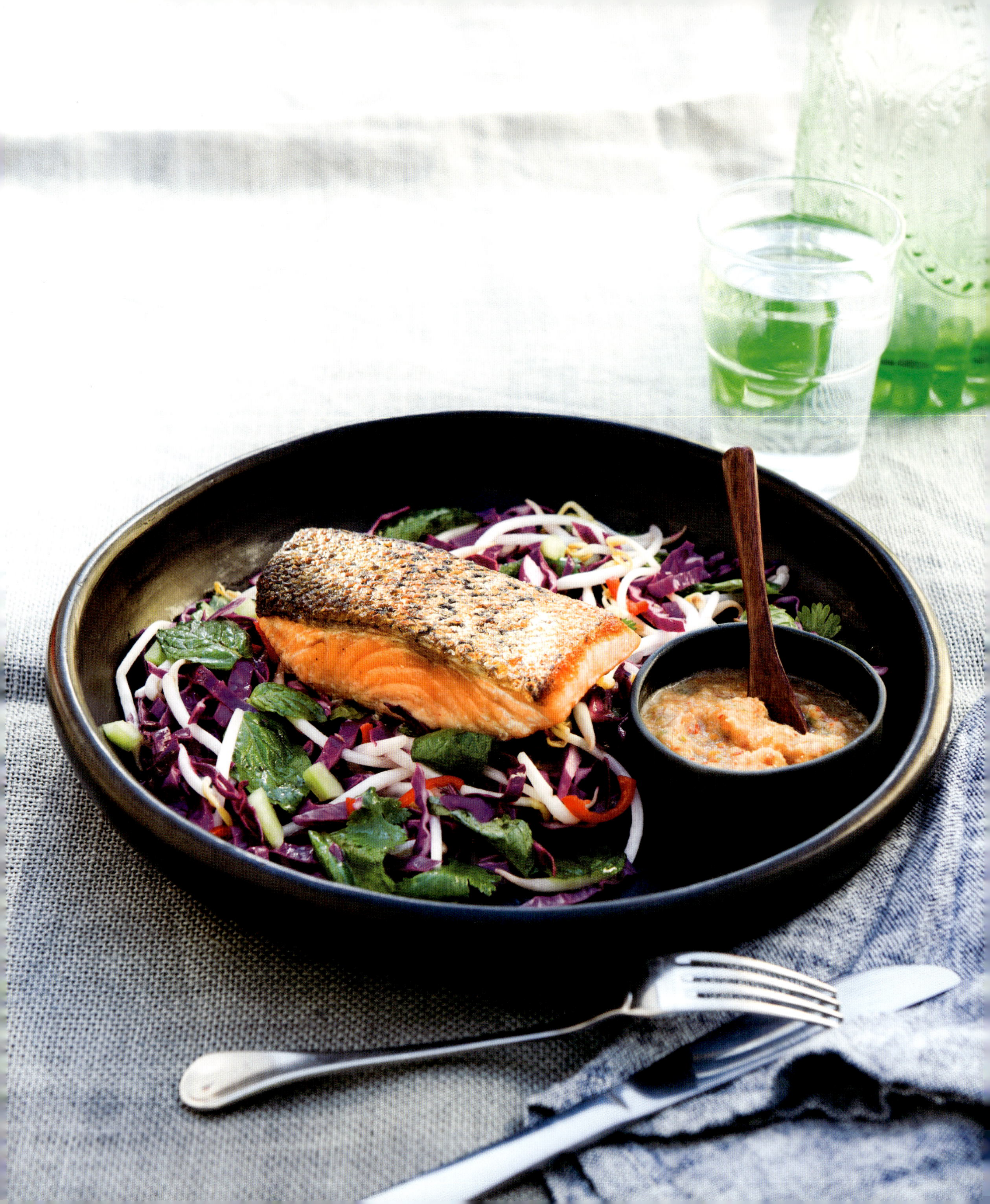

Crispy Skin Salmon with Asian Salad and Tomato Nahm Jim

We just love fresh salmon fillets. They are healthy, tasty and very simple to cook. They can be a bit expensive sometimes but make a great treat. We've given this recipe an Asian touch with the herbaceous salad and the wonderful spicy Nahm Jim sauce. This goes equally well on the BBQ and is sure to wow any guests lucky enough to come over.

Ingredients

4 salmon fillets, skin on
salt and pepper
2 tablespoons olive oil

Salad

½ cup mint leaves, loosely packed
½ cup fresh coriander (cilantro) leaves, loosely packed
1 cup red cabbage, thinly sliced
1 cup bean sprouts
1 fresh long red chilli, sliced thinly
1 cucumber, peeled, seeded and cubed

Dressing

75 ml/2½ fl oz lime juice
1 tablespoon fish sauce
2 tablespoons peanut oil
2 tablespoons palm sugar

Tomato Nahm Jim

2 garlic cloves
2 coriander (cilantro) roots, washed and coarsely chopped
1 long green and 1 long red chilli, seeded and coarsely chopped
1 bird's eye chilli, seeded and coarsely chopped (optional)
6 ripe cherry tomatoes
2 small red shallots, sliced thinly
2 tablespoons palm sugar
2 tablespoons fish sauce
60 ml/2 fl oz lime juice

Method

1. Remove any bones from the fish, then sprinkle the skin liberally with salt and pepper and refrigerate until ready to cook.
2. Mix the salad ingredients in a bowl. Whisk together the salad dressing ingredients in a separate bowl and pour over the salad. Toss gently to combine.
3. Combine the Tomato Nahm Jim ingredients in a food processor and process until blended.
4. Remove the fish from the refrigerator and pat the skin dry with paper towel. Heat the olive oil in a frying pan set over a medium heat. When hot, fry the fish, skin side down, for about 3 minutes, or until the skin is crispy.
5. Turn the fish over and cook for another 2 minutes, or as desired.
6. Serve the fish with Nahm Jim and dressed salad.

Caramel Pork

People often baulk at slow cooker recipes but they are actually very simple. This one has an Asian base that gives the dish a wonderful quality and the pork will just melt in your mouth. We often set a slow cooker up before work and when we arrive home, not only is dinner done, the house smells amazing too. This sort of meal is great for a busy family and there's likely to be leftovers for lunch.

Ingredients

- 1.8 kg/4 lb pork shoulder
- 3 tablespoons oil
- 2 spring onions (scallions), sliced
- 3 cm/1¼ in fresh root ginger, cut into matchsticks
- 2 garlic cloves, sliced
- 2 tablespoons sweet chilli sauce
- 175 ml/6 fl oz chicken stock
- 2 tablespoons lime juice
- 1 tablespoon fish sauce
- 60 ml/2 fl oz kecap manis (sweet soy sauce)
- 2 kaffir lime leaves, shredded

Method

1. Transfer the pork to the bowl of the slow cooker.
2. Heat the oil in a frying pan. Add the spring onions, ginger and garlic. Cook, stirring, for 3 minutes, or until softened. Transfer to the slow cooker.
3. Add the sweet chilli sauce, stock, lime juice, fish sauce, kecap manis and lime leaves. Stir to combine. Cover with a lid. Cook on low heat for 6 hours, or until the pork is very tender.
4. Remove the pork from the sauce and discard the fat. Roughly pull apart into large pieces. Serve with rice and your choice of steamed Asian greens. Drizzle with sauce.

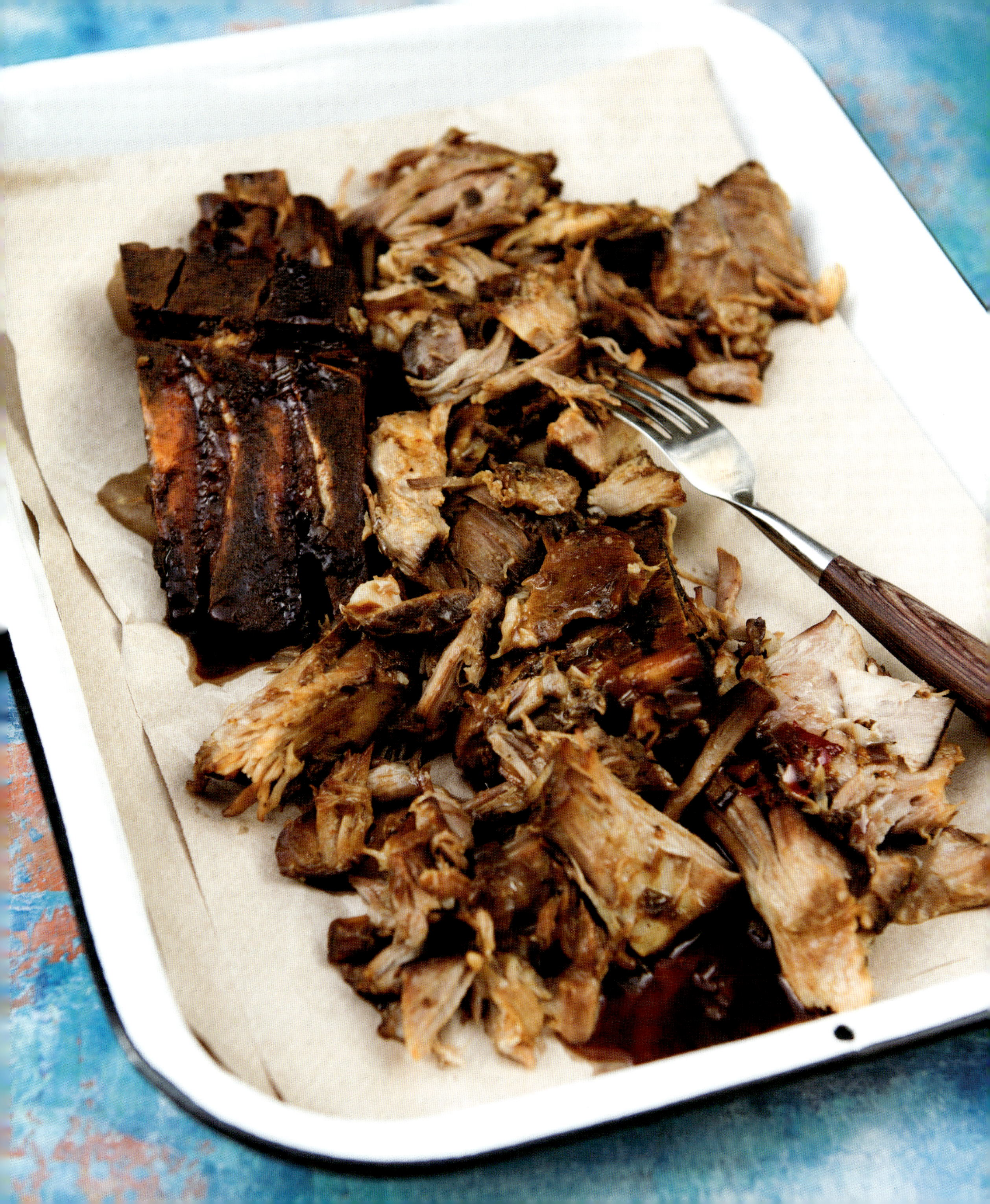

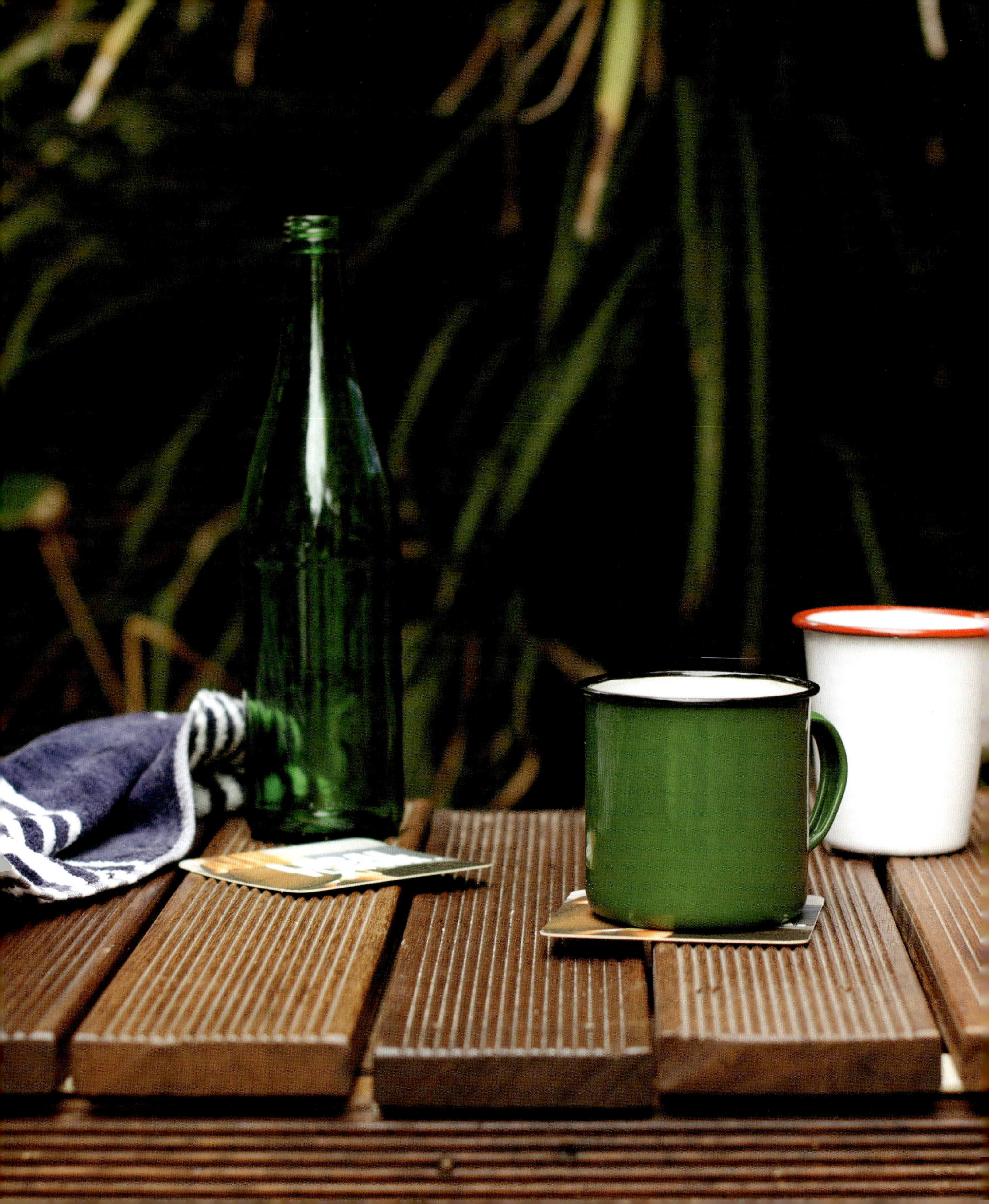

Fettuccine Marinara with Creamy White Wine and Tarragon Sauce

Creamy pasta is not something you will find at our tables often, so when you do you can bet it's worth the effort. Making your own pasta is a must and really isn't that hard.

The beautiful seafood and aniseed flavour in this dish are a marriage made in heaven. We have used Pernod but it can be left out if you prefer. This would make a great entrée but you can easily increase the portion size and serve a delicious seafood main.

Ingredients

1 tablespoon olive oil
4 large shrimp (prawns), shelled and deveined
8 scallops
flat-leaf parsley, chopped, to garnish
1 large red chilli, thinly sliced, to garnish

Pasta
400 g/14 oz '00' flour, plus extra for dusting
4 eggs
1 tablespoon oil

Creamy Sauce
2 tablespoons olive oil, plus extra for drizzling
3 garlic cloves, minced
1 medium onion, diced
4 thyme sprigs
175 ml/6 fl oz white wine
75 ml/2½ fl oz Pernod
8 mussels
180 ml/6 fl oz single (light) cream
1 tablespoon tarragon, chopped
3 bird's eye chillies
salt and pepper, to taste

Method

1. For the pasta, tip the ingredients into a food processor bowl and blend until a breadcrumb texture forms. Empty onto a lightly floured bench and bring together by kneading. Cut the mix into 6 equal portions. Roll one portion flat with a rolling pin. Roll through a pasta machine until the desired thickness is reached. Transfer through a fettuccine attachment and place on baking paper. Repeat for all pasta portions.
2. For the sauce, heat 2 tablespoons of oil in a frying pan over a medium heat. Add the garlic and onion and sauté until the onion is lightly browned. Add the thyme, wine and Pernod and bring to the boil. Reduce the heat to a simmer, add the 8 mussels and cover with a lid. When the mussels open remove from the pan and set aside to rest. Add the cream, tarragon and chillies. Cook until reduced by a quarter.
3. Meanwhile heat a frying pan over medium heat. Oil and season the shrimp and scallops in a bowl. Place both in the pan and cook through, turning once. Remove and set aside to rest. Turn the heat up to high. Place the scallops in pan and cook until slightly caramelised on both sides. Remove and rest. Before serving add the mussels, prawns and scallops to the sauce.
4. Bring a large pan of salted water to the boil. Add the pasta, bring back to the boil and cook until *al dente*. Pour into a colander and drizzle with oil.
5. To serve, place pasta in a bowl. Decorate the pasta with the seafood and pour a generous amount of sauce over both. Garnish with parsley and chilli.

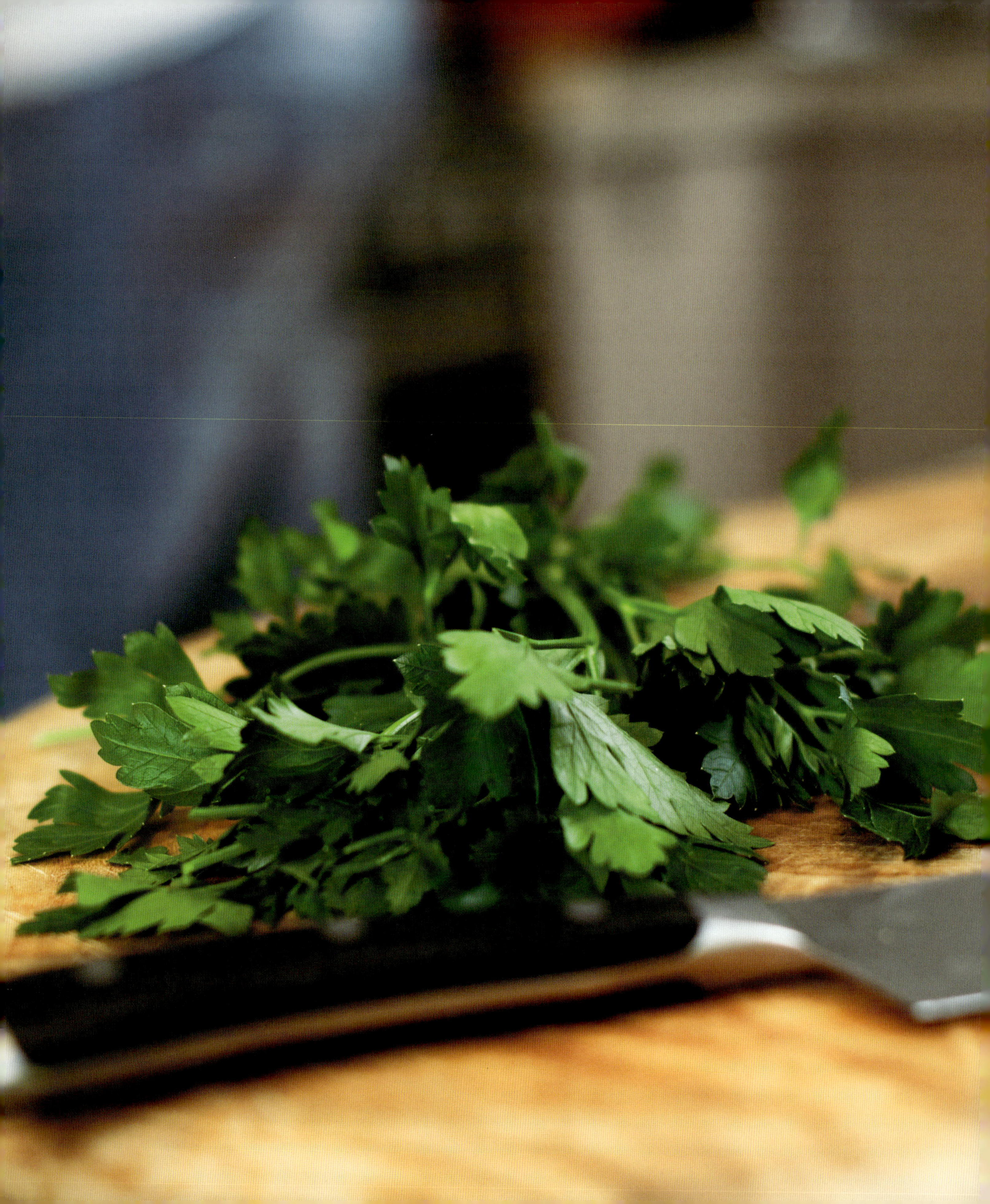

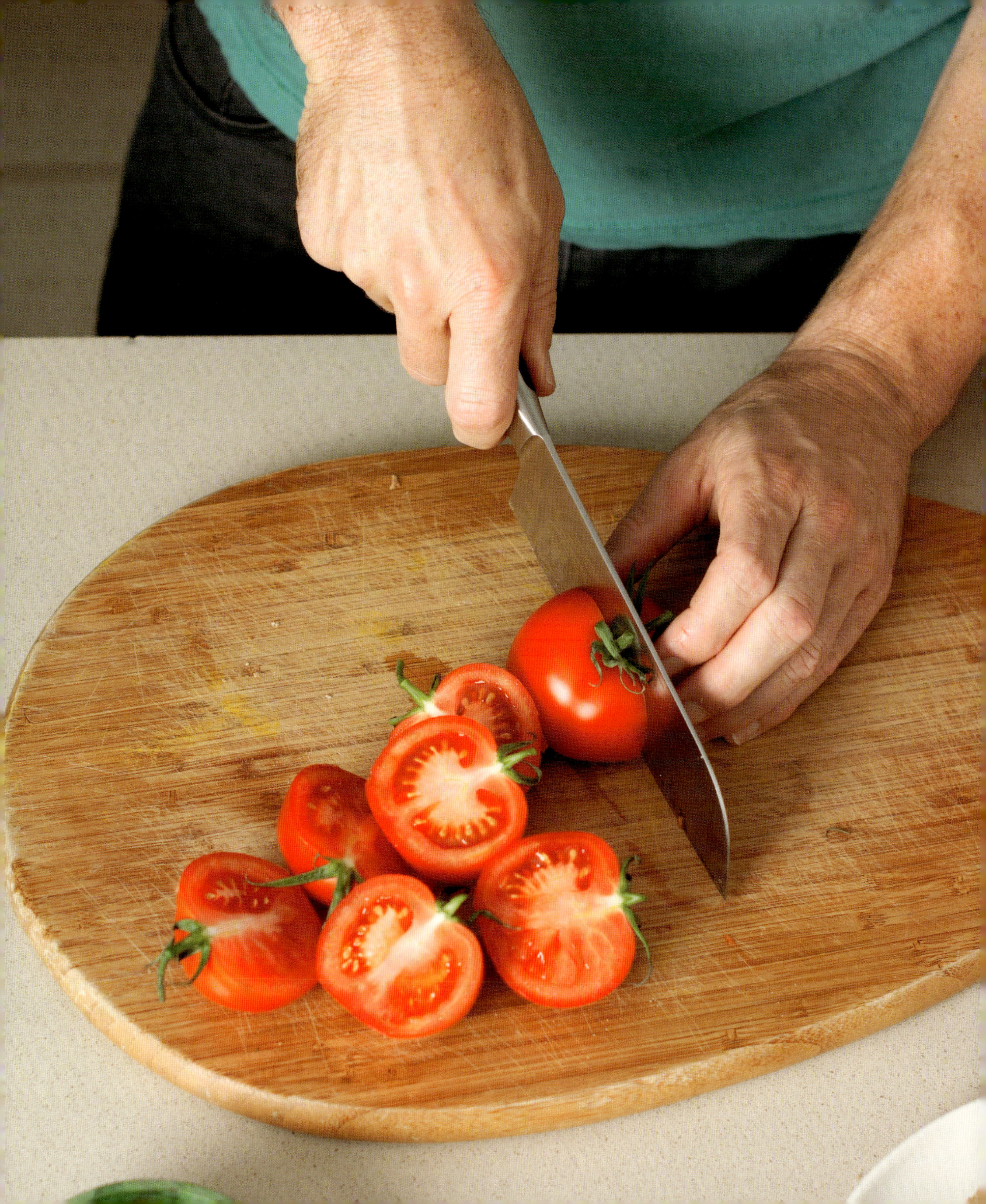

8-Hour Slow-cooked Beef Brisket

Slow-cooked meat sounds like hard work, but it's actually the opposite. The smoky taste and melt-in-your-mouth texture of this meat makes it hard to stop eating. This is the sort of dish you prepare when you know there is a group of people coming over for dinner and you want to impress. The leftovers make for amazing sliders too.

Ingredients

1 kg/2¼ lb beef brisket
1 tablespoon oil
salt and pepper, to taste
225 g/8 oz tomato purée
115 g/4 fl oz apple cider vinegar
500 ml/16 fl oz red wine
250 ml/8 fl oz beef stock
60 g/2 oz brown sugar
1 tablespoon Worcestershire sauce
1 tablespoon chilli powder
3 tablespoons smoky paprika
2 garlic cloves
1 large onion, chopped
1 cinnamon quill
2 star anise
cornflour (corn starch), to thicken
sugar (optional)

Method

1. Season the brisket with salt and pepper. Heat a large frying pan over a high heat, add the oil and when hot seal all sides of the brisket in the hot pan.
2. Add all the other ingredients to a large slow cooker and stir to combine. Add the sealed brisket and roll in the liquid to cover.
3. Cook on low heat for about 8 hours, turning the meat regularly. It should fall apart when ready.
4. After about 7 hours, remove about ¾ of the liquid and simmer it in a small pan until reduced by half. You may like to add some dissolved cornflour to thicken the sauce, add it 1 teaspoon at a time, and you can adjust the sweetness with sugar to taste, adding 1 teaspoon at a time.
5. Use a fork to break up the meat into small portions to serve. Serve the meat with the reduced sauce, roasted potatoes and steamed vegetables.

Seared Tuna with a Roasted Capsicum Salad

It wasn't that long ago that we would have never considered eating partly cooked tuna. That was until we tasted it! In this recipe we've coupled the fish with a spice rub that complements the tuna and the oven-roasted capsicum. Sashimi-grade tuna can be expensive, but as a treat it is money well spent.

Ingredients

450 g/1 lb fresh sashimi-grade tuna, cut into slices
300 g/10½ oz spinach
1½ tablespoons lemon juice

Capsicum Salad

1 red capsicum (bell pepper)
1 yellow capsicum (bell pepper)
1 tablespoon capers
12 pitted Kalamata olives, diced
1 tablespoon flat-leaf parsley, chopped
1 tablespoon red onion, finely chopped
150 ml/5 fl oz extra virgin olive oil
salt, to taste
fresh ground black pepper, to taste
½ teaspoon fennel seeds
1 tablespoon ground black pepper
1 teaspoon chilli flakes, crushed

Method

1. Preheat the oven to 200°C/400°F/Gas mark 6. Place the capsicums on a baking tray and roast in the oven, turning regularly, until the skins blister and then peel. When cool enough to handle, finely dice the capsicums into a bowl and mix with the capers, olives, parsley and red onion. Stir in half of the olive oil and season with the salt and pepper.
2. Dry-roast the fennel seeds in a pan over gentle heat until fragrant. Remove from the heat, leave to cool and then grind to a fine powder. Mix the ground fennel, ground black pepper and crushed chilli flakes, then sprinkle the mixture over the tuna to coat it lightly.
3. Wash the spinach and blanch in a pan set over moderate heat with just the water clinging to the leaves. Plunge the spinach into iced water to stop the cooking process, and then squeeze out the excess water.
4. Heat a frying pan over high heat, then add the remaining oil and sear the tuna briefly on both sides. The cooking should be fast with the fish remaining raw and glassy in the centre. Remove the tuna from the pan and rest briefly.
5. Toss the cooked spinach in the same pan until warmed through, and then add the lemon juice and season with a little salt and pepper.
6. Place the warmed spinach in the centre of each serving platter. Finely slice the tuna and pile it on top, then spoon the capsicum salad around the fish and serve immediately.

Green Chicken Korma

This dish is one of our most enjoyable Indian dishes. The beautiful fresh herbs impart a vibrant green tint. This is not meant to be a hot dish and the heat can be toned down for the kids, but you can also add more chilli if you like it hot. This meal is best served with your choice of rice or naan bread.

Ingredients

- 60 g/2 oz natural cashew nuts
- 6 tablespoons oil
- 4 medium onions, chopped
- 1½ cups coriander (cilantro) leaves, loosely packed
- ½ cup mint leaves, loosely packed
- 4 green chillies
- 2 bay leaves
- 6 green cardamom pods
- ½ cinnamon quill
- 3 cm/1¼ in ginger, peeled and chopped
- 4 garlic cloves, chopped
- 1 kg/2¼ lb chicken thighs
- 1 teaspoon ground coriander
- ½ teaspoon ground cumin
- salt, to taste
- 1 teaspoon sugar
- 2 teaspoons lime or lemon juice
- 60 ml/2 fl oz single (light) cream
- 1 tablespoon butter
- ¼ teaspoon mace powder

Method

1. Soak the cashews nuts in 200 ml/7 fl oz of water in a bowl, for at least 15 minutes.
2. Add 4 tablespoons of the oil to a frying pan and fry the onions over a medium heat until they are crispy brown, but not burnt at the edges, 20–30 minutes.
3. When the onions are cooked, tip them into a blender with the coriander, mint, green chillies, soaked and drained cashew nuts and 50 ml/1¾ fl oz water and purée.
4. In the same pan, heat the remaining oil over a low heat and add the bay leaves, cardamom pods, cinnamon, ginger and garlic. Increase the heat to medium, add the chicken pieces and sauté in the aromatic oil for about 5 minutes, or until the chicken is seared. Add the ground coriander and cumin. Sauté the chicken for 2 minutes, stirring so that the chicken doesn't stick to the pan. Add the cashew nut purée and sauté the chicken for another 2 minutes.
5. Add the salt, sugar, lime juice and 200 ml/7 fl oz water. Taste and adjust the seasoning. Now bring to the boil and simmer until the chicken is cooked, then add the cream and stir well.
6. Just before serving, heat a little butter in a ladle and put ¼ teaspoon of mace powder into the ladle. After 10 seconds put it into the pot and mix well.
7. Serve with your choice of rice or naan bread.

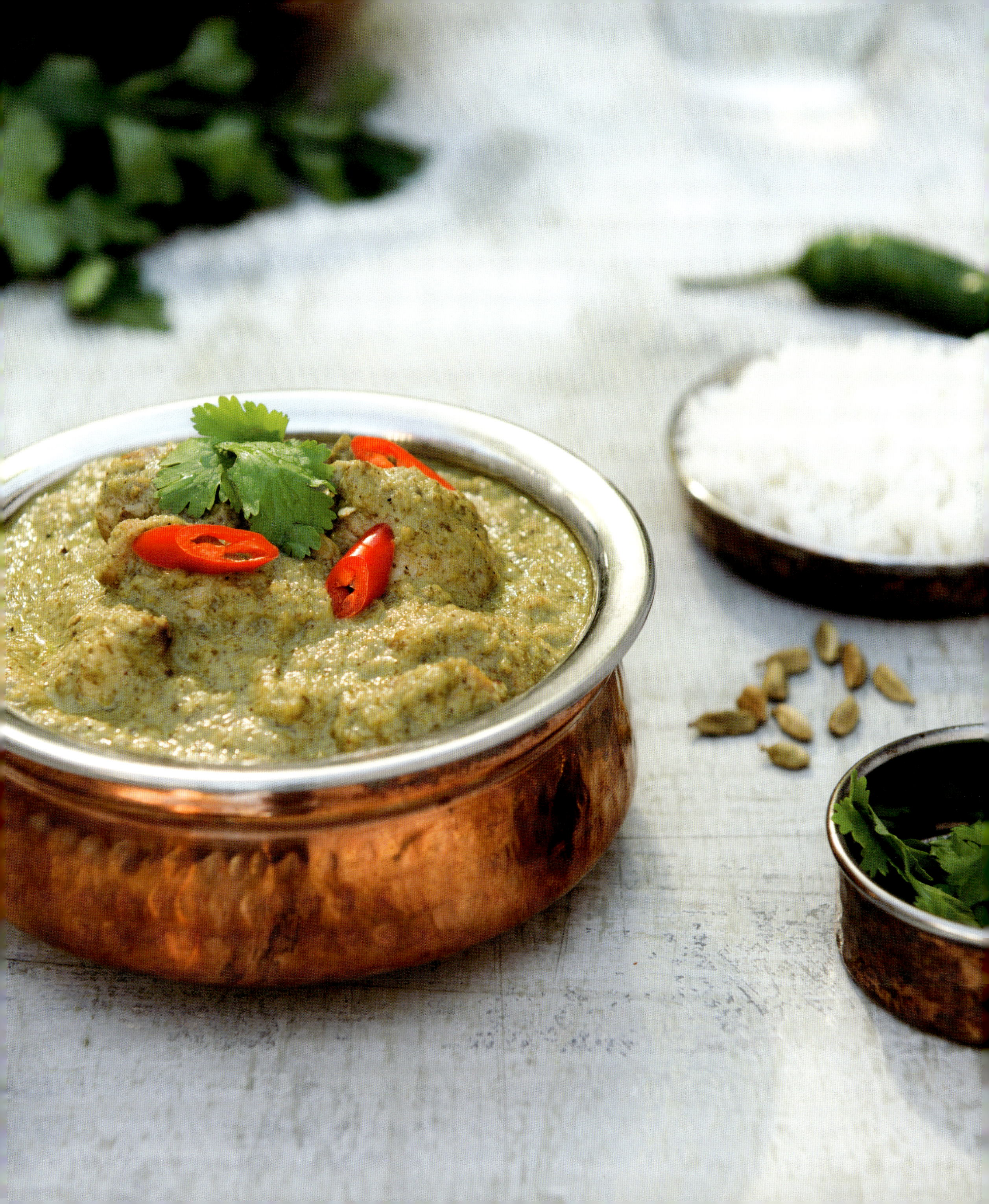

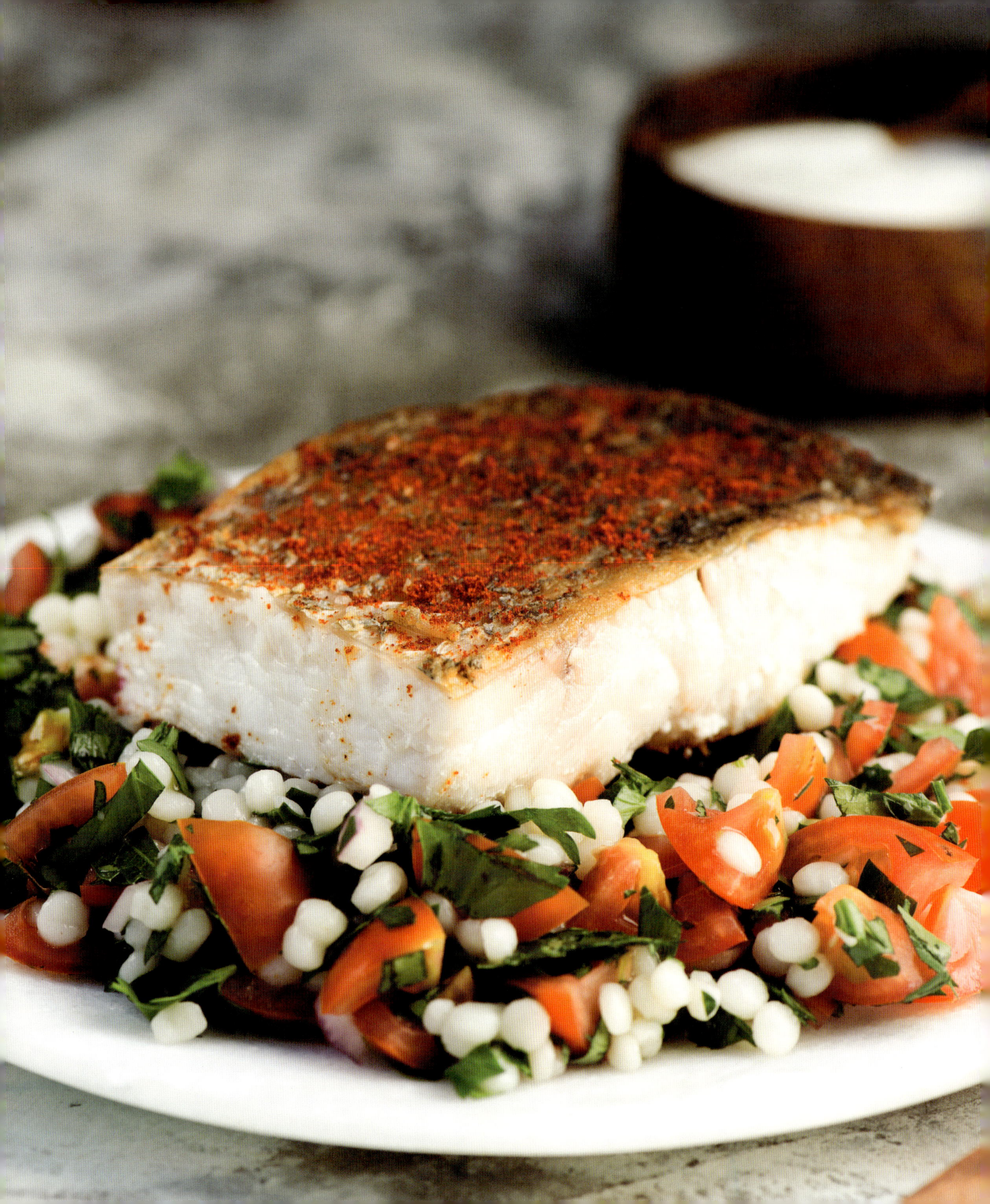

Middle Eastern Fish Fillets, Tabbouleh and Yogurt Sauce

This recipe works well for a number of fish types. You can use salmon, ocean trout, barramundi or snapper. You can also decide if you want the skin on or off. Versatile, tasty and healthy. What's not to like?

Ingredients

4 fish fillets, of your choice
2 teaspoons sumac
3 tablespoons olive oil
coriander (cilantro) leaves, to garnish

Tabbouleh

375 ml/12 fl oz water
85 g/3 oz pearl couscous
1 medium ripe tomato, chopped
2 spring onions (scallions), finely chopped
1 cup flat-leaf parsley, chopped
¼ cup mint leaves, chopped
1 tablespoon lemon juice

Yogurt Sauce

125 ml/4 fl oz Greek natural (plain) yogurt
1 tablespoon tahini
2 teaspoons lemon juice
1 garlic clove, crushed
salt, to taste

Method

1. Place the fish fillets, skin side up, on a lined baking tray. Liberally apply salt and pepper to the skin and refrigerate until ready to cook.
2. For the tabbouleh, bring the water to boil in a small pan. Add the couscous and cook for about 15 minutes, or until *al dente*.
3. Add the couscous to a large bowl and combine with the tomato, onions, parsley, mint and lemon juice. Mix to combine and add salt to taste.
4. For the yogurt sauce, whisk all the ingredients together in a bowl and season to taste.
5. Remove the fish from the refrigerator and pat the skin dry with paper towel. Sprinkle the skin with sumac.
6. Heat the oil in a frying pan over a medium flame. Place the fillets skin side down and cook for about 4 minutes, or until the skin is crispy. Turn the fish over and cook until the fillet is cooked through. The time will depend on the thickness of the fillet and how you like your fish cooked.
7. To serve, place the fish on top of some tabbouleh and add the yogurt dressing.

Kare Ayam (Balinese Chicken Curry)

If there is one meal we were inspired to cook from our trips to Bali, it's this one. There is just something about the smell, the look and the taste of this dish—there is nothing quite like it. The use of fresh galangal and turmeric make this dish what it is. Beautiful! We were so inspired by this curry we planted all the essentials in our gardens. However, you can access them now in most major grocery stores. It is lovely going to pick them fresh from your garden though. Serve with steamed rice and fried shallots.

Ingredients

5 tablespoons oil, for frying
6 kaffir lime leaves
1 stalk lemongrass
750 g/1 ½ lb chicken thighs, cut into large pieces
250 ml/8 fl oz water
400 ml/14 fl oz can coconut milk
salt, to taste
fried shallots, to garnish

Spice Mix
2 bird's eye chillies
4 large red chillies
2 red shallots, chopped
5 garlic cloves, chopped
1 tablespoon ginger, chopped
2 tablespoons galangal, chopped
1 tablespoon fresh turmeric, chopped
2 teaspoons tamarind purée
½ teaspoon shrimp paste
5 candle or macadamia nuts
2 teaspoons ground coriander
¼ teaspoon ground cumin
¼ teaspoon ground nutmeg
2 teaspoons palm sugar, grated
2 tablespoons oil

Sambal
2 tablespoons coconut oil
½ teaspoon shrimp paste, roasted
2 shallots, chopped
3 tablespoons chopped garlic
1 tablespoon bird's eye chillies
juice of 1 lime

Method

1. To make the spice mix, deseed the chillies. Place all the spice mix ingredients into the bowl of a food processor and pulse until well combined.
2. Heat the oil in a large wok and fry the spice mix over a medium heat until fragrant. Add 4 lime leaves and lemongrass and fry until coated with spices.
3. Add the chicken and fry for at least 3 minutes, or until the meat has changed colour. Add the water and simmer, uncovered, until the meat is tender. Be careful to not overcook the chicken or it will be dry.
4. Add sufficient coconut milk until the mixture is the level of 'soupiness' you desire.
5. For the sambal, heat the coconut oil in a small pan over a medium flame. Add the shrimp paste and a pinch of salt and fry for 30 seconds, stirring continuously. Add the shallots and garlic and cook until golden brown. Add the chillies and cook for another 2 minutes.
6. Tip the sambal into a small bowl and mix in the lime juice.
7. Serve with steamed rice and garnish with fried shallots and the remaining 2 lime leaves, shredded. Add sambal to taste.

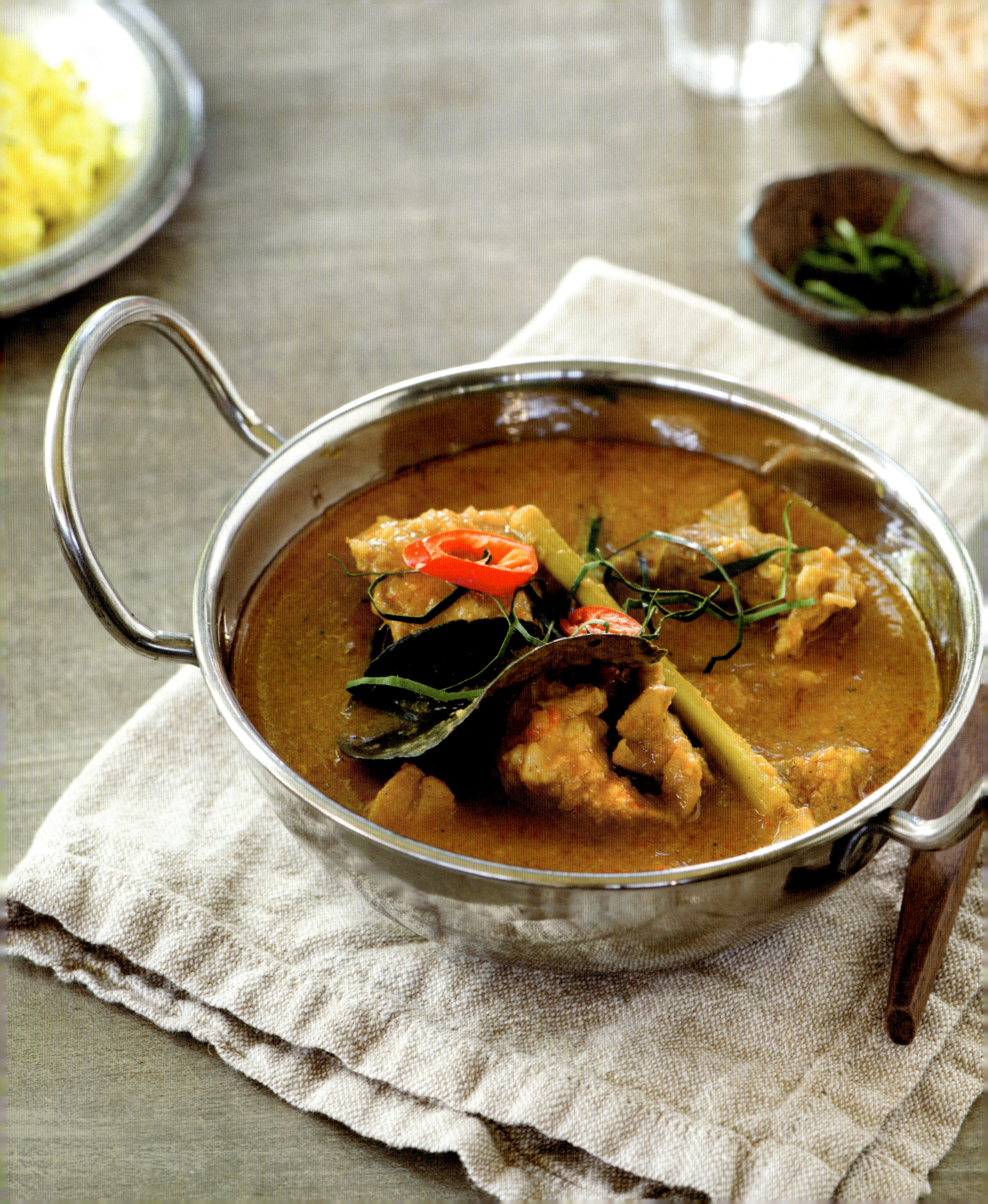

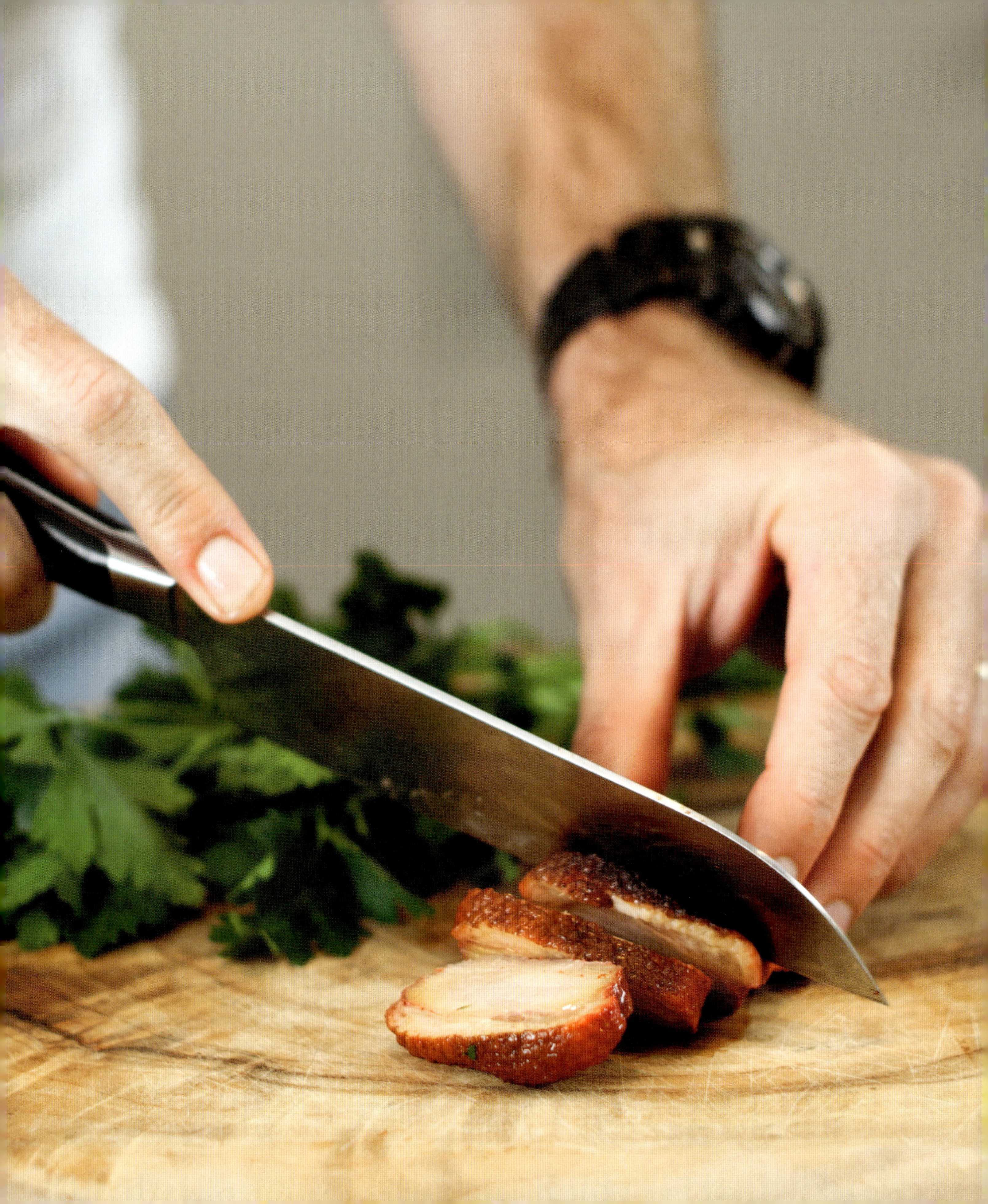

Duck with Scallops and Sichuan Pickled Cucumber

Duck is truly a beautiful meat to use and cook. The key to cooking this is to make sure you render the fat from under the skin as it gets crispy. The combinations of Asian spices, citrus and beautiful scallops make this quite a decadent dish that is sure to impress any dinner guest.

Ingredients

- 4 boneless duck breast, skin on
- 1 teaspoon five-spice powder
- ½ teaspoon salt
- zest and juice of 2 oranges
- 2 teaspoons honey
- 1 tablespoon soy sauce
- ¼ teaspoon cornflour (corn starch), dissolved in 1 teaspoon water
- 2 tablespoons olive oil
- 16 scallops, seasoned
- handful rocket (arugula) leaves

Method

1. To make the Sichuan pickled cucumber, discard the ends off the cucumbers and cut each in half lengthwise. Scrape out the seeds, then cut into 4–5 cm/1½–2 in batons. Place in a bowl and sprinkle with salt and stand for 1 hour. Squeeze the water out of cucumber and pat dry with a kitchen towel.
2. Heat the peanut oil in a wok over a medium heat and add the chillies, ginger, rice wine vinegar and ground Sichuan peppercorns and stir until aromatic. Remove from the heat and mix in a bowl with sugar and cucumber.
3. Preheat the oven to 190°C/375°F/Gas mark 5. Place the duck skin-side down on a cutting board. Trim off all excess skin that hangs over the sides. Turn over and make three parallel, diagonal cuts in the skin of each breast, cutting through the fat but not into the meat. Sprinkle both sides with five-spice powder and salt.
4. Place the duck skin-side down in an ovenproof skillet over a medium-low heat. Always start the cooking process with a cool skillet so as to not burn the skin. As the skillet heats the fat will render out and the skin will crisp up nicely. Cook until the fat is melted and the skin is golden brown, about 10 minutes. Transfer the duck to a plate; pour off all the fat from the skillet. Return the duck to the skillet skin-side up and transfer to the oven.

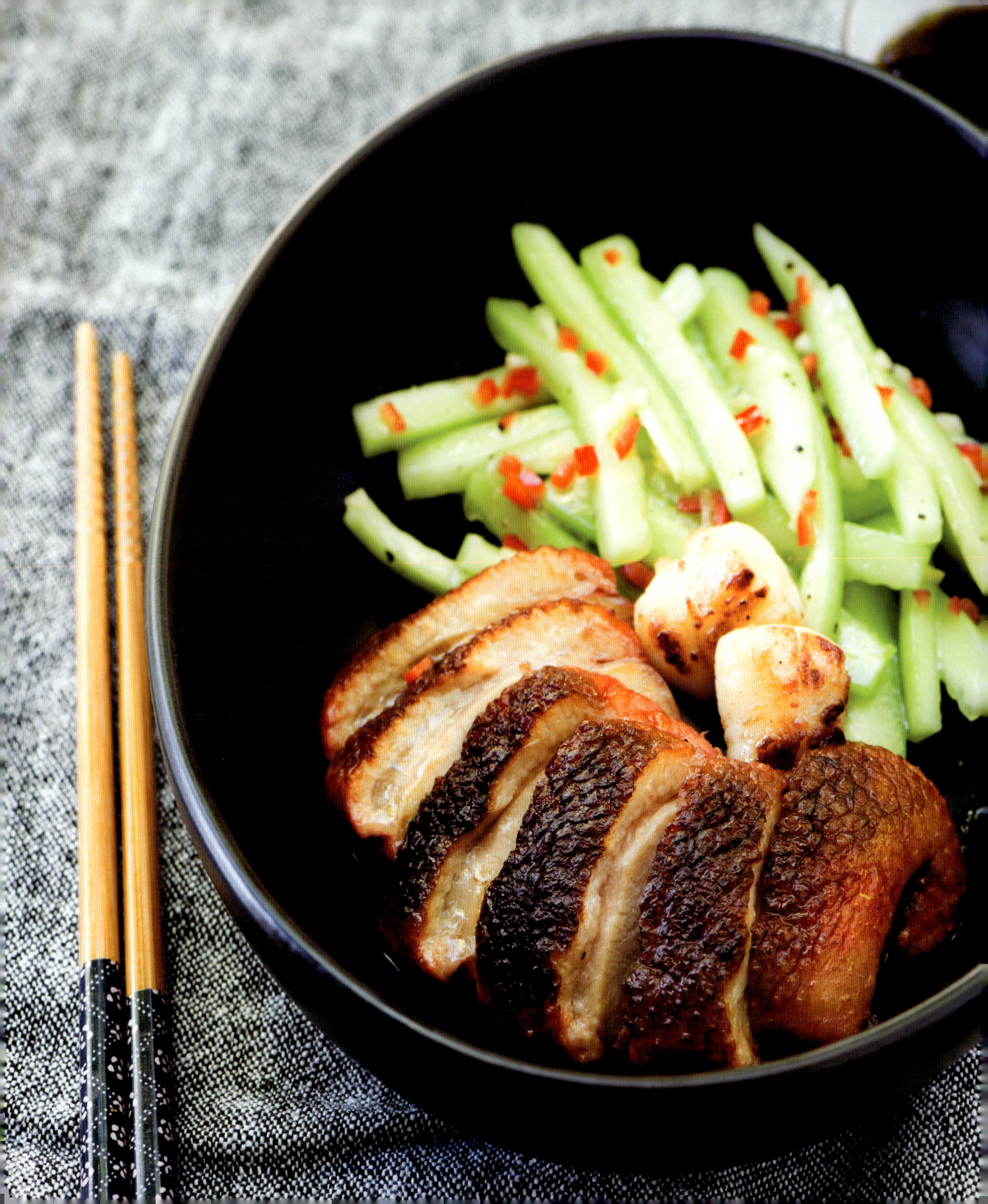

SICHUAN PICKLED CUCUMBER

8 continental cucumbers

50 g/1¾ oz salt

2 tablespoons peanut oil

8 long red chillies

2 knobs ginger, julienned

150 ml/5 fl oz rice wine vinegar

1 tablespoon Sichuan peppercorns, roasted and ground

120 g/4 oz palm sugar

5. Roast the duck for 10–15 minutes for medium cooked, depending on the size of the breast and reserve the cooking liquid. Transfer the meat to a cutting board; let rest for 5 minutes.

6. Pour off any fat remaining in the pan (take care, the handle will still be hot); place the pan over a medium-high heat and add the orange juice and honey. Bring to a simmer, stirring to scrape up any browned bits. Add the orange zest and soy sauce and continue to cook until the sauce is slightly reduced. Stir the cornflour mixture then whisk it into the sauce; cook, stirring, until slightly thickened,

7. Heat some oil in a frying pan until it is smoking and sear the scallops. Work in 2 or 3 batches. They should have a firm crust but still be translucent (nearly raw) inside. Set aside in a warm place.

Duck with Scallops

Cont.

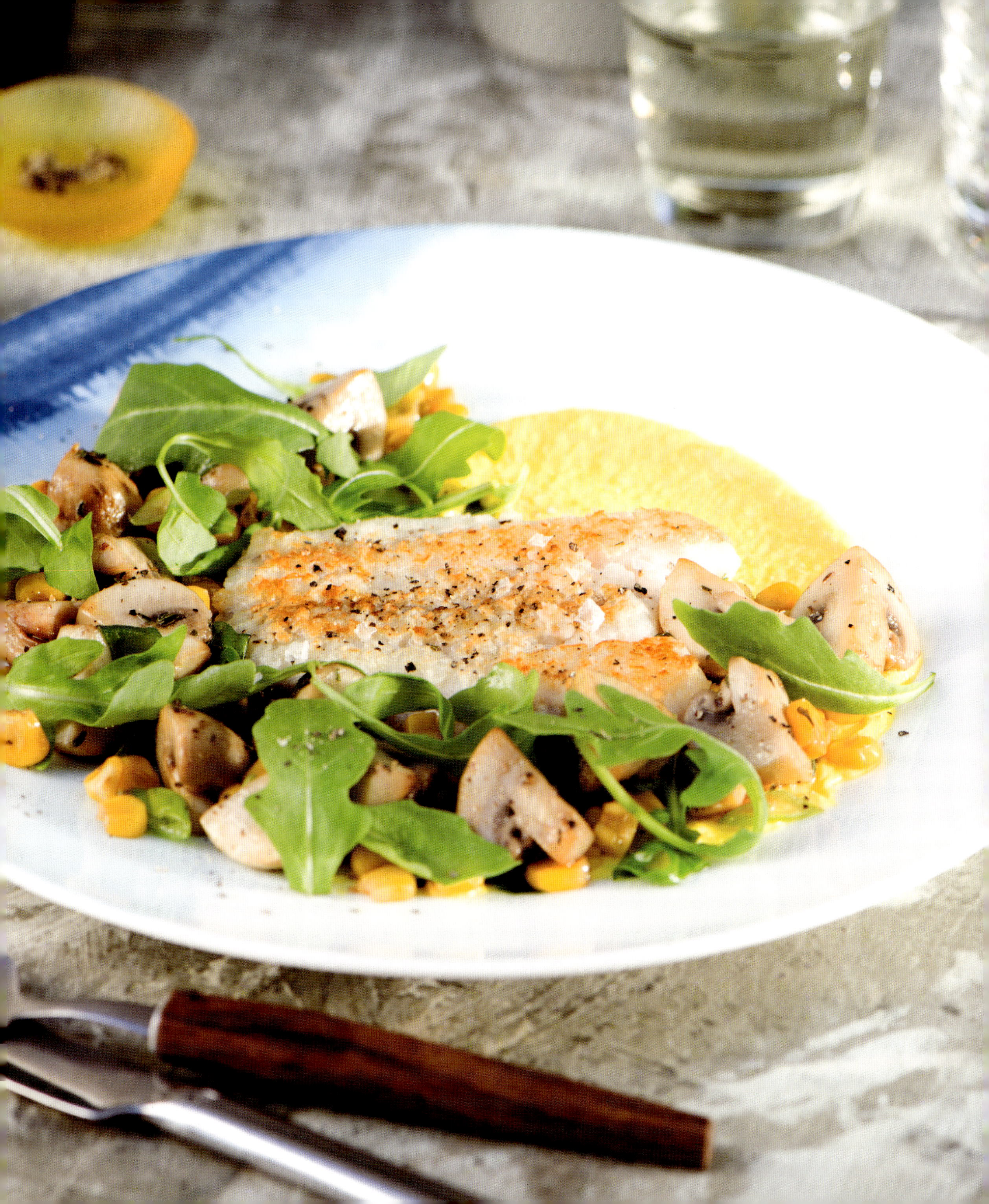

Snapper and Warm Mushroom Salad with Corn Purée

This dish uses a tried-and-true combination of fish, corn and red wine vinaigrette. You can use any firm white fish instead of snapper. The use of tarragon in the mushroom salad brings a lovely aniseed flavour to the dish. You can substitute the tarragon with dill, if you like. The lovely burst of yellow from the corn also makes this an attractive dish. Remember we eat with our eyes first.

Ingredients

4 snapper fillets, skin removed
30 g/1 oz plain (all-purpose) flour
2 tablespoons oil

Corn Purée

2 corn cobs
30 g/1 oz butter
2 red shallots, sliced
150 ml/5 fl oz chicken stock
150 ml/5 fl oz single (light) or cream

Mushroom Salad

200 g/7 oz button (white) mushrooms, peeled and quartered
45 g/1½ oz corn kernels (reserved from the corn cobs)
1 thyme sprig, leaves only
1 garlic clove, crushed
1 spring onion (scallion), thinly sliced
50 ml/1¾ fl oz olive oil
salt and pepper, to season
2 shallots, finely chopped
½ bunch of tarragon, leaves only
1 small handful of rocket (arugula)

Red Wine Vinaigrette

30 ml/1 fl oz red wine vinegar
1 teaspoon Dijon mustard
1 teaspoon seeded mustard
salt and pepper, to taste
60 ml/2 fl oz olive oil

Method

1. For the corn purée, cut the kernels from the cobs, reserving 45 g/1½ oz of the kernels for the salad. Heat the butter in a frying pan over a medium heat and sauté the shallots until soft. Add the corn and cook for about 10 minutes, stirring occasionally. Add the stock and simmer for 5 minutes. Add the cream and simmer for another 5 minutes, then season to taste. Blend the mixture and pass through a sieve so that the purée is smooth.
2. For the mushroom salad, toss the mushrooms, reserved corn, thyme, garlic, spring onion and oil in a bowl. Season to taste, cover and refrigerate for 30 minutes. Remove from the refrigerator and strain using a colander. Heat a large frying pan over a medium heat and cook the strained mixture for about 4 minutes, stirring occasionally. Drain and stir in the shallots, tarragon and rocket.
3. For the red wine vinaigrette, whisk together the vinegar and mustards, then season with salt and pepper. Whisking constantly, slowly pour in the olive oil until combined.
4. Dry the snapper fillets and coat lightly in flour. Heat 2 tablespoons of oil in a frying pan over a medium heat. Cook the fillets on one side for 4 minutes. Turn and cook for another 3 minutes. Remove from the heat and set aside for 4 minutes.
5. To serve, place a tablespoon of purée on the plate and use the back of the spoon to smear across the plate. Place a fillet overlapping the purée. Serve the salad beside the fillet and drizzle with vinaigrette.

Lamb Tagine with Dates

We have only recently discovered the wonders of Moroccan food. The divine combinations of dry spices, fruit, nuts and citrus just dance on your tongue. The use of a slow-cooking method also ensures the lamb just falls off the bone. Don't be put off by the number of ingredients—it is worth the effort. This makes a beautiful winter dinner for the family or when friends come over.

Ingredients

- 1 kg/2¼ lb boneless lamb
- 45 g/1½ oz butter
- 1 onion, finely chopped
- 1 teaspoon ground ginger
- 1 teaspoon ground cinnamon
- ½ teaspoon ground black pepper
- 55 g/2 oz dried dates, pitted and chopped
- Pinch of ground saffron threads
- 2 tablespoons honey
- 2 tablespoons lemon juice
- 200 g/7 oz fresh dates
- ½ preserved lemon
- 40 g/1½ oz slivered almonds

Couscous

- 2 tablespoons olive oil
- 1 onion, finely chopped
- grated zest of 1 orange
- 115 g/4 oz currants
- 2 teaspoons ground cumin
- 250 ml/8 fl oz orange juice
- 15 g/½ oz butter
- 350 g/12 oz couscous
- 2 tablespoons coriander (cilantro) leaves, chopped

Method

1. Trim the lamb and cut it into 2.5 cm/1 in cubes. In a large heavy pan, melt 30 g/1 oz of the butter over low heat, add the onion and cook gently until softened.
2. Sprinkle in the ground ginger, cinnamon and black pepper and stir for 1 minute. Increase the heat to high, add the lamb and stir until the colour of the meat changes.
3. Reduce the heat, add 375 ml/13 fl oz water, the chopped dates and saffron and season to taste. Reduce the heat, cover and simmer for 1½ hours, stirring occasionally to prevent the sauce sticking as the chopped dates cook to a purée.
4. Stir in the honey and lemon juice and adjust the seasoning. Put the whole dates on top, cover and simmer for 10 minutes, or until the dates are plump.
5. Meanwhile, rinse the preserved lemon under cold running water, remove and discard the pulp. Drain the zest, pat dry with kitchen paper and cut into strips. Melt the extra butter in a small frying pan, add the almonds and brown lightly, stirring often. Tip immediately onto a plate to prevent burning.
6. For the couscous, heat the oil in a pan over a low flame. Add the onion, orange zest, currants and cumin. Cook, stirring occasionally, for 10 minutes, or until the onion is soft.
7. In a separate pan, bring the juice, butter and 250 ml/8 fl oz of water to the boil, then slowly add the couscous. Remove from the heat and stand, covered for 5 minutes. Fluff with a fork, then stir in the onion mixture and coriander leaves.
8. Remove the whole dates from the top of the lamb and set them aside with the almonds. Ladle the meat into a serving dish or tagine and scatter the dates on top, along with the lemon strips and roasted almonds. Serve hot with couscous.

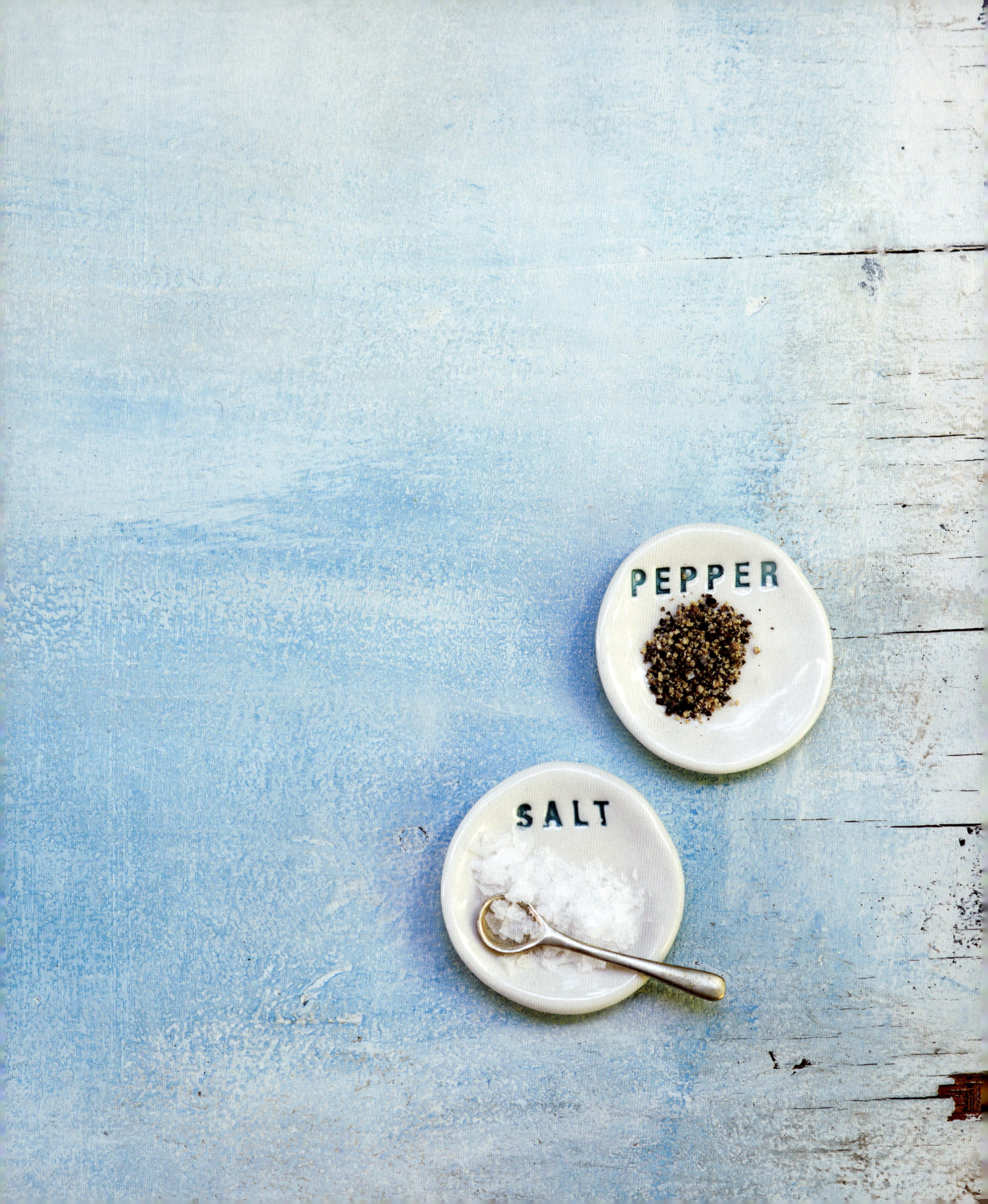
PEPPER
SALT

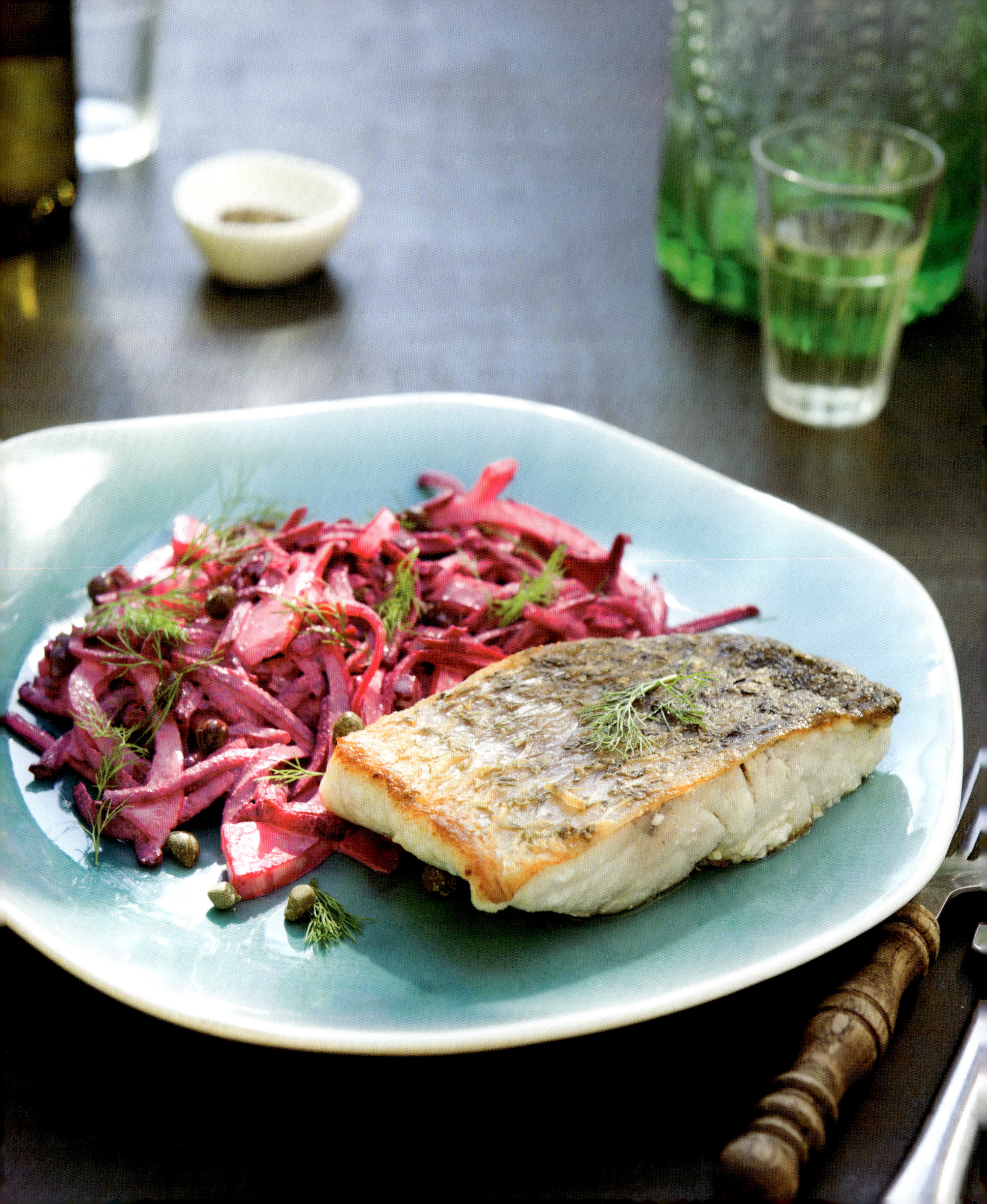

Pan-Fried Fish with Fennel and Beetroot Remoulade

For this dish, any ocean-going variety of fish is suitable. We like to use Spanish mackerel or barramundi. Both fish are a prized addition to any meal. We are lucky to have a mate who catches them regularly and sometimes gives us fresh fish fillets and this is the way we love to serve them. The combination of fennel and beetroot go beautifully with any slightly oily fish.

Ingredients

- 4 firm, oily fish fillets, skin on (we use Spanish mackerel)
- sea salt
- freshly ground black pepper
- extra virgin olive oil
- lemon wedges, to serve

Mayonnaise
- 2 egg yolks
- 3 teaspoons lemon juice
- pinch of salt
- 200 ml/7 fl oz olive oil
- freshly ground white pepper

Remoulade
- 2 baby fennel bulbs, trimmed, thinly sliced
- 2 baby beetroot, thinly sliced
- 60 g/2 oz mayonnaise (see recipe above)
- 60 ml/2 fl oz lemon juice
- 4 sweet gherkins, finely chopped
- 2 tablespoons capers, drained and chopped
- 3 teaspoons wholegrain mustard

Method

1. To make the mayonnaise, place the egg yolks, lemon juice and salt in a large bowl and whisk until the mixture thickens. Add the oil to the mixture slowly, whisking constantly. Stir in pepper. Mayonnaise can also be made using a food processor.
2. Season the fish skin with salt and pepper, cover and refrigerate for 10 minutes. Remove from the refrigerator and pat dry with paper towel.
3. Heat the oil in a non-stick pan over a medium flame. Cook, skin side down, for about 4 minutes, or until the skin is crispy. Turn and cook until firm.
4. For the remoulade, combine the fennel and beetroot, mayonnaise, lemon juice, gherkin, capers and mustard in a large bowl.
5. Divide the remoulade among the plates and top with mackerel. Serve with lemon wedges.

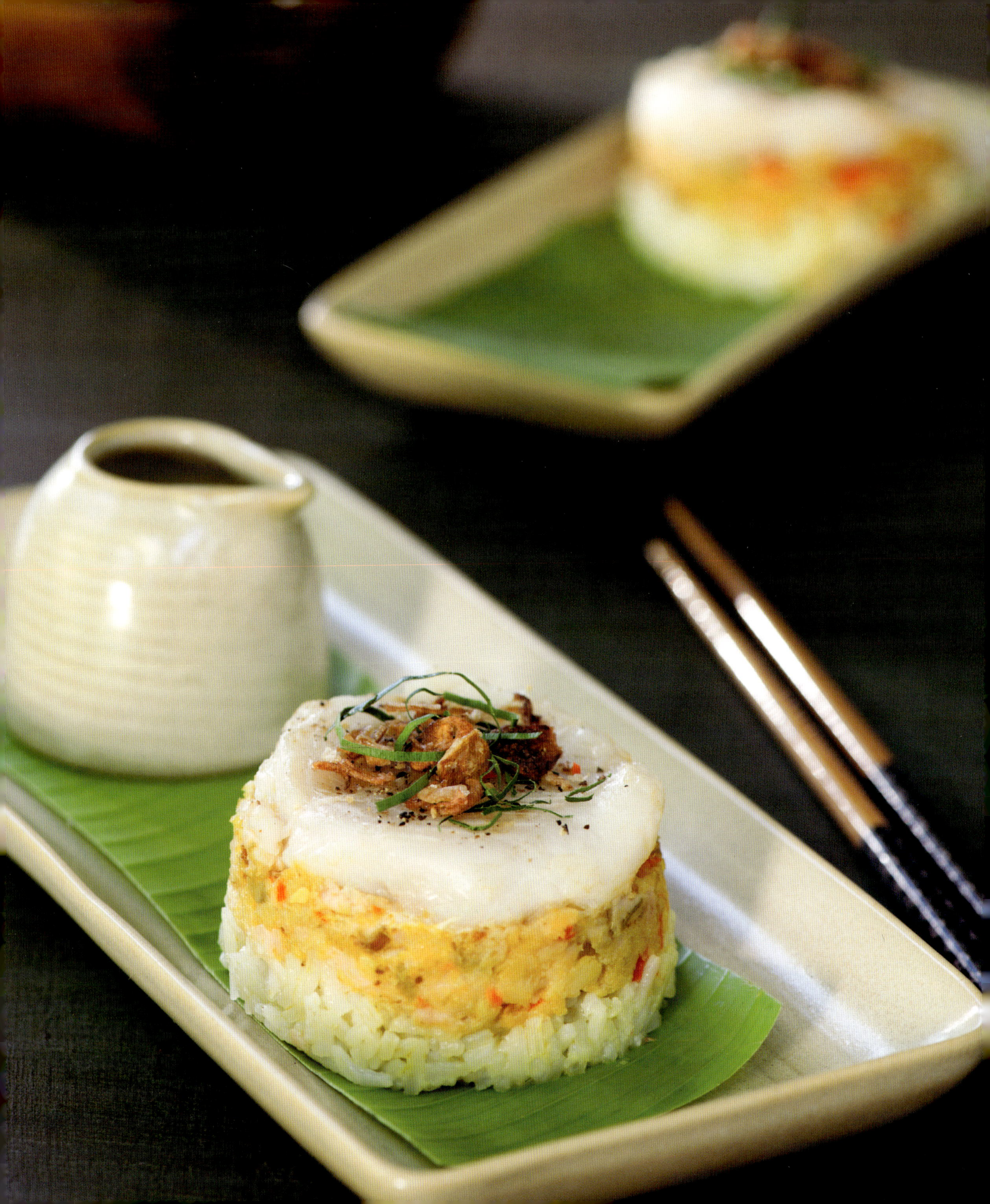

Spicy Fish Stack with Coconut Dressing

This is a dish we came up with to give a restaurant feel to baked fish. There is a fair bit of work involved here but we think it is worth it. The end result is visually appealing and the taste is spectacular. If you are feeling lazy, the dressing goes really well over a piece of baked fish too.

Ingredients

200 g/7 oz jasmine rice
1 teaspoon ground turmeric
4 x 100 g/3½ oz pieces snapper
salt and pepper, to taste
300 g/10½ oz chicken mince
1 tablespoon oil
1 shallot, finely sliced
3 shredded kaffir lime leaves, shredded, to garnish

Spice Paste
3 garlic cloves
4 cm/1½ in piece turmeric
4 cm/1½ in piece galangal
1 tablespoon ground coriander
1 lemongrass (white stalk only)
1 red shallot
3 large red chillies
1 tablespoon kaffir lime leaves, finely chopped
15 ml/½ fl oz fish sauce
½ tablespoon coconut oil, for frying

Dressing
150 ml/5 fl oz coconut milk
40 ml/1½ fl oz white wine vinegar
60 ml/2 fl oz lime juice
20 ml/⅔ fl oz ginger juice
40 ml/1½ fl oz fish sauce
3 tablespoons brown sugar
1 large green chilli, finely chopped
2 tablespoons coriander (cilantro) leaves

Method

1. Preheat the oven to 180°C/350°F/Gas mark 4.
2. Cook the rice flavoured with the turmeric in a rice cooker.
3. Cut each portions of snapper using a large food ring. Season with salt and pepper. Process the remaining fish in a food processor to a fine mince.
4. Add the spice paste ingredients to the bowl of a food processor and blend to a paste. Fry the paste in the coconut oil until aromatic. Set aside to cool.
5. In a large bowl, mix together the chicken mince, minced fish and cooked spice paste until combined.
6. On separate sheets of baking paper, form each stack using the large food ring as a guide. Layer the cooked rice, compress it firmly, then add the chicken and fish mixture. Top with the fish round. Each layer should be approximately 2 cm/¾ in thick.
7. Wrap each stack in the baking paper and tie off using kitchen string. Place each parcel on a wire rack in a baking tray that has been filled to a depth of 2.5 cm/1 in with water and bake for 18–20 minutes, or until cooked through.
8. Meanwhile, heat the oil in a small frying pan and fry the sliced shallot until cooked through.
9. Place all the dressing ingredients except for the coriander leaves into a bowl and whisk until combined. Stir the coriander leaves gently through.
10. Unwrap the stacks, discarding the baking paper and transfer to serving plates. Spoon the dressing over the stacks and garnish with fried shallots and shredded kaffir lime leaves.

Spiced Chicken, Chickpea Salad and Minted Yogurt Dressing

Some people will caution against cooking chicken breast and say it is hard to cook without drying it out. Try this method and you will be glad you did. It will be moist and tender and low on fat. The spices and yogurt also work well with lamb fillet.

Ingredients

100 ml/3½ fl oz grape-seed oil
2 teaspoons ground coriander
1 teaspoon ground cumin
¼ teaspoon ground turmeric
chilli flakes, to taste
zest of ½ lemon
4 x 200 g/7 oz chicken breasts, skinned
3 garlic cloves, crushed

Chickpea Salad
1 x 400 g/14 oz can chickpeas
¼ teaspoon ground chilli
¼ teaspoon ground coriander
juice of ½ lemon
2 tablespoons olive oil
2 tablespoons coriander (cilantro) leaves
1 tablespoon mint leaves, chopped
salt and pepper, to taste

Minted Yogurt Dressing
3 garlic cloves, crushed
¼ cup mint leaves, chopped
50 ml/1¾ fl oz olive oil
300 ml/10½ fl oz natural (plain) yogurt
salt and pepper, to taste

Method

1. Preheat the oven to 180°C/350°F/Gas mark 4.
2. Combine the grape-seed oil with the ground spices, chilli and lemon zest in a large bowl. Add the chicken and coat the surface evenly and leave to marinate in a non-metallic dish for about 1 hour.
3. For the chickpea salad, put the chickpeas on an oven tray and bake for about 15 minutes, or until they are crunchy. Toss the chickpeas and remaining salad ingredients into a bowl and mix together.
4. To make the minted yogurt dressing, place all the ingredients in a blender and process on a medium speed until combined.
5. To cook the chicken, heat a large frying pan over medium heat and cook the breasts on each side until golden brown. Remove from the pan and place on a lined baking tray then place in the oven for about 5 minutes, or until cooked through. The cooking time will depend on the thickness of the meat.
6. To serve, place a portion of the salad on the plate. Slice the chicken into thick pieces and arrange on top. Add a good dollop of the yogurt dressing and season with salt and pepper.

Scallop, Chorizo and Fennel Salad

Ingredients

2 baby fennel, fronds attached
1 Granny Smith apple, cored, halved and sliced
2 shallots, sliced
1 radicchio, torn
30 g /1 oz pine nuts, toasted
3 tablespoons olive oil
2 dried chorizo, sliced
20 scallops, roe removed
lime wedges, to serve

Dressing

juice of 2 limes
2 tablespoons olive oil
2 teaspoons Dijon mustard
½ teaspoon sweet paprika
1 teaspoon caster (superfine) sugar
60 ml/2 fl oz olive oil
salt and pepper, to taste

Method

1. Thinly slice the fennel and roughly chop the fennel fronds.
2. To make the dressing, put the lime juice, fennel fronds, mustard, paprika, sugar and 60 ml/2 fl oz oil in a small bowl. Whisk to combine and season with salt and pepper.
3. Combine the sliced fennel, apple, shallots, radicchio and pine nuts in a large bowl with the dressing.
4. Heat 1 tablespoon of the oil in a large frying pan over a high heat. Add the chorizo and cook for 1 minute on each side, or until golden. Combine the chorizo and the pan juices with the salad. Return the frying pan to the stove top.
5. Heat the remaining 2 tablespoons of oil in the pan and sear the scallops on each side, or until golden and almost cooked through. Add the scallops to the salad, toss gently to combine and season with salt and pepper.
6. Serve the salad with lime wedges.

This dish uses three beautiful ingredients and is an example of simple and tasty food. You can replace the chorizo with bacon but it is never as good. This is an easy meal to put together but the complex flavours will make this a real standout!

Tip
If you can't find radicchio, don't stress—you can replace it with watercress.

Crunchy Fish

Everyone has fond memories of fish and chips. This dish is inspired by a mate of ours, Sean, a keen fisherman on the Gold Coast. He regularly heads out into the blue yonder and rarely misses out. This is the way he serves the small fillets to the kids. They really are crunchy and the kids will devour them.

Ingredients

- 4 fillets white fish, skin off, sliced into equal portions
- 30 g/1 oz plain (all-purpose) flour
- 60 g/2 oz cornflakes, lightly crushed
- 1 lemon, quartered
- salt and pepper, to season

Batter

- 500 ml/17 fl oz crushed ice and water
- 270 g/9½ oz plain (all-purpose) flour, plus 50 g/1¾ oz extra for coating

Mayonnaise

- ¼ teaspoon mustard powder
- ¼ teaspoon salt
- ¼ teaspoon caster (superfine) sugar
- ¼ lemon zest
- 1 egg
- 1 tablespoon white vinegar
- 1 small pickle
- 1 sprig dill
- 250 ml/8 fl oz vegetable oil

Method

1. Preheat the deep fryer to 180°C/350°F. If you don't have a deep fryer, fill a frying pan with oil, 5 cm/2 in deep. To test if the oil is hot enough, toss in a cube of bread and if it browns in about 15 seconds the oil is ready.
2. For the mayonnaise, process all the ingredients, except for the oil, in the bowl of a food processor until blended. Gradually add the oil while pulsing the processor until the mayonnaise starts to thicken. Transfer to a sealed container and refrigerate until needed.
3. For the batter, mix the ingredients gently in a bowl using chopsticks or a fork. Be careful not to over-mix. It is important to have the batter cold.
4. Tip the flour onto a plate, and put the crushed cornflakes on another. Roll the fish pieces in flour, then dip each piece into the batter before coating with crushed cornflakes. Fry the fish for 4 minutes until golden brown. Remove and place on some paper towel.
5. Serve a few pieces of the fish with a lemon wedge and a dollop of the mayonnaise. Season with salt and pepper.

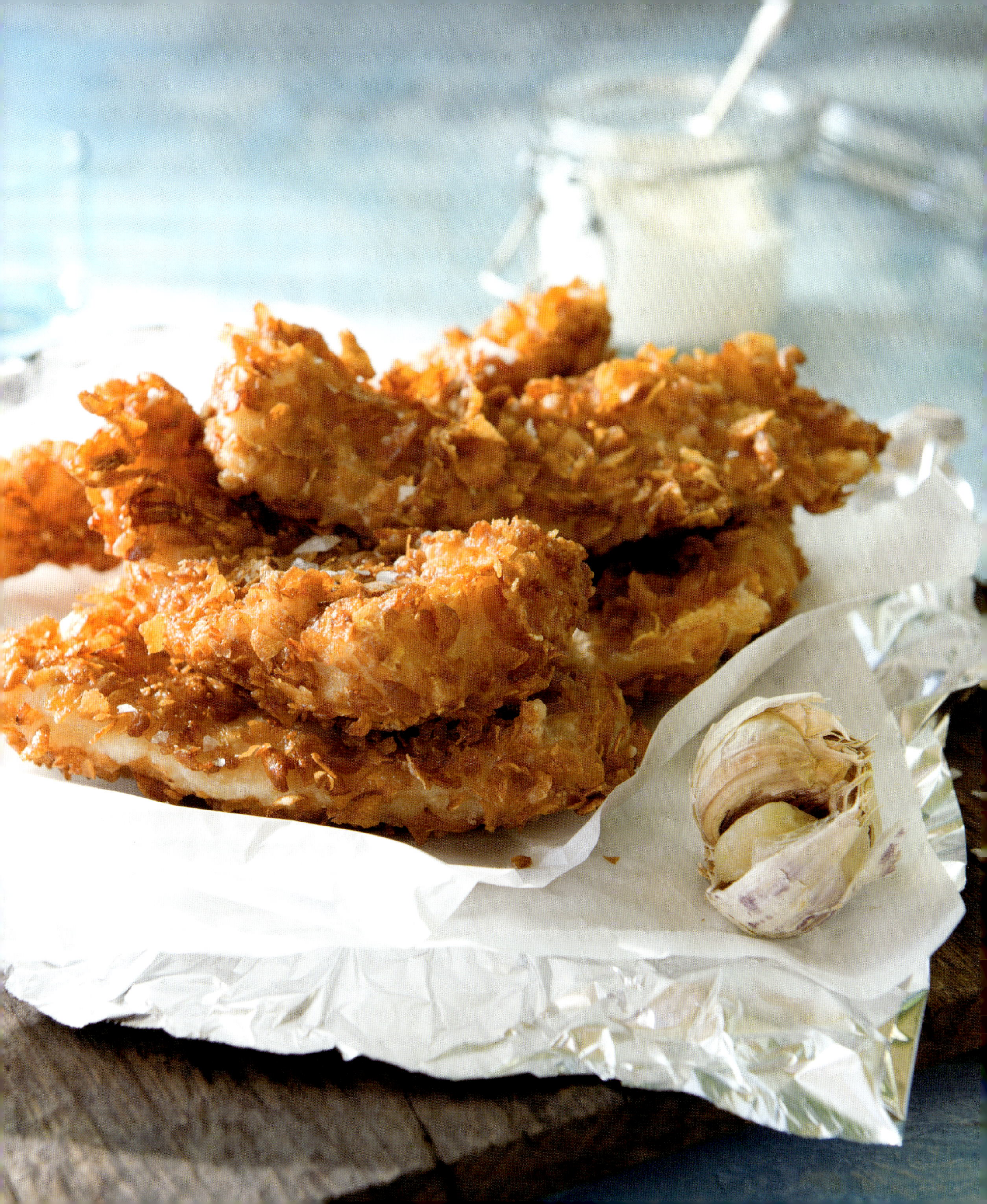

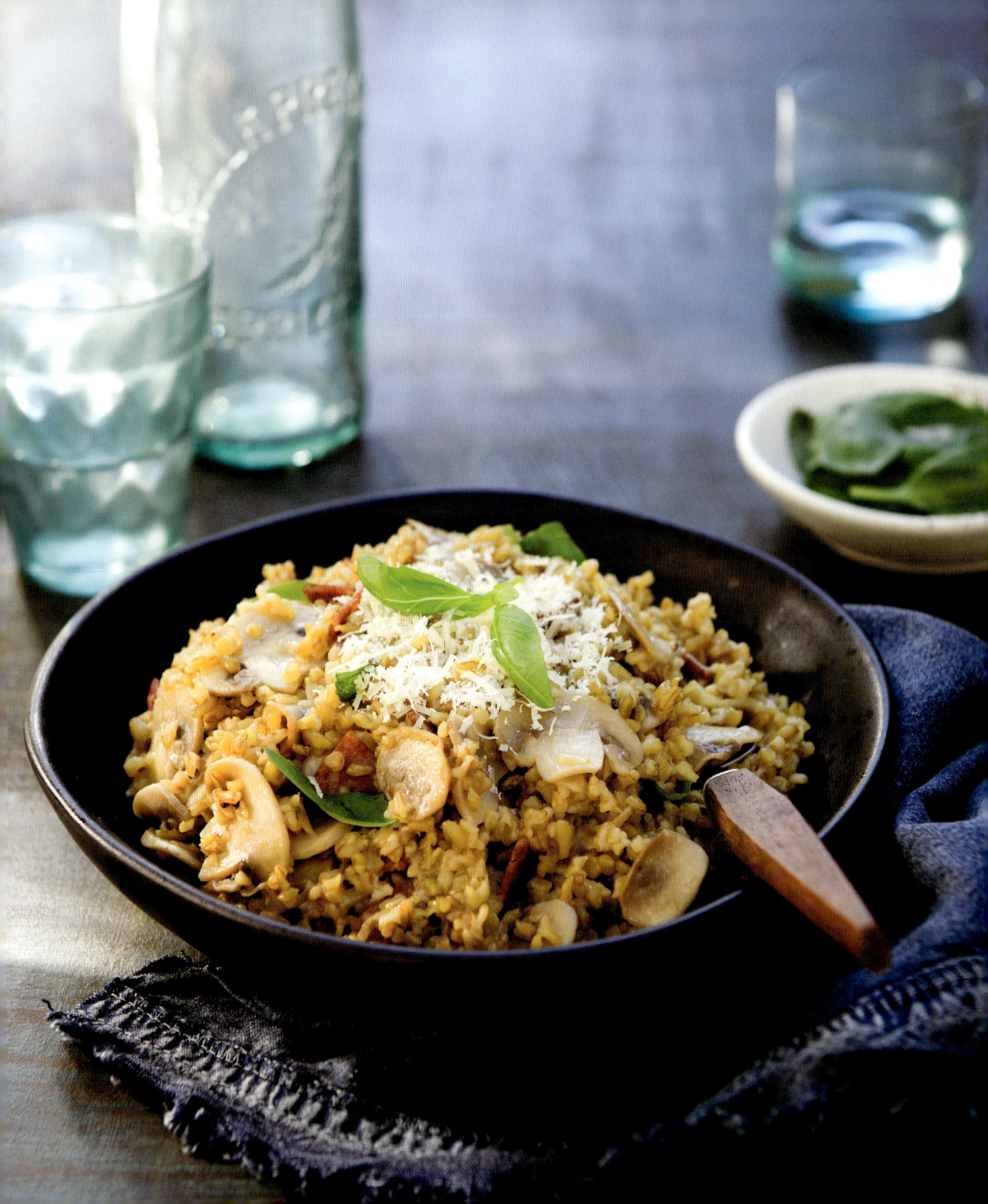

Mushroom and Leek Freekeh Risotto

Who doesn't love a good risotto? Well, here's a low GI (glycaemic index) alternative to using arborio rice. Freekeh has a higher nutrient level than mature wheat and has nearly four times the fibre content of brown rice. You simply replace the rice with freekeh and cook it the same way.

Ingredients

- 1 litre/1¾ pints chicken stock
- 30 g/1 oz butter
- 2 tablespoons olive oil
- 1 brown onion, diced sliced
- 2 garlic cloves, crushed
- 1 leek, white part only, thinly sliced
- 3 rashers (strips) bacon, diced
- 350 g/12 oz field (portobello) mushrooms,
- 2 cups freekeh, rinsed and drained
- 125 ml/4 fl oz dry white wine
- 60 g/2 oz Parmesan cheese, grated (shredded)
- 1 tablespoon basil, chopped, to serve

Method

1. Bring the stock to the boil in a medium pan then reduce to a simmer.
2. In a large, deep frying pan melt the butter. Add the oil, onion, garlic, leek and bacon, and cook over a medium heat until the bacon is crispy. Add the mushrooms and cook for another 3 minutes.
3. Add the freekeh and cook for a few minutes until it is coated in the butter and oil.
4. Add the wine and cook until it has been absorbed. Add the simmering stock with a ladle, about a ladleful at a time, making sure it is absorbed before adding more.
5. Continue until the freekeh is tender. It will still retain a slight crunch and the whole mixture should be slightly creamy.
6. To serve, stir through the Parmesan cheese and add the basil.

Dukkah-crusted Chicken on Red Quinoa Salad

The diversity of grains available today is amazing. We have embraced quinoa in our cooking as an alternative to rice and couscous because of its added nutritional values. One such value is that quinoa is a protein-enriched food that contains all nine essential amino acids. In this dish, the quinoa is complemented by the nut and spice blend of dukkah. Two food worlds collide in this dish and will not disappoint.

Ingredients

4 chicken thigh fillets
1 tablespoon oil

Quinoa Salad
1 tablespoon oil
3 garlic cloves, finely chopped
2 shallots, finely sliced
1 white or green zucchini, quartered and chopped
½ large red chilli, seeded and sliced finely
1/3 cup red quinoa
250 ml/8 fl oz beef stock

Dukkah Crust
45 g/1½ oz hazelnuts
½ cup sesame seeds
2 tablespoons coriander seeds
2 tablespoons cumin seeds
1 teaspoon flaked sea salt
1 teaspoon ground black pepper

Tip
You can serve this dish with a simple dressing of natural yogurt combined with lemon juice and seasoning.

Method

1. Preheat the oven to 180°C/350°F/Gas mark 4 and line a baking sheet with baking paper.
2. For the dukkah crust, roast the hazelnuts on another baking sheet for 4–5 minutes, or until toasted. Remove and rub between a tea towel to remove as much skin as possible. Place the toasted hazelnuts into a food processor and pulse until roughly chopped. Transfer to a large bowl.
3. Heat a frying pan over a medium heat. Add the sesame seeds and cook for 2 minutes, stirring continuously until golden brown. Combine with the hazelnuts.
4. Heat the same frying pan over a medium flame. Add the coriander and cumin seeds and cook, string continuously, until aromatic and the seeds begin to pop. Crush finely using a mortar and pestle or coffee grinder. Add to the bowl with the hazelnuts and season with salt and pepper. Mix well.
5. Add the thigh fillets to the bowl one at a time and coat with the dukkah crust. Heat 1 tablespoon of oil in a frying pan over a medium heat and fry the fillets for 2 minutes on each side. Place the fillets on the lined baking tray and bake for 20 minutes, or until cooked through.
6. For the quinoa salad, heat 1 tablespoon of oil in a frying pan over a medium heat. Add the garlic and shallots and cook until golden brown. Add the zucchini and chilli, cooking for another 3 minutes. Remove from the heat and set aside.
7. Rinse the quinoa thoroughly, then soak for 15 minutes in water. Drain and add the quinoa to a medium pan with the beef stock. Bring to the boil, then cover and simmer for about 15 minutes, or until the stock is absorbed. Remove from the heat and stand for 5 minutes. Stir in the onion mixture.
8. To serve, thinly slice the chicken fillets and place on top of a serving of quinoa salad.

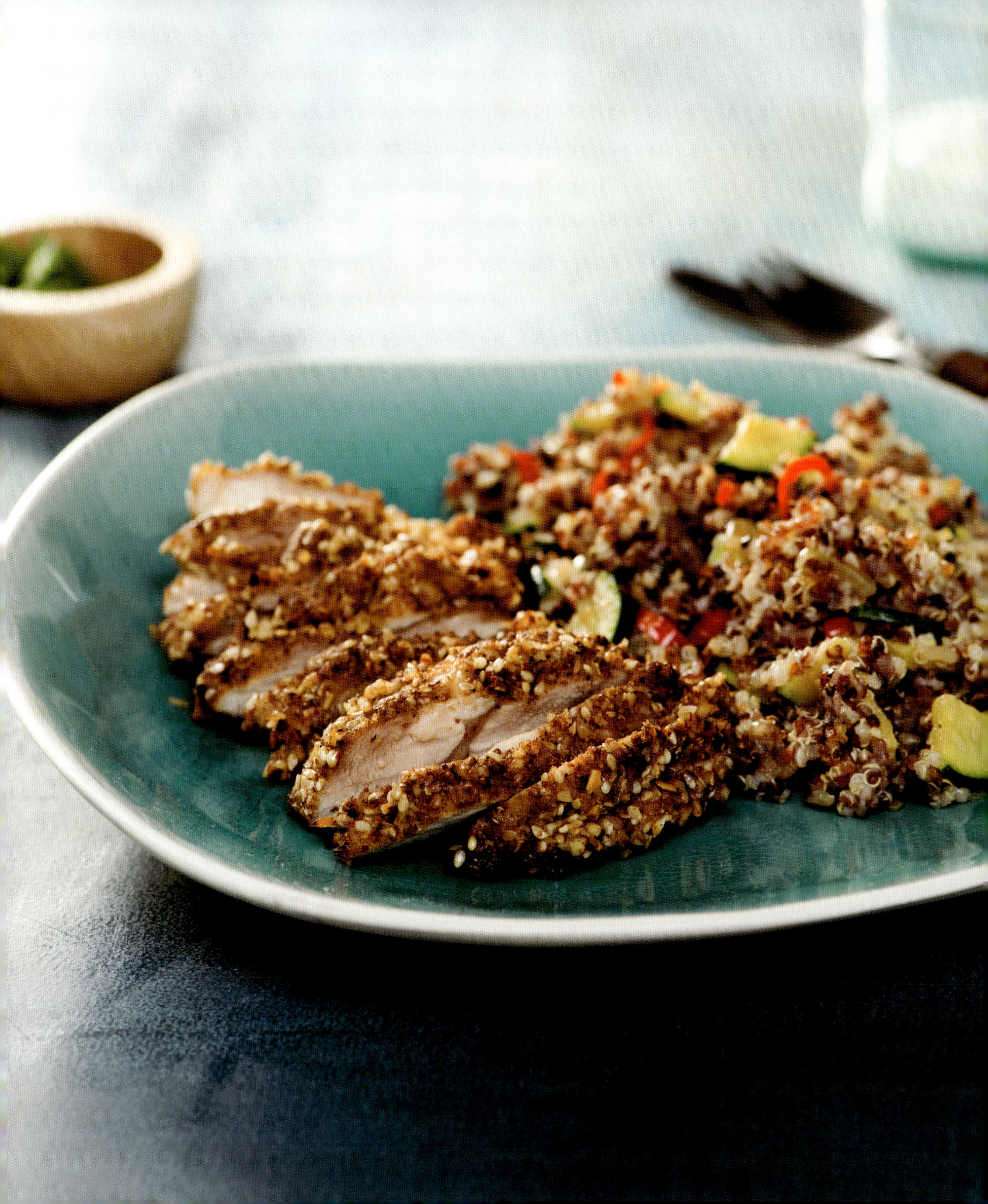

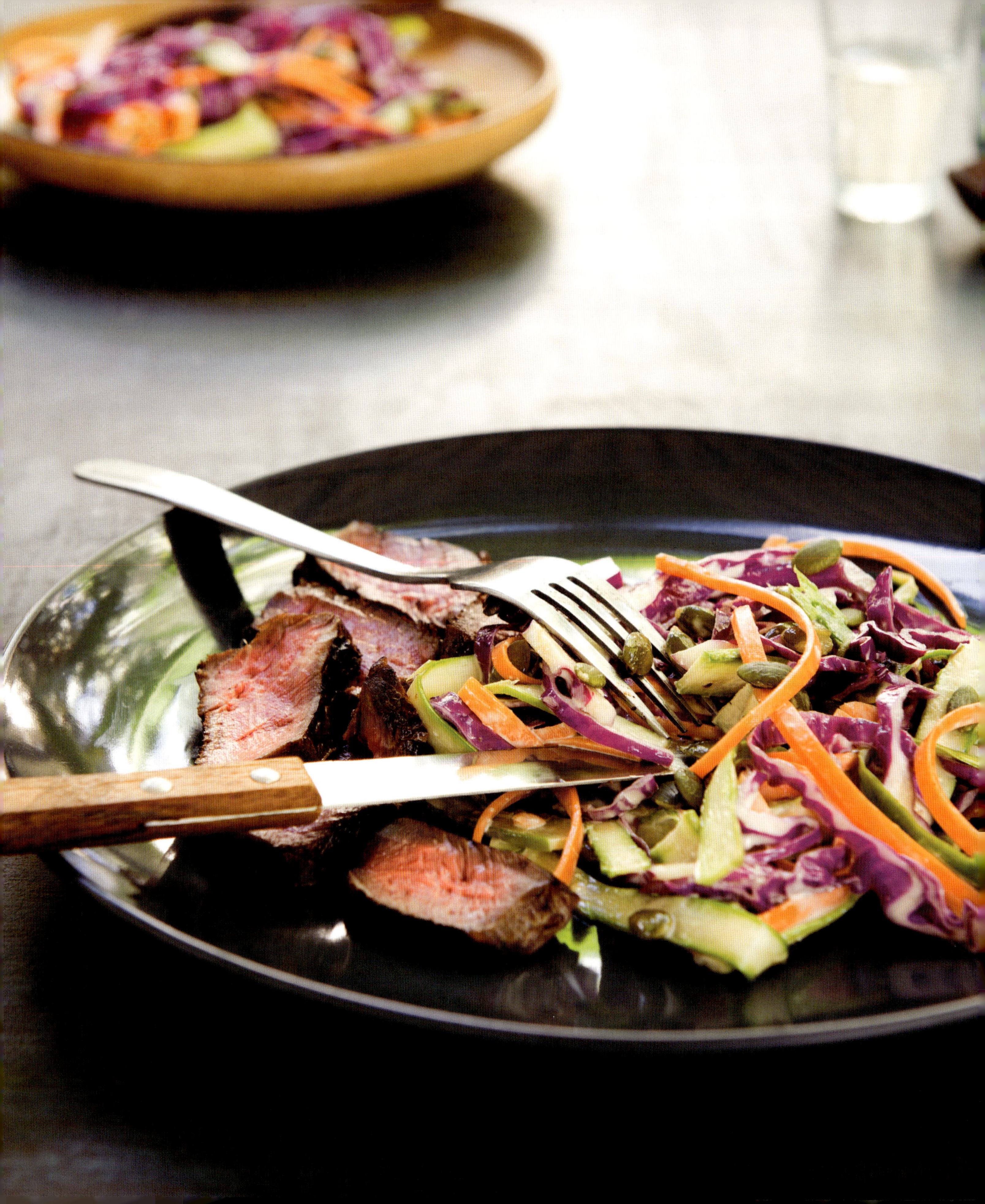

Marinated Steak on Asparagus Slaw

Ingredients

4 steaks, cut of your choice
1 tablespoon oil

Marinade

60 ml/2 fl oz soy sauce
60 ml/2 fl oz balsamic vinegar
60 ml/2 fl oz grape-seed oil
1 large red chilli, seeded, finely chopped
1 bird's eye chilli, seeded, finely chopped
60 ml/2 fl oz honey
2 garlic gloves, minced
1 cm/½ in piece of root ginger, finely shredded

Slaw

½ red cabbage, sliced thinly
5–7 asparagus stalks, ends removed, peeled
2–3 small carrots, peeled and sliced
50 g/1¾ oz pepita seeds (pumpkin), roasted
2–3 tablespoons whole egg mayonnaise (see recipe below)

Whole Egg Mayonnaise

2 eggs
1 teaspoon Dijon mustard
juice of 1 lemon
500 ml/17 fl oz grape-seed oil
salt and pepper, to taste

Method

1. For the whole egg mayonnaise, place the eggs, mustard and lemon juice into the bowl of a food processor and pulse until combined.
2. Drizzle in the oil while pulsing until it thickens to an emulsion. Season with salt and pepper to taste.
3. Transfer to a airtight container with a lid and store in the refrigerator for up to 2 weeks.
4. For the marinade, combine all the ingredients in a bowl and stir. Place the steaks into a casserole dish and pour the marinade over. Cover with cling film (plastic wrap) and refrigerate for at least 1 hour. Remove from the refrigerator and allow the steak to reach room temperature.
5. For the slaw, combine all the ingredients in a large bowl and stir in 2–3 tablespoon of the mayonnaise.
6. Heat the oil in a frying pan or on a barbecue plate over a high heat. Drain the excess marinade from the steak and cook for 3 minutes on each side, or until cooked to your liking. Remove and cover with aluminium foil for 5 minutes. Slice the steak thinly just prior to serving.
7. Serve with asparagus slaw topped with slices of marinated steak.

Tip
After peeling the carrots, continue to peel to get crunchy thin ribbons for your slaw.

Marinating is a great way of add extra taste to inexpensive cuts of meat – the longer you marinate the steak, the more flavour you will infuse. We find that it is best to get the meat ready in the morning before heading off for the day. The fresh Asian qualities in this marinade accompany the slaw brilliantly. This is a quick, easy meal to prepare that will rival any steak and salad meal.

Burgers

Mediterranean Burger

The burger has passed the taste test time and again. More recently it has become a hip and happening meal in pubs and cafes in the form of the 'slider'. Just like most blokes, we love a good burger. Here are some of the best, with a twist, from our pantry.

Ingredients

4 Turkish bread rolls, toasted and buttered
1 handful rocket (arugula) leaves
2 tablespoons olive oil

BURGER PATTY
85 g/3 oz chickpeas, drained, rinsed and patted dry
½ teaspoon ground cumin
½ teaspoon cayenne pepper
½ teaspoon sea salt
30 g/1 oz multi-grain breadcrumbs
1 egg, lightly beaten
350 g/12 oz lamb mince
115 g/4 oz feta, crumbled
2 garlic cloves, crushed
30 g/1 oz pitted Kalamata olives, finely chopped
½ cup mint leaves, finely chopped
½ red onion, finely chopped

YOGURT DRESSING
150 g/5 oz Greek natural (plain) yogurt
1 garlic glove, crushed
1 tablespoon finely chopped mint leaves
1 tablespoon lemon juice
salt and pepper, to taste

Method

1. To make the dressing, mix all of the ingredients in a small bowl, season to taste and refrigerate until needed.
2. For the burger patty, pulse the chickpeas in a food processor until roughly chopped. Add the cumin, cayenne pepper, salt, breadcrumbs and egg and process until well combined.
3. Tip into a large bowl and add all the remaining patty ingredients. Mix until well combined. Divide the mixture into 6 equal patties and shape into rounds. Cover and refrigerate for 20 minutes.
4. Heat the oil in a frying pan or barbecue plate over medium heat. Cook the patties for 4–5 minutes on each side or until cooked through. Cover to keep warm.
5. Put the rocket onto the bread roll bases, top with patty, yogurt dressing and bread tops.

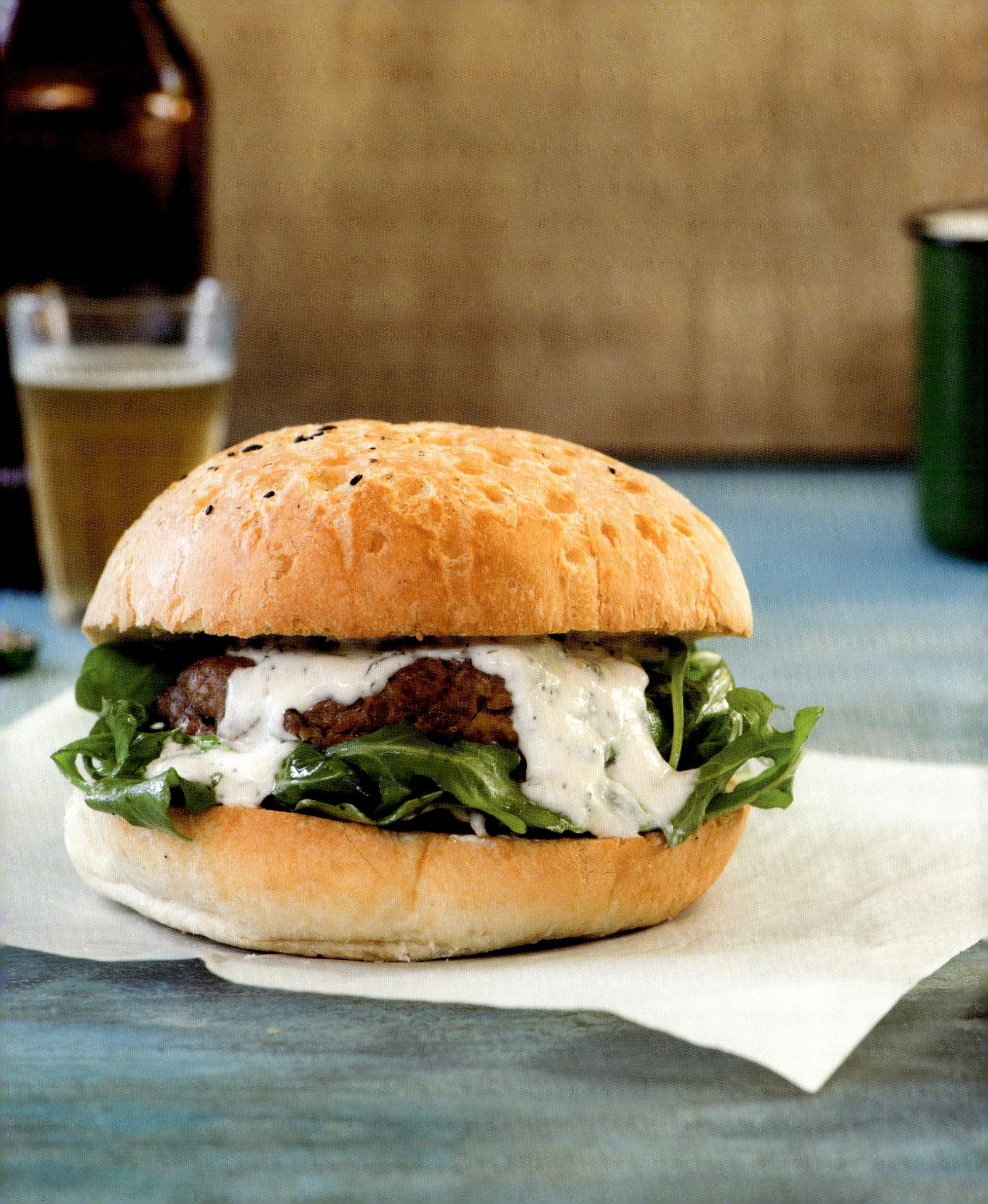

Open Salmon Burger

Ingredients

1 quantity Yogurt Flat Bread Pizza Bases (see recipe, p. 93)
2 tablespoons oil
4 salmon fillets, skinned
salt and pepper, to taste
½ cup coriander (cilantro) leaves
¼ cup Thai basil
¼ cup mint leaves
¼ cup beansprouts

Sweet Chilli Dressing

1½ tablespoons sweet chilli sauce
1½ tablespoons lemon juice
3 teaspoons fish sauce
2 teaspoons brown sugar

Crème Fraîche Spread

4 tablespoons crème fraîche
zest of 1 lemon
salt and pepper, to taste

Method

1. Make the yogurt flat bread and dry fry in a frying pan, set over medium heat, for 1 minute on each side, or until slightly char-grilled. Make 1 large flat bread per serving.
2. Heat the oil in a frying pan over a medium heat. Season the salmon fillets and fry each for 2–3 minutes on each side. Set aside for 5 minutes to rest before flaking the flesh into large chunks.
3. To make the sweet chilli dressing, combine all the ingredients in a small bowl and set aside.
4. Combine the coriander, basil, mint and beansprouts in a bowl. Dress the herbs and beansprouts with the sweet chilli dressing and toss to cover evenly.
5. For the crème fraîche spread, combine all the ingredients together in a small bowl.
6. Serve as an open burger. Top the flat bread with crème fraîche spread, flaked salmon and dressed salad.

Pulled Pork Burger

Ingredients

2 tablespoons paprika
1 tablespoon salt
1 teaspoon pepper
½ teaspoon cayenne pepper
2 garlic cloves, crushed
60 ml/2 fl oz honey
2 tablespoons red wine vinegar
1 tablespoon olive oil
1 kg/2¼ lb pork shoulder
1 onion, sliced
125 ml/4 fl oz chicken stock
4 panini rolls, sliced in half, toasted and buttered

Fennel and Apple Slaw

2 or 3 tablespoons whole egg mayonnaise (see Marinated Steak on Asparagus Slaw page 85)
2 Granny Smith apples, grated or julienned
1 fennel bulb, thinly sliced
salt and pepper, to taste

Method

1. In a small bowl, mix together the paprika, salt, pepper and cayenne. Add the garlic, honey, red wine vinegar and oil and mix to form a paste. Cover the pork with the paste.
2. Place the onion in the base of a slow cooker and top it with the pork. Pour in the stock. Turn the slow cooker onto low and cook the pork for 6–8 hours, or until the meat is tender enough to shred with a fork.
3. To make the fennel and apple slaw, mix the ingredients together in a small bowl.
4. Place the pulled pork on panini roll base. Top with pork with slaw and bread top.

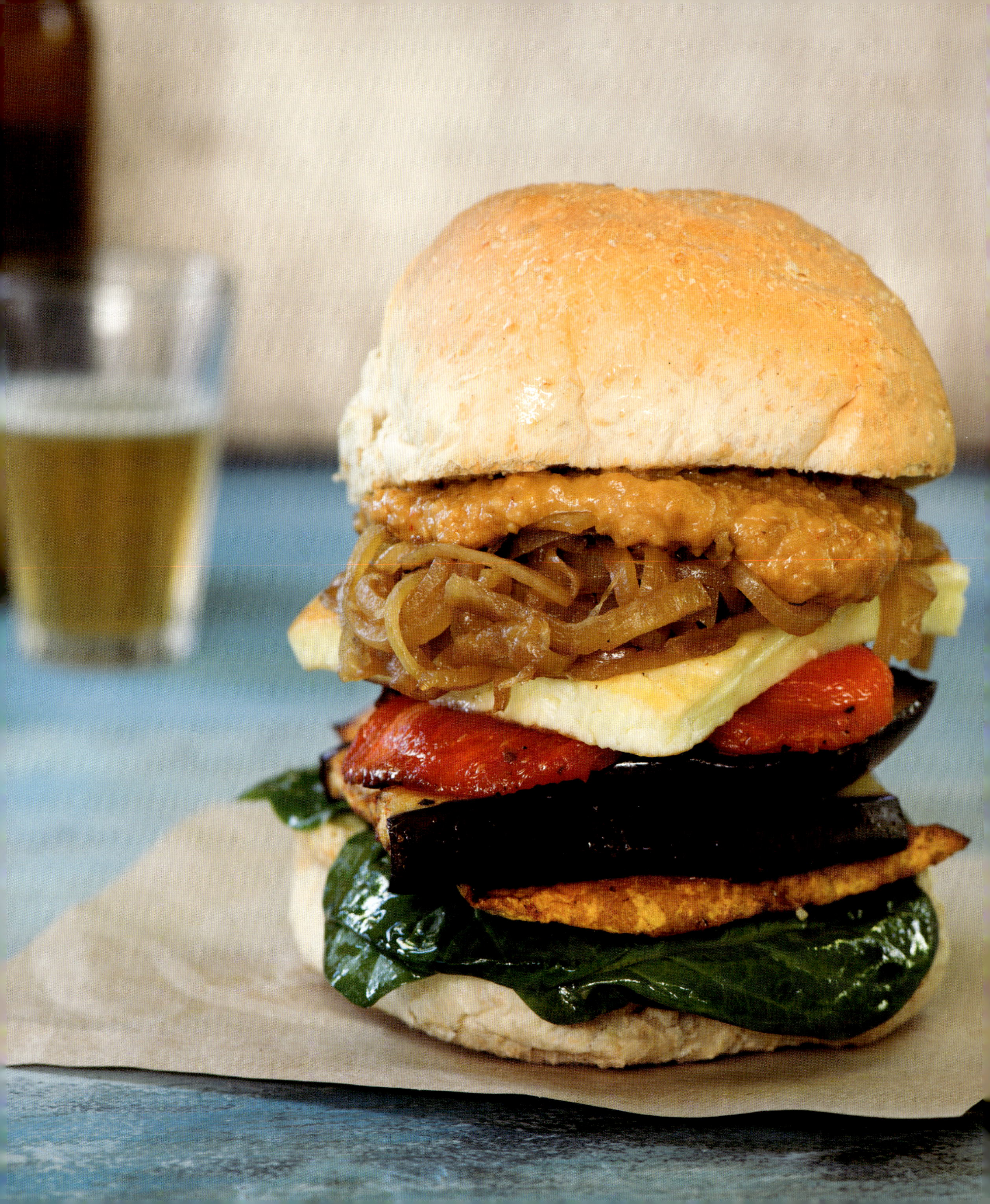

Veggie Stack Burger

Ingredients

¼ butternut pumpkin, peeled and cut into 0.5 cm/¼ in slices
2 capsicums (bell peppers), halved and seeded
½ eggplant (aubergine), cut into 0.5 cm/¼ in slices
3 tablespoons oil
¼ teaspoon paprika
¼ teaspoon cayenne pepper
salt and pepper, to taste
90 g/3 oz halloumi, sliced
4 multi-grain rolls, halved, toasted and buttered
1 handful of baby spinach leaves

Caramelised Onions
40 g/1½ oz butter
2 onions, sliced
½ teaspoon salt
½ teaspoon sugar
1 teaspoon balsamic vinegar

Spicy Satay Sauce
1 tablespoon peanut oil, for frying
150 g/5 oz raw peanuts
½ teaspoon shrimp paste
1 large chilli, seeded and sliced
2 bird's eye chilli, seeded and sliced
4 cloves garlic
¼ tomato, chopped
1 tablespoon brown sugar
2 teaspoons kecap manis
2 kaffir lime leaves, finely cut

Method

1. Preheat the oven to 180°C/350°F/Gas mark 4. Place the pumpkin, capsicum and eggplant pieces in a large bowl. Toss with 2 tablespoons of the oil, paprika, cayenne pepper, and salt and pepper. Place vegetables on a baking tray lined with baking paper. Bake for 20–30 minutes, or until tender. Remove the skin from the capsicum when cool enough to handle.

2. For the spicy satay sauce, heat the oil in a pan over a medium heat. Fry the peanuts until golden brown. Tip onto kitchen paper. In the same pan, fry the shrimp paste for 30 seconds. Add the shrimp paste, 125 ml/4 fl oz water, and all the remaining ingredients except for the peanuts, to the bowl of a food processor and blend. Add the peanuts and blend until fairly smooth. Add more water if necessary.

3. For the caramelised onions, melt the butter in a frying pan over a medium heat. Add the onions and stir to coat evenly. Fry for 10 minutes, stirring occasionally. You may need to reduce the heat to prevent the onions burning or drying out. Add a little water if necessary.

4. After 10 minutes, sprinkle with salt and sugar and cook for another 10 minutes, or until onions are a rich brown colour. Add the balsamic vinegar to deglaze the pan.

5. Heat the remaining oil in a frying pan over a medium heat. Cook the halloumi pieces for 2 minutes on each side until lightly browned and gently crisp.

6. Place the baby spinach onto the bread bases and top with slices of pumpkin, eggplant and capsicum. Add halloumi slices, caramelised onion and spiced satay sauce. Finish off with the bread tops.

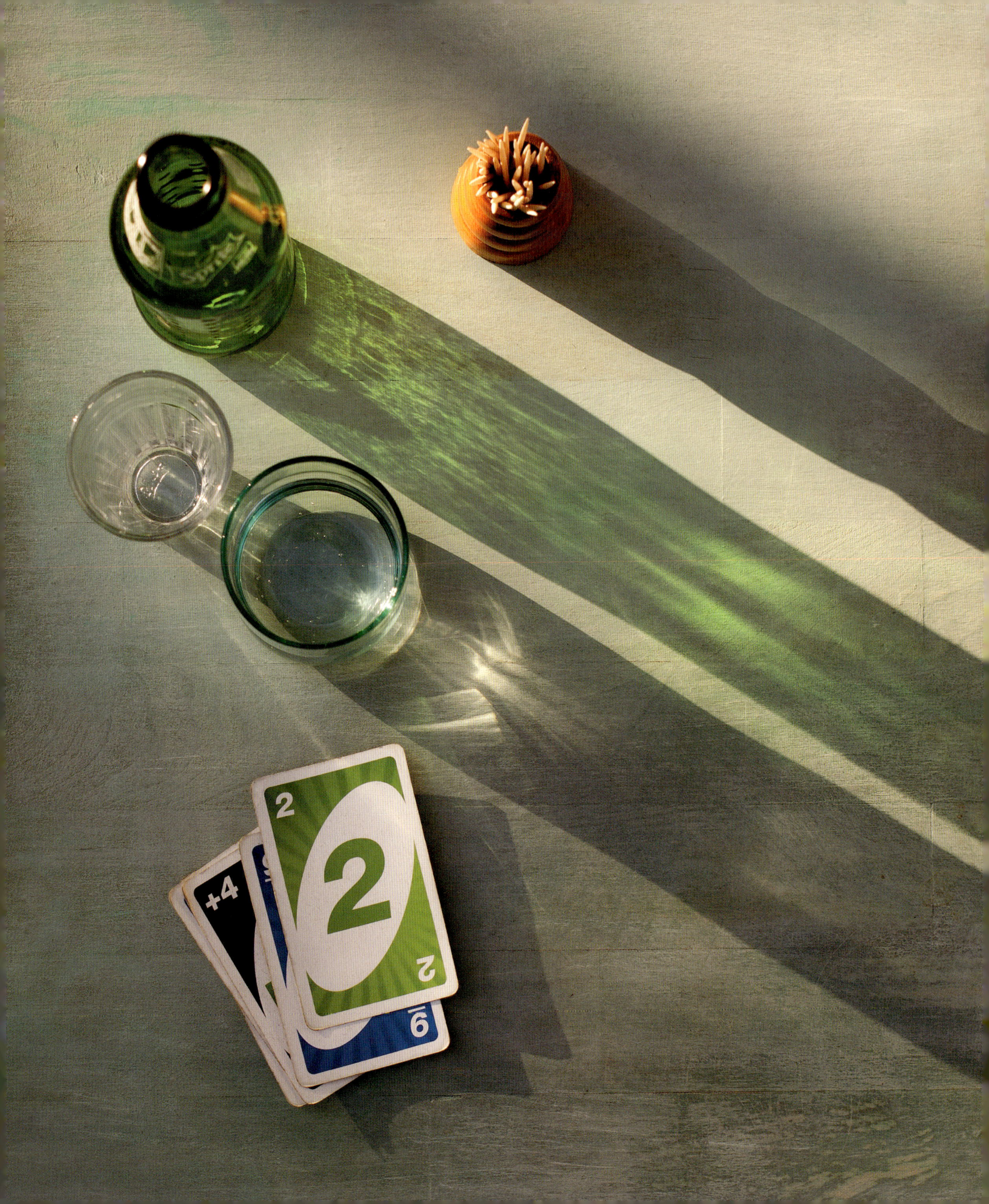
2
2
+4

Pizza Dough

Makes 3 medium pizza bases

Ingredients

375 ml/12 fl oz warm water

2 teaspoons dried yeast

450 g/1 lb plain (all-purpose) flour, plus extra for dusting

¼ teaspoon caster (superfine) sugar

1 teaspoon salt

60 ml/2 fl oz olive oil, plus extra for greasing

Method

1. To make the pizza dough, combine the water, yeast and flour in a large bowl. Set aside for about 5 minutes. Tip all the ingredients into the bowl of a food processor and pulse until a dough ball forms. Tip out the dough onto a lightly floured bench and use your hands to bring the dough together. Knead for about 10 minutes, or until the dough is smooth and elastic.
2. Brush a bowl lightly with olive oil and put the dough inside. Turn the dough to cover evenly with oil. Cover with cling film (plastic wrap) and set aside in a warm, draught-free place for 30 minutes. The dough should double in size.
3. Remove the dough and divide the mixture into three balls, or as required. On a lightly floured bench, roll out the dough into a round flat pizza base.
4. Unused bases can be stored in the freezer.

Yogurt Flat Bread Pizza Base

Ingredients

350 g/12 oz self-raising (self-rising) flour, plus extra for dusting

350 g/12 oz Greek natural (plain) yogurt

2 teaspoons salt

2 teaspoons baking powder

Method

1. To make the yogurt flat bread pizza base, put all the ingredients into the bowl of a food processor and pulse until a dough is formed. If the dough is too wet, sprinkle with flour and pulse again.
2. Tip out the dough onto a lightly floured bench and knead for 3 minutes.
3. Divide into three equal size pieces and roll out each using a floured rolling pin.
4. Unused bases can be stored in the freezer.

Basic Tomato Paste

1. Combine tomato purée/paste with dried oregano leaves, salt and pepper.

Tip

A variety of herbs can be added to the flat bread for extra taste, including dill and tarragon.

Pizza Time

Traditional pizza nights offer a perfect solution for feeding the family. For years now we have been making our own pizzas, starting with store-bought bases and, more recently, making the bases from scratch. Pizzas are amazing because of the diversity of toppings that can be arranged on top. If you want to have a crack at pizza bases, we have provided a classic pizza dough and a quicker yogurt flat bread that can be used. Here are some ideas to get you started.

Pear, Bacon and Blue Cheese Pizza

Ingredients
- 1 quantity pizza bases (see p. 93)
- 3 tablespoons olive oil
- 115 g/4 oz bacon, diced
- 2 ripe pears, sliced
- 60 g/2 oz Gorgonzola blue cheese
- 45 g/1½ oz Parmesan cheese, shaved
- handful of rocket (arugula) leaves, to serve

Method
1. Preheat the oven to 200°C/400°F/Gas mark 6.
2. Put the pizza bases on baking trays and brush with the olive oil. You can make the pizzas into any shape and size you want.
3. Fry the bacon on a preheated pan until mostly cooked.
4. Arrange pear slices evenly on the bases. Distribute the cooked bacon around the pizza.
5. Top with blue cheese and Parmesan, then bake for about 20 minutes, or until cooked to your liking.
6. Cut the pizzas to serve and add the rocket before eating.

Vegetarian Pizza

Ingredients

1 quantity pizza base (see recipe p. 93)
1 quantity Basic Tomato Paste (see recipe p. 93)
2 red capsicums (bell peppers), halved, seeds removed, and thinly sliced
200 g/7 oz field (portobello) mushrooms, sliced
1 red onion, halved and sliced
2 small zucchinis, sliced diagonally
½ cup sun-dried tomatoes
150 g/5 oz feta, crumbled
225 g/8 oz mozzarella cheese, grated (shredded)
1 handful of rocket (arugula), washed
1 tablespoon lemon juice
1 tablespoon olive oil
salt and pepper, to taste
chilli flakes (optional)

Method

1. Preheat the oven to 180°C/350°F/Gas mark 4. Place the pizza bases on baking paper or pizza trays and cover with basic tomato paste.
2. Layer the capsicums, mushrooms, onion, zucchini, tomatoes and cheeses onto the pizza bases.
3. Cook for about 20 minutes, or to your liking.
4. Place the rocket in a small bowl, add the lemon juice, oil and seasoning and toss gently.
5. Remove the pizzas from the oven and slice. Plate up and arrange the dressed rocket over the pizza slices. Sprinkle with chilli flakes if you like it hot.

Roasted Vegetables with Goat's Cheese and Caramelised Onion Pizza

Ingredients

1 quantity pizza base (see recipe p. 93)
250 g/9 oz sweet potato, sliced
250 g/9 oz pumpkin, sliced
3 tablespoons olive oil
1 large red onion, sliced
2 garlic gloves, crushed
2 tablespoons pine nuts, toasted
1 tablespoon rosemary, chopped
225 g/8 oz mozzarella, grated (shredded)
150 g/5 oz goat's cheese
handful of rocket (arugula) leaves, washed

Method

1. Preheat the oven to 200°C/400°F/Gas mark 6.
2. Place the sweet potato and pumpkin slices on a baking tray. Brush with olive oil and bake for about 20 minutes, or until they start to get some colour.
3. Cook the onions in a little olive oil in a preheated pan over medium heat. Add a drizzle of water to the onions and continue to cook until the onions are soft and caramelised.
4. Combine the garlic and remaining olive oil, then brush over the pizza bases.
5. Add the pumpkin and sweet potato to the pizza bases. Top with onion, pine nuts and rosemary being careful to evenly distribute the toppings. Add the cheeses and bake for about 20 minutes, or until cooked through.
6. Cut the pizzas and serve with rocket leaves.

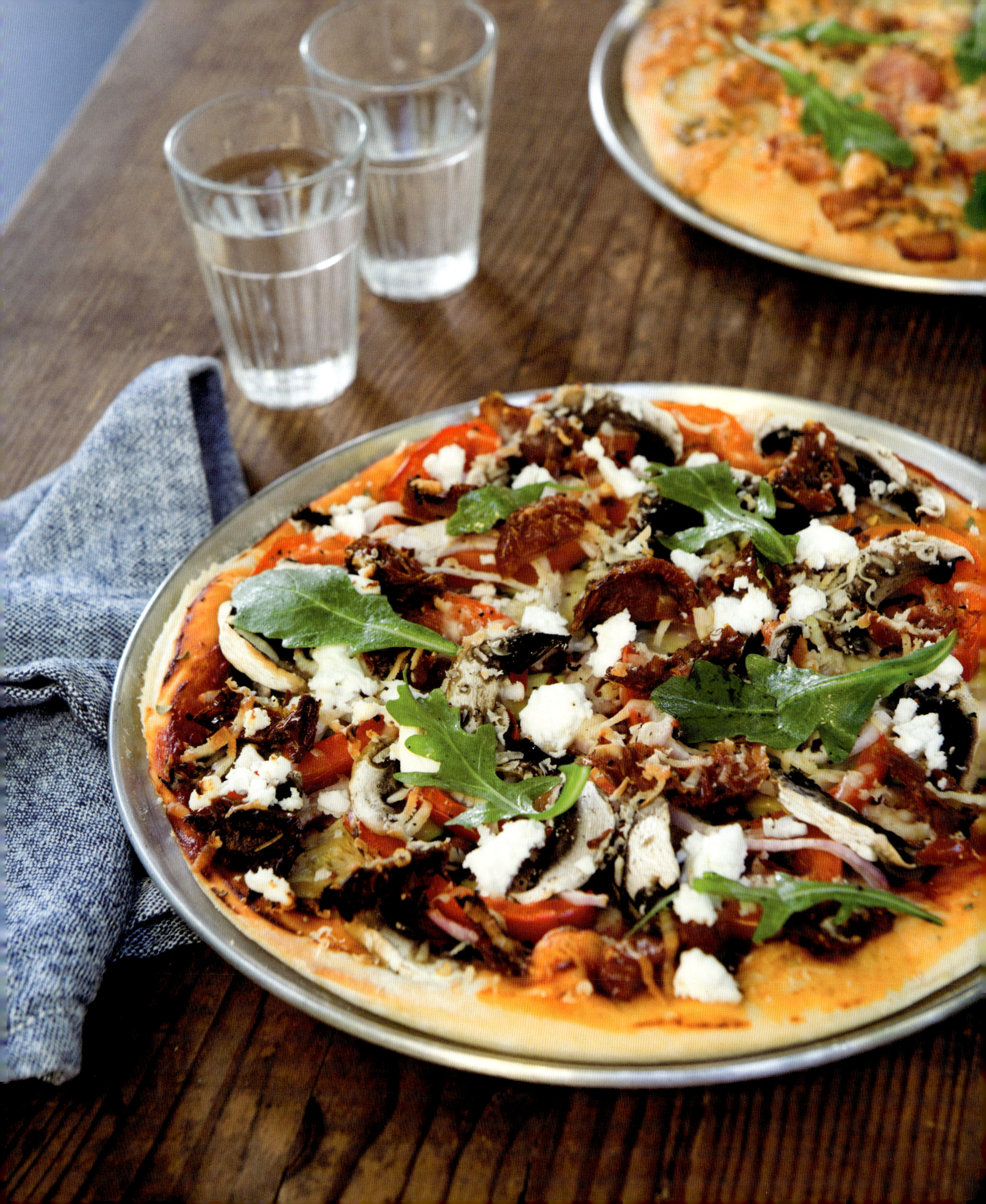

Hot and Spicy Pizza

Ingredients

1 quantity pizza base (see recipe p. 93)
1 quantity basic tomato paste (see recipe p.93)
18 slices pepperoni
1 chorizo, sliced diagonally
12 slices prosciutto
2 red capsicums (bell pepper), cored and thinly sliced
1 red onion, halved and sliced
3 large red chillies, seeded, halved and thinly sliced
18 pitted Kalamata olives, halved
225 g/8 oz mozzarella, grated (shredded)

Method

1. Preheat the oven to 180°C/350°F/Gas mark 4. Place the bases on baking paper or pizza trays and cover with basic tomato paste.
2. Layer the ingredients onto the pizza bases. Top with grated cheese.
3. Bake for about 20 minutes, or until cooked to your liking.
4. Remove the pizzas from the oven and slice.

Ingredients

1 tablespoon olive oil

3 tablespoons Sichuan pepper

2 tablespoons flaked salt

450 g/1 lb centre cut sashimi-grade tuna

40 g/1½ oz white sesame seeds

40 g/1½ oz black sesame seeds

2 green apples, halved, cored and thinly sliced into crescents

2 small cucumbers, thinly sliced

50 g/1¾ oz snow pea (sugar snap) shoots

1 avocado, peeled and diced

3 spring onions (scallions), finely sliced

3 teaspoons pickled ginger

2 tablespoons coriander (cilantro) leaves

Miso Dressing

3 tablespoons white miso paste

3 tablespoons mirin

1½ tablespoons rice wine vinegar

½ teaspoon sesame oil

2 tablespoons honey

Method

1. Heat the oil in a frying pan over a high heat. Meanwhile, mix the pepper and salt together and rub on the tuna, coating it evenly. Add the tuna to the pan and sear for 1 minute on each side. Transfer to a clean plate until cool enough to handle.
2. Combine the sesame seeds on a clean flat surface and roll the cooled tuna on the sesame seeds to coat. Wrap with cling film (plastic wrap) and refrigerate.
3. Combine all the miso dressing ingredients in a bowl and whisk lightly.
4. Remove the tuna from the refrigerator and slice into 2.5 cm/1 in pieces. To serve, plate the ingredients in a line in the following order; tuna, apple and cucumber. Build around these ingredients using snow pea shoots, avocado dice, onions, pickled ginger and coriander leaves. Drizzle with dressing.

Sesame Seared Tuna and Apple Salad with Miso Dressing

This recipe uses sashimi-grade tuna. You can halve the recipe to serve as a small starter to make an expensive ingredient go further, if you like. The Japanese-inspired flavours and fresh ingredients make the whole dish so tasty. If you haven't tried Japanese food this is a really easy and healthy recipe to begin with.

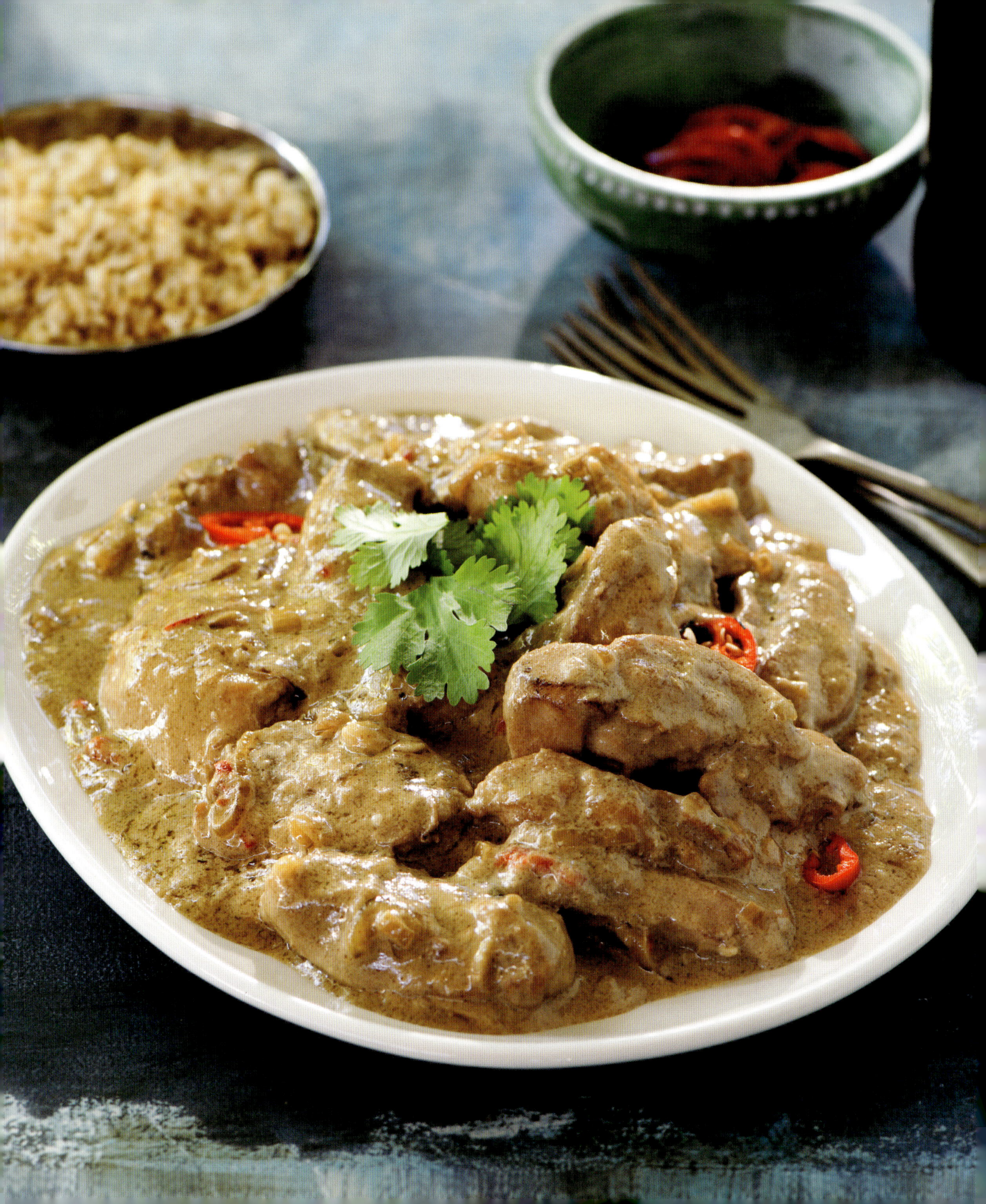

Creamy Balinese Chicken

Ingredients

6 tablespoons oil
4 shallots, 2 halved and finely sliced and 2 finely chopped
1 kg/2¼ lb chicken thigh fillets, cut into large pieces
3 garlic gloves, minced
2.5 cm/1 in piece of galangal, peeled and grated
1 tablespoons ground coriander
1 teaspoon ground cumin
½ teaspoon shrimp paste
6 macadamia nuts, crushed
3 tablespoons kecap manis
450 ml/16 fl oz coconut cream
1 large chilli, seeded and chopped
salt and pepper, to taste

Method

1. In a frying pan, heat half the oil over a medium flame and fry the sliced shallots until browned. Remove from the pan and set aside. In the same oil, fry the thigh pieces until evenly coloured, then remove.
2. In a large pan, heat the remaining oil over medium heat. Fry the chopped shallots until browned. Add the garlic and galangal, frying briefly before adding the coriander, cumin and shrimp paste. Cook, stirring constantly for 3 minutes.
3. Add the crushed nuts, kecap manis, coconut cream and chilli, and bring to the boil. Add the partly cooked chicken, seasoning and reduce the heat to a simmer for about 30 minutes, string occasionally. Just before serving, add the fried sliced shallots and stir in.
4. Serve with white rice.

The food of Bali is very easy to fall in love with. Whether it's a fast mie goreng to fill an empty stomach after a morning surfing or a satay stick when walking the streets during a shopping spree. The Balinese even have the perfect condiment for every meal ... that's right, a cold Bintang. This is one of many meals we replicated when we came home.

Tip
Chicken legs can replace thigh fillets for variety.

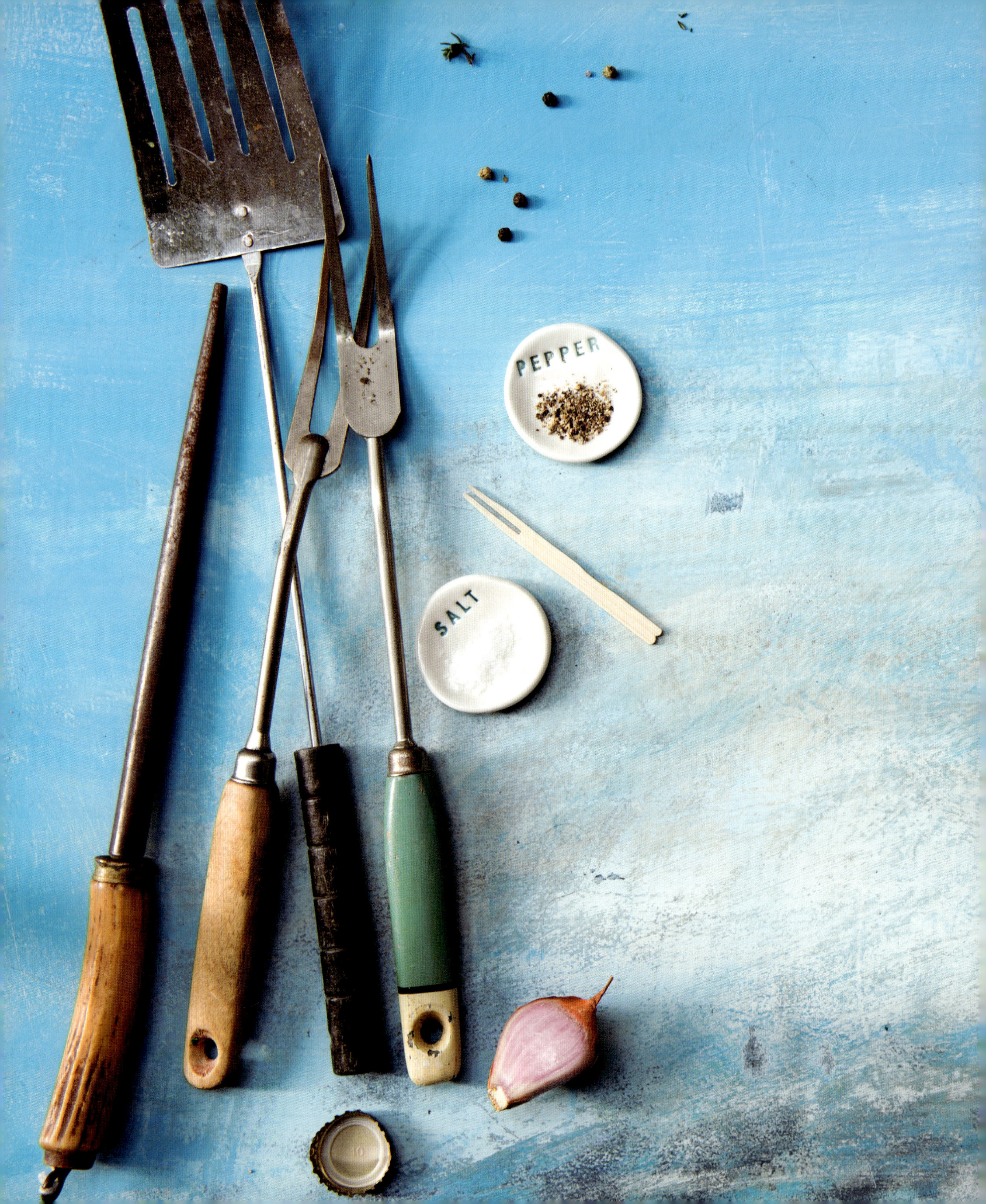
PEPPER
SALT

The BBQ

Some things just taste better on the barbecue. There is something special about this method of cooking; it's an Australian tradition. We like to use the 'barbie' a few times a week and there is no limit to the type of meal you can put together. Whether it's a humble steak or a beautiful piece of fish, with a little preparation you can really impress your family and friends. The recipes we have included in this chapter are some of our best-loved things to cook. With a beer in one hand and a pair of tongs in the other, it doesn't get any better.

Indonesian Chicken Drumsticks

Drumsticks are one of the cheapest cuts of the chicken and, in our humble opinion, one of the tastiest. This dish requires the chicken to be poached, you can simply marinate and barbecue it, but it isn't as good. We recommend you take the little extra time to poach it and get the benefit of the sauce also. This is a great dish to put down in front of a group of hungry people and just let them help themselves.

Ingredients

- 1.5–2 kg/3 lb 5 oz–4 lb 6 oz chicken drumsticks
- 1 x 400 ml/14 oz can coconut milk
- 1 stalk lemongrass, white part only, bruised
- 4 kaffir lime leaves
- 3 tablespoons kecap manis
- coriander (cilantro) leaves, to serve
- chopped chilli, to serve
- 1 tablespoons lime juice

Marinade

- 3 small shallots, chopped
- 4 garlic cloves, chopped
- 2 bird's eye chillies, chopped
- 3 cm/1¼ in piece turmeric, chopped
- 3 cm/1¼ in piece galangal, chopped
- 6 candlenuts (use macadamias, if not available), toasted, chopped
- 1 stalk lemongrass, white part only, bruised and chopped
- 1 teaspoon ground coriander
- ½ teaspoon ground cumin
- 2 tablespoons vegetable oil

Method

1. To make the marinade, process all the ingredients in the bowl of a food processor until finely chopped. Tip the marinade into a large bowl and rub the drumsticks all over to coat. Cover with plastic wrap and refrigerate for at least 30 minutes to marinate.
2. Put the coconut milk, lemongrass and the kaffir lime leaves in a large pan over a low flame and bring to a simmer. Stir in the marinade from the drumsticks. Cover and simmer for 15 minutes. Add the marinated chicken drumsticks and simmer, covered, for 20 minutes or until cooked through. Remove the drumsticks and pour the poaching liquid into the bowl of a food processor or blender and process, then strain through a fine sieve into a jug.
3. Brush the chicken drumsticks with kecap manis and place on a heated barbecue over a medium flame. Cook until a lovely dark brown colour. Be careful not to have the barbecue too hot or you will burn the chicken.
4. To serve, place the chicken in a large tray or bowl and sprinkle with coriander leaves and chopped chilli, then drizzle with lime juice. This is meant as a shared plate and people can then add the sauce or simply squeeze lime juice on them.

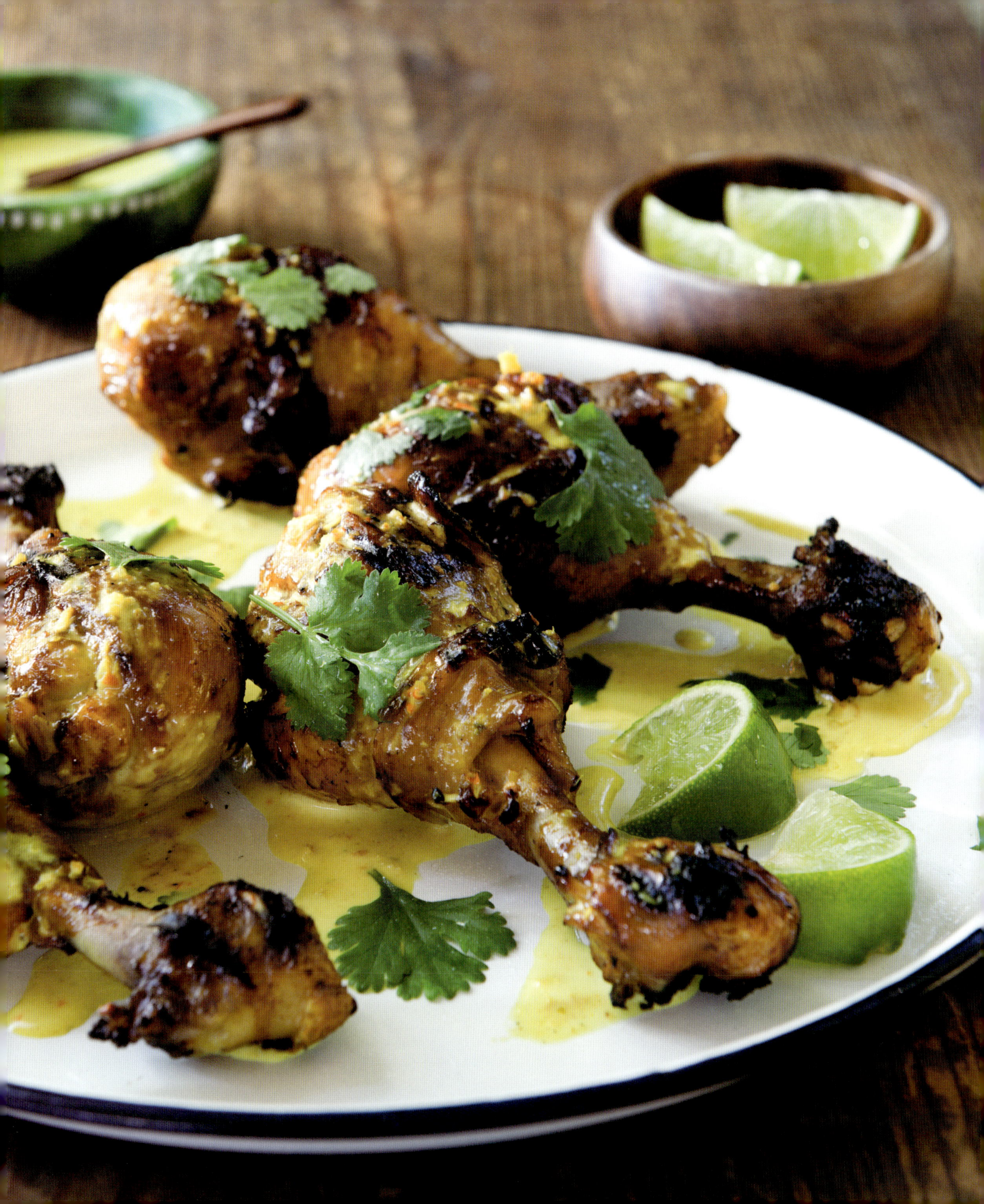

Warm Seafood Salad with Citrus Dressing

This is a tasty and refreshing meal for seafood lovers. Seafood and citrus are a great combination when cooking. This meal can be used as a starter or part of a main meal. Be sure to get good quality produce when cooking seafood.

Ingredients

200 g/7 oz calamari hoods, cleaned
2 fillets firm white fish, skin off
750 g/1½ lb uncooked shrimp (prawns), shelled and deveined
Oil, for cooking
1 tablespoon coriander (cilantro) leaves, chopped
1 tablespoon mint, chopped

Citrus Dressing
juice of 2 lemons
2 tablespoons orange juice
175 ml/6 fl oz olive oil
½ teaspoon finely grated lemon zest
½ teaspoon finely grated orange zest
1 teaspoon palm sugar
1 clove garlic, minced
salt and pepper, to taste

Method

1. For the citrus dressing, put all the ingredients in a small bowl and whisk until combined.
2. Cut the calamari in half lengthwise. Score the inside of in a criss-cross pattern.
3. Combine all the seafood in a large bowl with half of the citrus dressing. Cover and refrigerate for a couple of hours or overnight.
4. Oil the barbecue plate and preheat over a high flame. Drain the seafood using a colander and cook in batches until lightly browned and the shrimp have changed colour.
5. Toss the seafood with the citrus dressing and the herbs and serve warm.

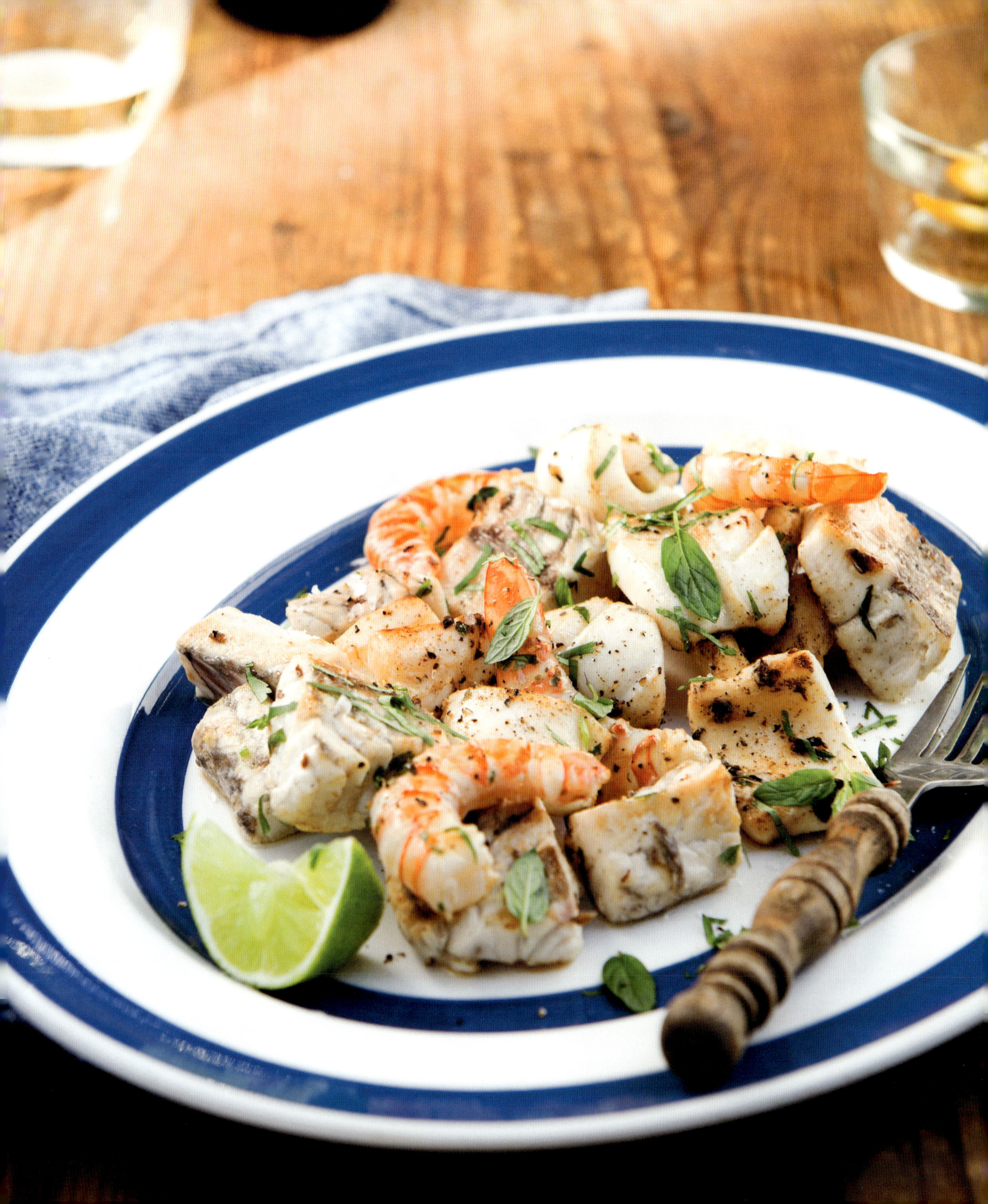

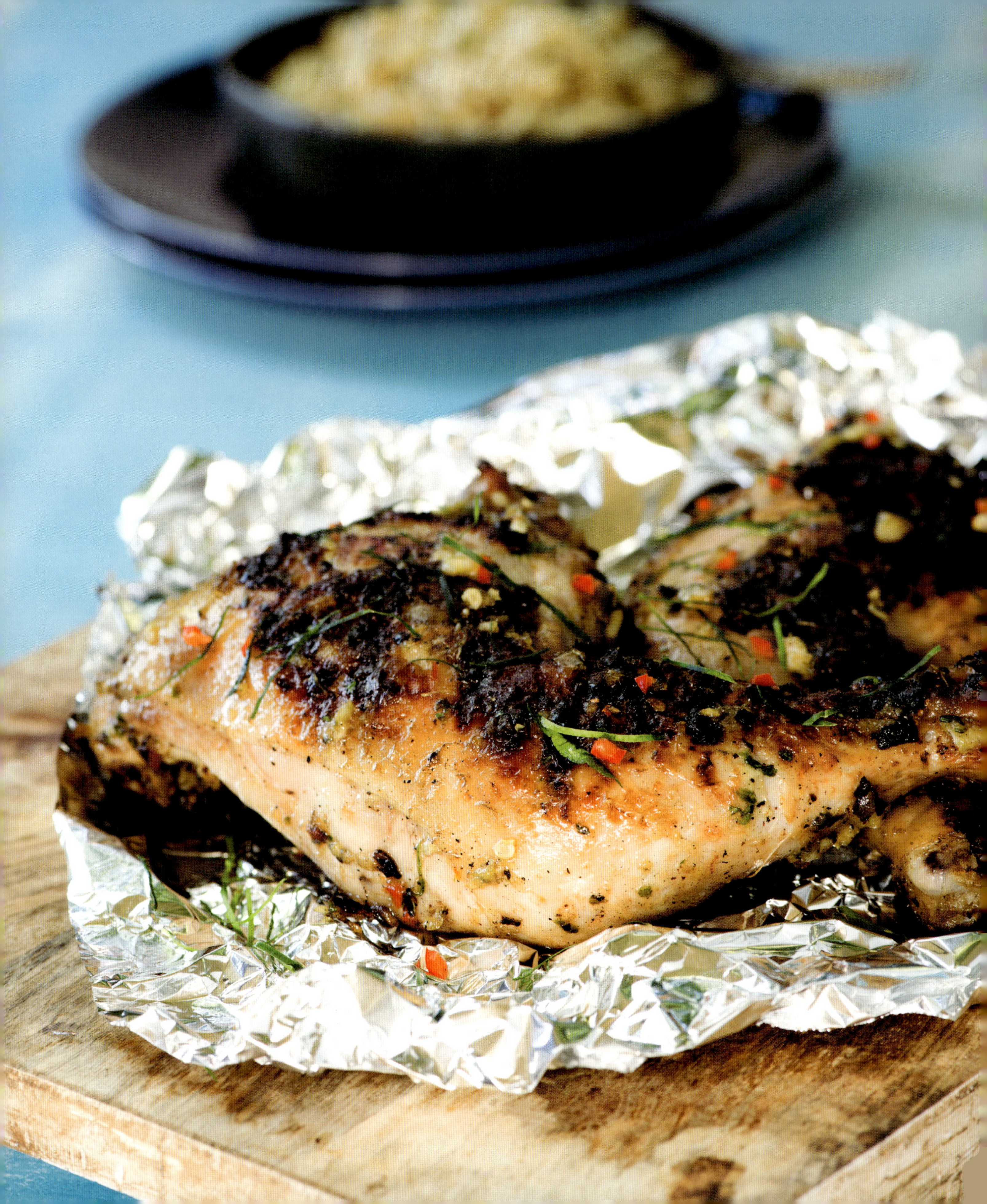

Thai Chicken with Fragrant Rice

This dish is a great combination of fresh Thai flavours with the char-grill of the barbecue. It's sure to surprise people when plated up straight from the grill. People love this fragrant rice when served up at our places and always ask after the recipe.

Ingredients

4 chicken Maryland (thighs and drumsticks), skin on)
salt and pepper
lime wedges, to garnish

Marinade
1 tablespoon oil
3 cm/1½ in piece galangal, peeled and grated (shredded)
4 garlic cloves, minced
4 shallots, finely chopped
1 large red chilli, seeded and finely chopped (retain the seeds if you like some heat)
½ cup coriander (cilantro) leaves, chopped
150 ml/5 fl oz coconut cream

Rice
2 tablespoons oil
200 g/7 oz jasmine rice, rinsed
2 teaspoons cumin seeds
100 ml/3½ fl oz coconut milk
350 ml/12 fl oz hot water
3 kaffir lime leaves, middle stem removed, rolled and thinly sliced

Method

1. Rub the chicken pieces with salt and pepper and place in a shallow dish.
2. For the marinade, place the oil, galangal, garlic, shallots, chilli and coriander leaves into a food processor and blend to a paste. Alternatively, use a mortar and pestle, if you like. Scrape the paste into a small bowl and mix in the coconut cream. Pour the marinade over the chicken, cover and refrigerate for at least 2 hours, but overnight is best.
3. For the rice, heat the oil in a large pan on a medium heat and add the cumin seeds. Stir until fragrant. Add the rice, stirring continually for 2 minutes. Next add, the coconut milk, water and seasoning. Bring to the boil.
4. Cover, then reduce the heat and simmer for 10 minutes, or until the liquid is absorbed by the rice. Remove from the pan and allow to stand for 10 minutes. Before serving, fluff the rice with a fork and mix in the shredded lime leaves.
5. Remove the chicken from the marinade and place on a barbecue grill or plate over a medium heat. Cook for about 25 minutes, turning regularly and basting with the remaining marinade. Allow the chicken to rest for 5 minutes before serving.
6. Serve with rice and garnish with a lime wedge. A sweet chilli sauce is a perfect condiment for this meal.

Tip
The chicken is properly cooked when clear juices run out after a skewer is inserted into the leg.

Satay Sticks

Anyone who has traveled to Asia will have tried various forms of satay sticks. Chicken, beef, pork or minced seafood are placed on sticks and grilled over burning coconut husks, then served with a peanut sauce. No trip to Bali is complete without buying satay sticks from the street vendors. The taste of the marinade mixed with that authentic sauce is just beautiful. Chicken satay for us was the first dish that our boys would eat in Bali, and it is still a family favourite. There are two ways to make satay sticks. One is to thread small pieces of marinated meat onto sticks and the other is to combine minced meat with a spice paste and wrap them onto lemongrass stalks. We have included one of each for you here.

Ingredients

CHICKEN
- 12 wooden satay sticks
- 300 g/10½ oz chicken thigh fillets
- 3 garlic cloves, minced
- 3 tablespoons oil
- 2 shallots, sliced and fried
- 1 teaspoon soy sauce
- 2 tablespoons kecap manis (sweet soy sauce)
- 2 teaspoons cracked black pepper
- 2 kaffir lime leaves, shredded

SPICY SATAY SAUCE
- 2 tablespoons oil, for frying peanuts
- 150 g/5 oz raw peanuts
- ½ teaspoon shrimp paste
- 1 teaspoon salt
- 1 large chilli, seeded and chopped
- 2 bird's eye chilli, seeded and chopped
- 4 garlic cloves
- 4 cherry tomatoes, chopped
- 1 tablespoon brown sugar
- 2 teaspoons kecap manis (sweet soy sauce)
- 2 kaffir lime leaves, finely cut
- 125 ml/4 fl oz water

Method

1. For the chicken satay sticks, soak the wooden sticks in water for about 30 minutes.
2. Slice the chicken into small, equal-sized pieces. Mix the rest of the ingredients in a bowl and combine with the chicken. Coat it evenly, cover and leave for about 20 minutes in the refrigerator.
3. Thread the chicken pieces onto the sticks and then barbecue or grill them for about 5 minutes, or until cooked. You can baste the chicken with the marinade as the skewers cook to avoid them drying out.
4. Serve with boiled rice and spicy satay sauce.

Spicy Satay Sauce

1. For the spicy satay sauce, heat the oil in a frying pan over medium heat. Fry the peanuts until golden brown. Transfer the peanuts onto paper towels.
2. In the same pan, fry the shrimp paste for 30 seconds.
3. Place the remaining ingredients in a food processor and blend until combined. Add the peanuts and blend until fairly smooth. Add a little water, if necessary. Return to the frying pan and set over a low heat if you want to serve the sauce warm.

Seafood

200 g/7 oz firm white fish (such as mackerel, snapper, flathead etc.)
100 g/3½ oz prawn (shrimp) meat
4 kaffir lime leaves
60 ml/2 fl oz coconut milk
2 teaspoons palm sugar
salt, to taste
lemongrass stalks, or skewers soaked in water

Spice Paste

¼ teaspoon shrimp paste
2 teaspoons tamarind puree
5 cloves garlic
¼ teaspoon pepper
2 small red shallots, sliced
1 tomato
2 stalks lemongrass (white part only), chopped
3 large red chillies
2 small red chillies
2 teaspoons palm sugar
2 teaspoons turmeric, chopped
2 teaspoons ginger, chopped
1 tablespoon galangal, chopped
½ teaspoon ground coriander
¼ teaspoon black pepper

1. For the spice paste, put the spice paste ingredients in the bowl of a food processor and blend to a smooth paste. Scrape out into a large bowl.
2. Place the seafood into the bowl a food processor and pulse until minced, then transfer to the bowl along with the spice paste. Mix all the ingredients together, then add the lime leaves, coconut milk and palm sugar.
3. Take a tablespoon of the mixture and mould onto the thick end of a lemongrass stalk.
4. Cook each stick on the grill (broiler), turning regularly to brown each evenly.
5. Serve the sticks on steamed rice with Spicy Satay Sauce.

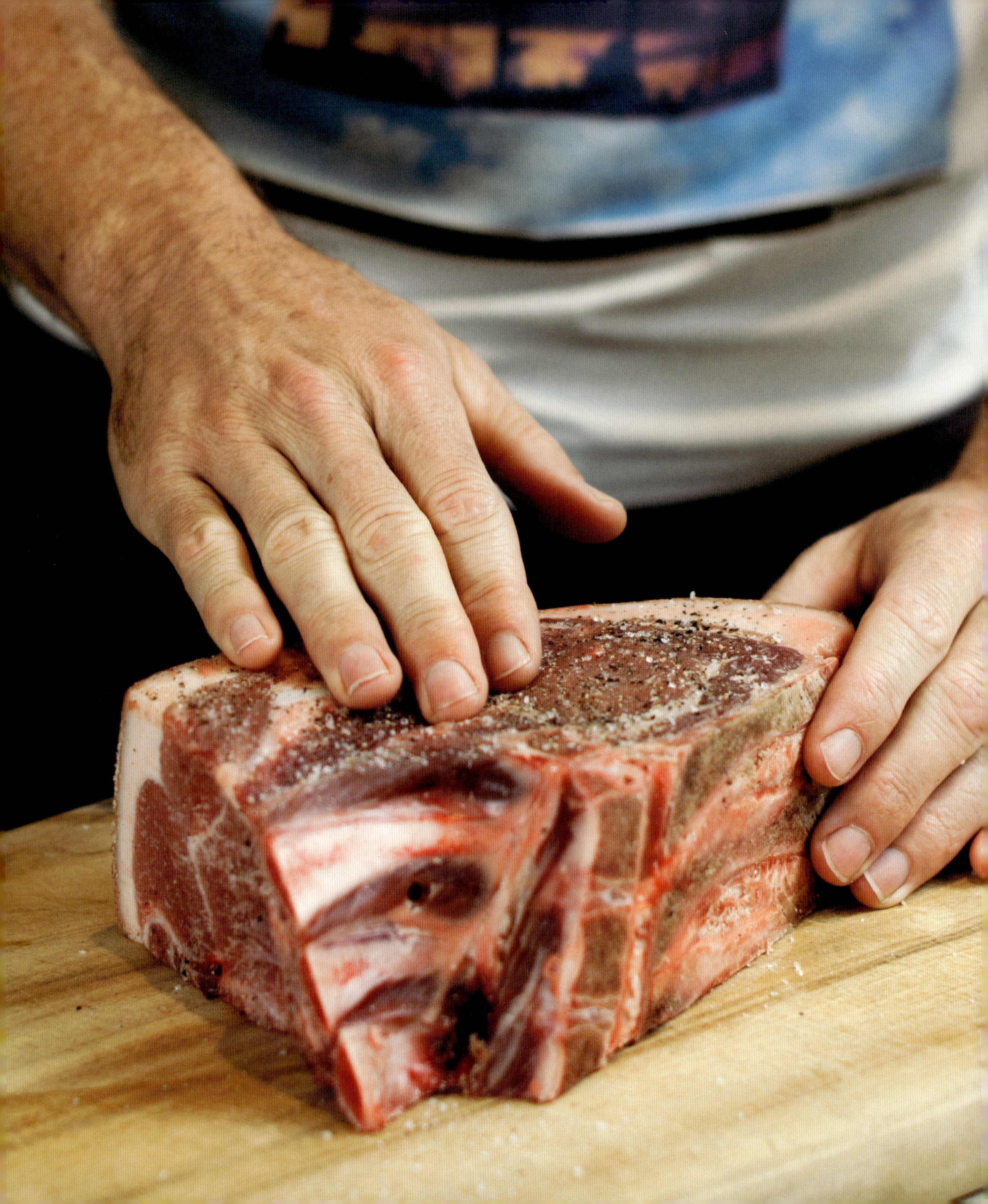

Peppercorn Beef Fillet, Grilled Sweet Potato and Field Mushrooms

There's nothing wrong with the classic meat and vegetable meal. If it ain't broke, don't try to fix it. We love this dish because it's no fuss, and the whole thing can be cooked on the barbecue.

The addition of some fresh herbs and spices to all elements of the meal will impress all who taste it. The only thing left out of the ingredients is the couple of beers needed when cooking the meal.

Ingredients

1 tablespoon black peppercorns
1 teaspoon cumin seeds
salt, to taste
4 beef fillet steaks
3 tablespoons olive oil

Sweet Potato
1 large sweet potato, peeled and cut into 1 cm/½ in slices
1 teaspoon fresh thyme leaves
½ teaspoon dried chilli flakes
2 tablespoons olive oil

Field Mushrooms
250 g/9 fl oz field (portobello) mushrooms, halved
2 tablespoons balsamic vinegar
1 teaspoon fresh thyme leaves
2 garlic cloves, minced
2 tablespoons olive oil
salt and pepper, to taste
1 handful rocket (arugula) leaves, washed

Method

1. For the field mushrooms, toss the mushrooms, balsamic, thyme, garlic and oil together in a non-metallic medium bowl. Season to taste. Cover and leave to marinate for at least 1 hour.
2. In a small frying pan, dry roast the peppercorns and cumin seeds for about 1 minute on a medium heat. Remove from the heat and crush in a mortar and pestle, or pulse in a spice grinder. Add some salt and rub the mixture into the fillets. Drizzle the fillets with oil and rub in. Set aside until ready to cook.
3. Boil the sweet potato in a pan of water until just tender, then drain. Combine the thyme, chilli flakes and oil in a medium bowl. Add the drained sweet potato and gently toss to coat. Preheated the barbecue grill or plate over a medium flame and cook the sweet potato until browned, turning once. Set aside and keep warm.
4. Increased the heat to a high flame and cook the prepared mushrooms for 4 minutes, turning continuously. Remove from the heat and allow to cool slightly. Mix the rocket leaves with the mushrooms.
5. For the steaks, brush the barbecue hot plate with oil and cook the steaks for 3–5 minutes on each side, or until cooked to your liking. Allow the steaks to rest for 5 minutes before serving. Serve with grilled sweet potato and mushroom salad.

Tip: After resting the steak, place on paper towel for 10 seconds before serving. This stops excess juices from pooling on your plate.

Pork Fillet with Sweet Chilli Sauce

This is another Balinese-inspired dish that goes well with any grilled meat or fish. You could substitute the pork for chicken, beef or even a nice fillet of fish. The authentic flavours in the sauce coupled with the coconut rice and beans will be dancing on your tongue.

Ingredients

Marinade

- 1 kg/2¼ lb pork fillet
- 4 tablespoons kecap manis
- 2 garlic cloves, minced
- 2 kaffir lime leaves, shredded plus extra shredded, to garnish
- 4 tablespoons oil
- 1 lemongrass stalk, bruised
- ¼ teaspoon salt
- 250 ml/9 fl oz water
- toasted coconut, to garnish

Spicy Sauce Paste

- 8 garlic cloves, chopped
- 1 tomato, diced
- 3 red shallots, diced
- 1 tablespoons ginger, chopped
- 3 large red chillies, seeded and chopped
- 4 red bird's eye chillies
- 1 stalk of lemongrass, white part only
- 2 teaspoons brown sugar
- ½ teaspoon shrimp paste
- ¼ teaspoon white pepper

Coconut Rice

- 250 ml/9 fl oz water
- 250 ml/9 fl oz coconut milk
- 200 g/7 oz jasmine rice

Method

1. Marinate the pork fillets in a bowl with 2 tablespoons kecap manis, garlic and kaffir lime leaves. Cover and refrigerate for 30 minutes.
2. For the spicy sauce paste, place all of the ingredients into the bowl of a food processor and blend.
3. Heat 2 tablespoons of the oil in a frying pan over a medium heat and fry off the paste mix until aromatic. Add the bruised lemongrass stalk, kecap manis and salt. Add the water, reduce the heat and simmer, covered, for 30 minutes, stirring occasionally. Remove the lemongrass stalk prior to serving.
4. For the jasmine rice, bring the water and coconut milk to the boil. Add the rice, bring back to the boil before reducing the heat. Simmer, covered, for 15 minutes, stirring occasionally, or until the liquid has been absorbed by the rice. Remove from the heat and allow to rest for 5 minutes covered.
5. Heat 2 tablespoons of oil on flat plate of a barbecue over a medium heat. Sear the pork fillets and then cook for 7 minutes on each side, or until cooked through. Remove, cover in aluminium foil and rest for 5 minutes.
6. To serve, place the rice in middle of plate using a presentation ring and top with sliced pork fillet. Ladle sauce around the coconut rice. Garnish the pork with toasted coconut and shredded lime leaves.

Tip: Add some green to this dish by serving with blanched snake or green beans.

Jamaican Jerk Pork Chops with Mango Salsa

Jerk food is traditionally Jamaican. The word 'jerk' refers to the way the protein is seasoned and cooked. The flavouring may vary, but usually includes onion, chillies, thyme and allspice. Traditionally, the meat is marinated for hours with a marinade or paste before being slowly smoked to enhance the flavours. Our version of this dish will get the tastebuds dancing.

Ingredients

4 thick pork chops
oil, for greasing the barbecue plate

Marinade

2 shallots, peeled and chopped
2 garlic cloves, minced
1 tablespoon kecap manis
1 tablespoon lime juice
1 tablespoon thyme leaves, chopped
2 large red chillies, seeded and chopped
½ teaspoon ground allspice
2 tablespoons olive oil
salt and pepper, to taste

Salsa

2 tablespoons lime juice
1 tablespoon oil
salt and pepper, to taste
1 mango, peeled and diced
1 cucumber, peeled, seeded and diced
1 red capsicum (bell pepper), diced
1 tomato, diced
1 small red onion, diced
handful coriander (cilantro) leaves, chopped

Method

1. Place the chops in a shallow dish. For the marinade, blend all the ingredients in a food processor until smooth. Rub the marinade onto the pork, pressing in well. Marinate for at least 2 hours in the refrigerator, preferably overnight.
2. Make the salsa by mixing the lime juice, oil and seasoning together in a small bowl. Put the rest of the salsa ingredients in a medium bowl and toss gently with the dressing. Cover and refrigerate until ready to serve.
3. Preheat and oil a barbecue plate over a medium flame. Cook the marinated chops for 15 minutes, turning once, or until cooked through. Serve immediately with a side of mango salsa.

Tip: Watermelon can replace the mango in the salsa for variety.

Spiced Lamb and Pearl Couscous

This dish uses the wonderful combination of lamb and char-grilled eggplant. It's a classic Mediterranean combination that will have people begging for more. You can use a cheaper cut of lamb but we recommend you use fillet if possible; it will give a much better result.

Ingredients

8 lamb fillets (about 1 kg/2¼ lb)
oil, for greasing
salt and pepper, to season
coriander (cilantro) leaves, to garnish

Lamb Rub
1 teaspoon ground cumin
1 teaspoon salt
½ teaspoon pepper
1 teaspoon garam masala

Pearl Couscous
2 tablespoons oil
1 shallot, sliced
1 garlic clove, minced
250 g/9 oz pearl couscous
500 ml (17 fl oz) vegetable stock
2 tablespoons dried cranberries (pomegranate flavoured recommended)
⅓ cup mint, chopped
zest and juice of 1 lemon

Method

1. Preheat the oven to 180°C/350°F/Gas mark 4.
2. For the pearl couscous, heat the oil in a frying pan over a medium flame and cook the shallots until golden brown. Add the garlic and couscous and cook for 5 minutes, stirring occasionally, until the couscous is lightly browned.
3. Pour in the stock and simmer for 8–10 minutes, covered, or until the liquid is absorbed. Remove from the heat and transfer to a large bowl. Add the cranberries, mint, zest and lemon juice and stir to mix.
4. For the lamb rub, mix all the ingredients together in a bowl.
5. Lightly oil and season the fillets with the lamb rub. Sear the fillet in a frying pan so it is still rare. Place in a lined baking tray and oven roast for 8 minutes. Remove and rest in foil for 5 minutes.
6. To serve, place couscous on a large flat plate and top with sliced fillet. Season with salt and pepper and garnish with coriander leaves.

Tip
Add texture to this meal with crunchy oven-roasted chickpeas.

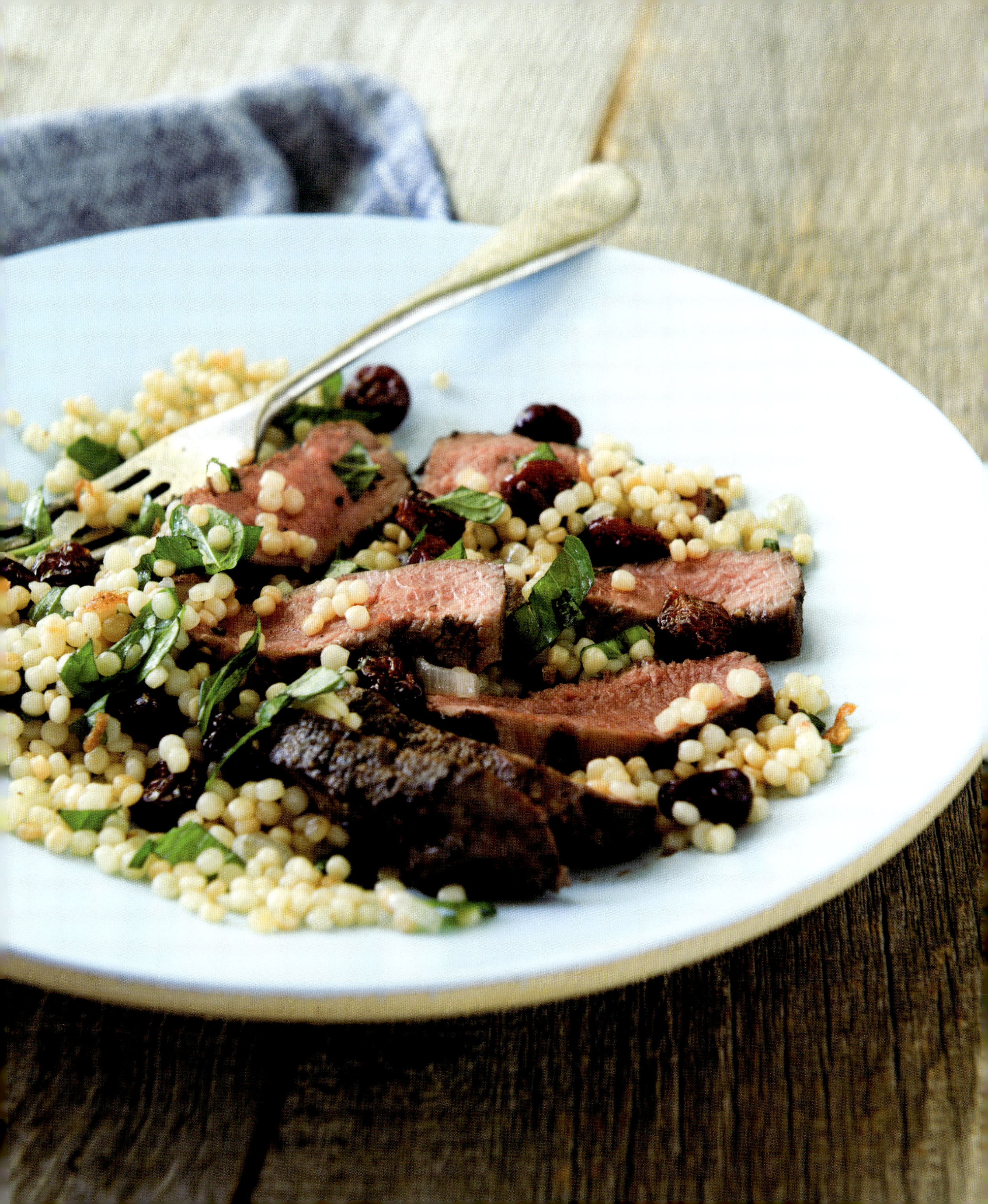

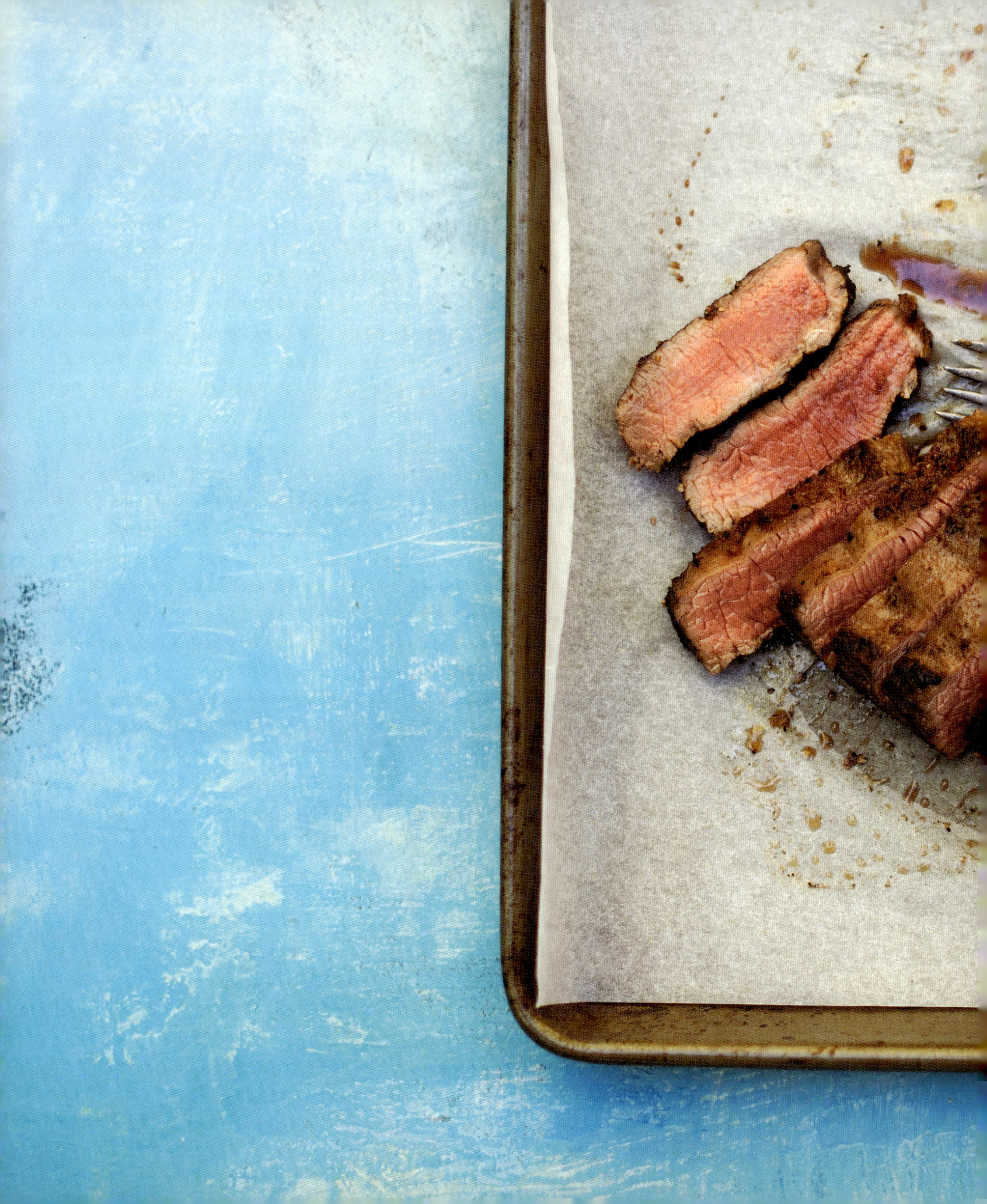

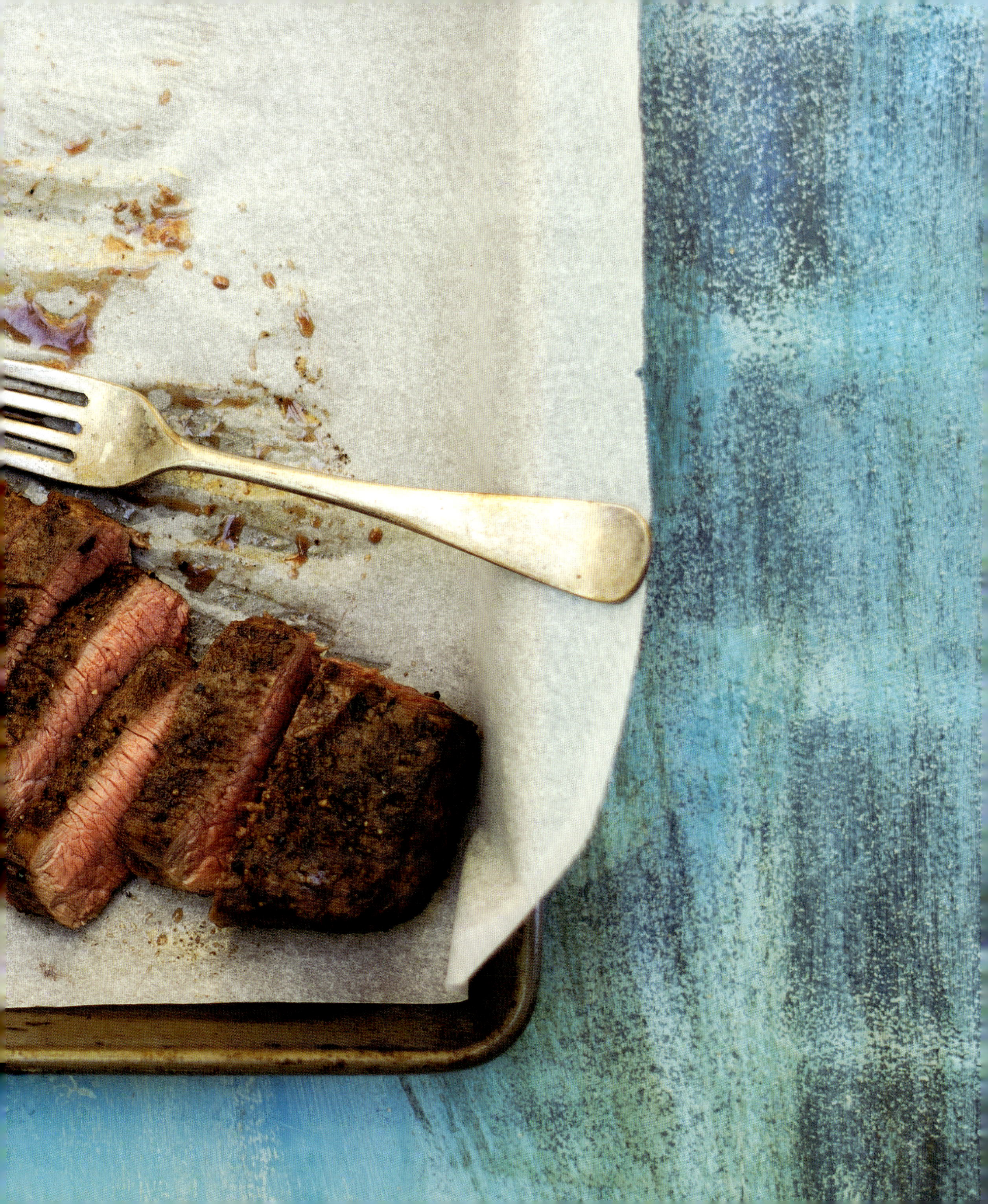

The Perfect Steak and Chimichurri Sauce

How many times have you been to someone's place for a barbecue and watched them take a beautiful piece of steak and turn it into a dry burnt offering? We hope after looking at this recipe you will never suffer that fate! Cooking a steak on a barbecue is easy once you know what you're after. We recommend cooking to medium-rare, but everyone has their own preference. Adding the perfect accompaniment? It's very hard to beat a good chimichurri.

Ingredients

4 x 200 g/7 oz steaks
salt and pepper
olive oil

Chimichurri Sauce

1 cup packed continental parsley
½ cup packed coriander (cilantro) leaves
2 garlic cloves, minced
125 ml/4 fl oz extra virgin olive oil
2 tablespoons red wine vinegar, plus extra, if needed
½ teaspoon chilli flakes
½ teaspoon ground cumin
salt, to taste

Method

1. To make the chimichurri sauce, place all the ingredients in a food processor and pulse to a smooth consistency. You may like to add more red wine vinegar to suit your taste.
2. Season the steaks liberally with salt and pepper just before cooking as the salt can draw out moisture from the meat. Heat a barbecue grill over a medium-high flame.
3. Place the seasoned meat on the barbecue and cook until you see blood coming through. Turn the meat and season. Cooking times here will vary depending on the thickness of your meat. You need to turn it only once and only after you see blood coming from the top surface of the meat. This should give you medium-rare every time.
4. Remove the steak again when you see blood coming to the top surface. Place the steaks on a plate and cover in foil and rest for about 5 minutes.
5. Serve your steak with your favourite side and top each with a good spoonful of the chimichurri.

Tip
Use eye fillet, rib fillet, porterhouse, rump or T-bone depending on your budget and tastes.

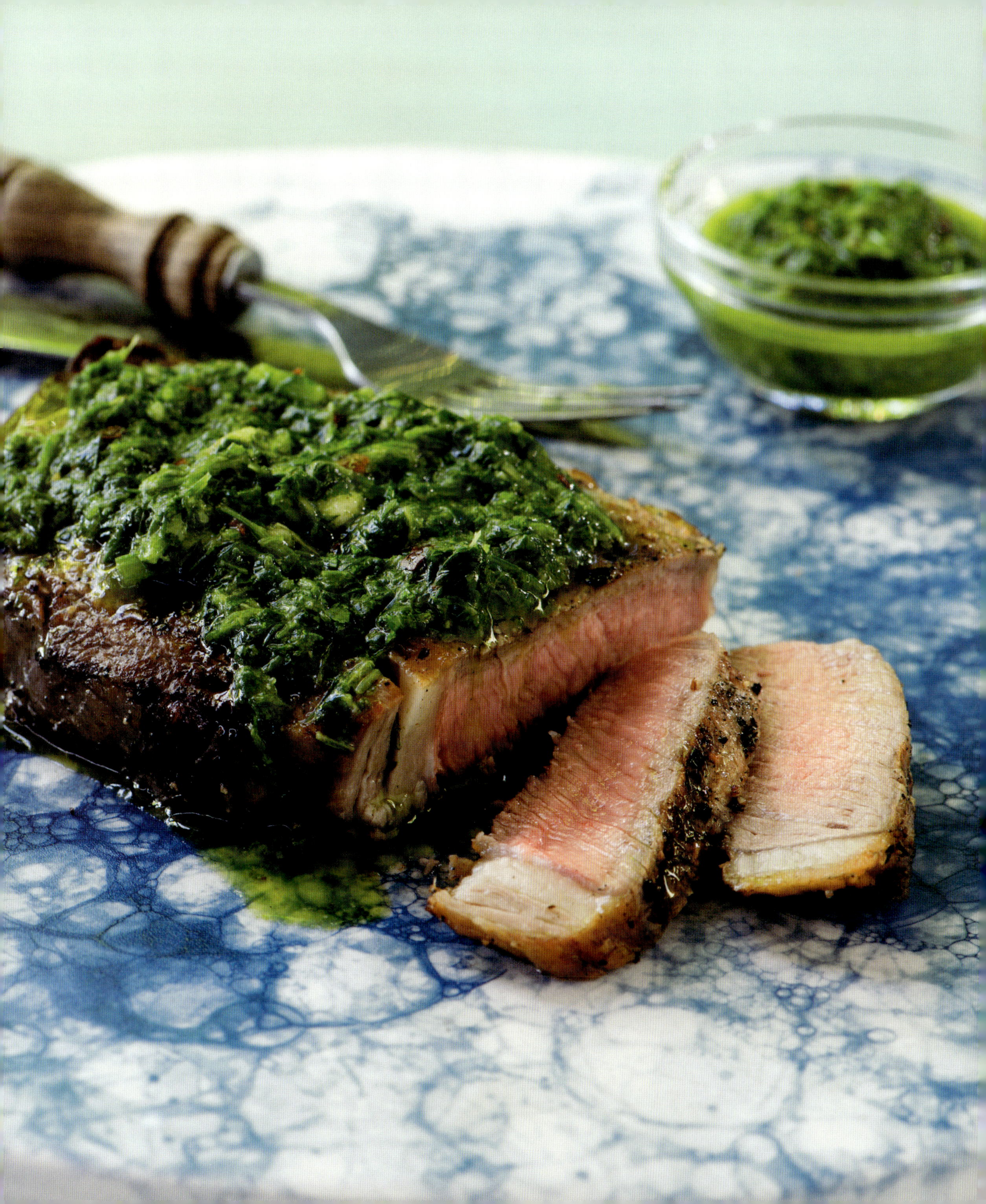

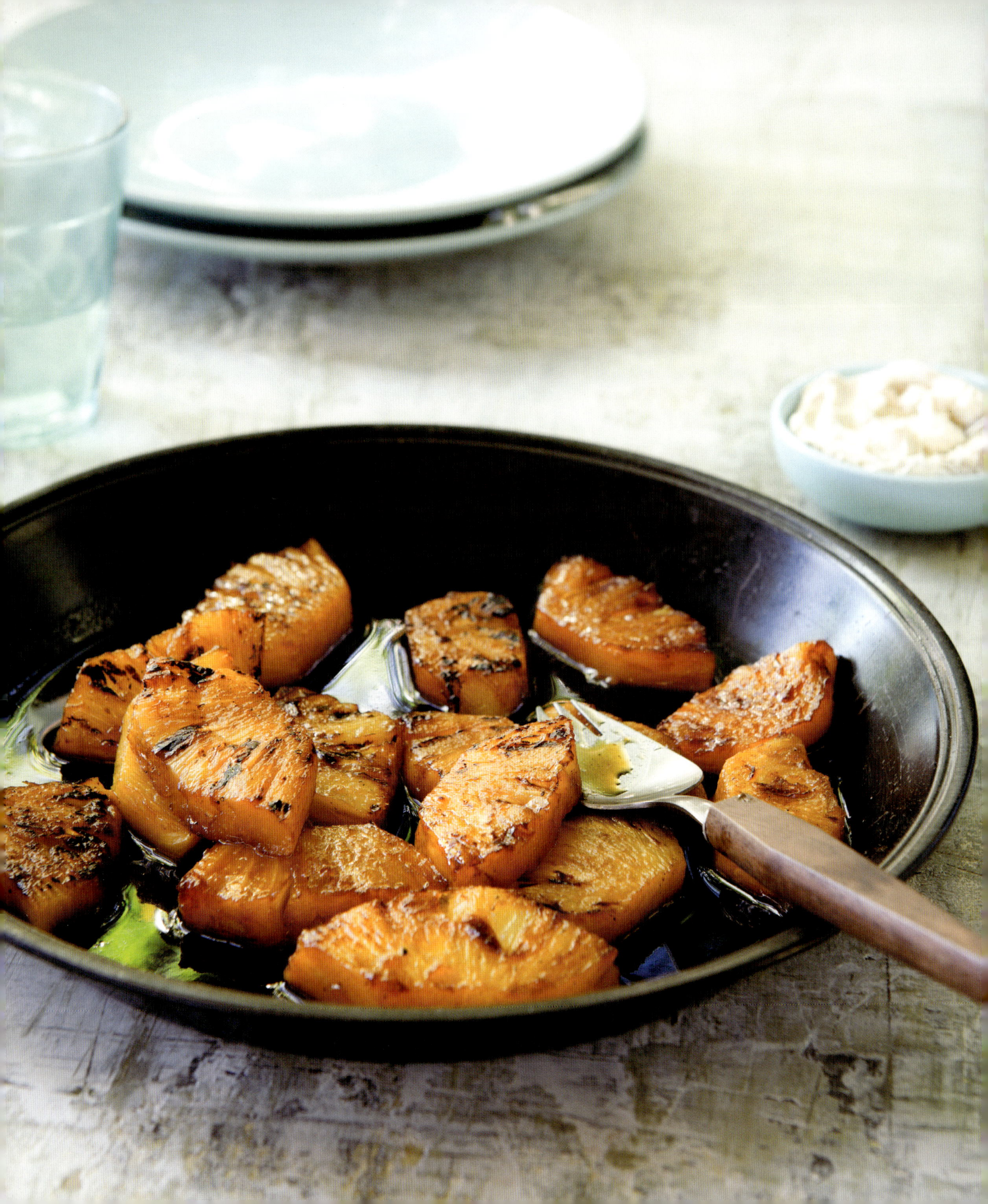

Caramelised Pineapple with Spiced Mascarpone and Lemon Syrup

Many people only think of the barbecue as a tool for producing starters and mains but you can produce a delicious and easy dessert. Caramelising fruit enables the natural sugars of the fruit to provide a sweet and slightly nutty taste. Other fruits you can try with this technique are bananas and peaches.

Ingredients

1 pineapple, skin removed and cut into 1 cm/½ in slices
4 tablespoons brown sugar
50 g/1¾ oz butter
2 tablespoons desiccated (dry, unsweetened, shredded) coconut

Spiced Mascarpone
115 g/4 oz mascarpone
½–1 teaspoon allspice

Lemon Syrup
250 g/9 oz caster (superfine) sugar
250 ml/9 fl oz water
1 star anise
1 cinnamon quill
2 cloves
juice of 1 lemon
1 lemon, thinly sliced

Method

1. For the lemon syrup, place all the ingredients into a small pan over a low heat. Stir until the sugar dissolves and then increase the heat and simmer for about 20 minutes, or until the liquid has reduced by half. Remove from the heat, strain and place in a heatproof dish or sauce container. Serve warm or cool.
2. For the spiced mascarpone, mix the mascarpone and allspice in a small bowl using a metal spoon. Cover and refrigerate until ready to serve.
3. Remove the core of the pineapple slices using a cookie cutter or small knife. Quarter the slices. Heat the barbecue flat plate over a medium-high flame. Place half the pineapple segments on the plate until they start to brown. Sprinkle half the brown sugar on the pineapple. When the sugar begins to caramelise, add half the butter. Continually move and flip the pineapple segments on the hotplate for 10 minutes, or until they soften. Repeat with the rest of the pineapple.
4. Clean the barbecue plate, reduce the heat to low flame and toast the coconut.
5. Serve pineapple segments with a dollop of spiced mascarpone. Drizzle with lemon syrup and sprinkle with toasted coconut.

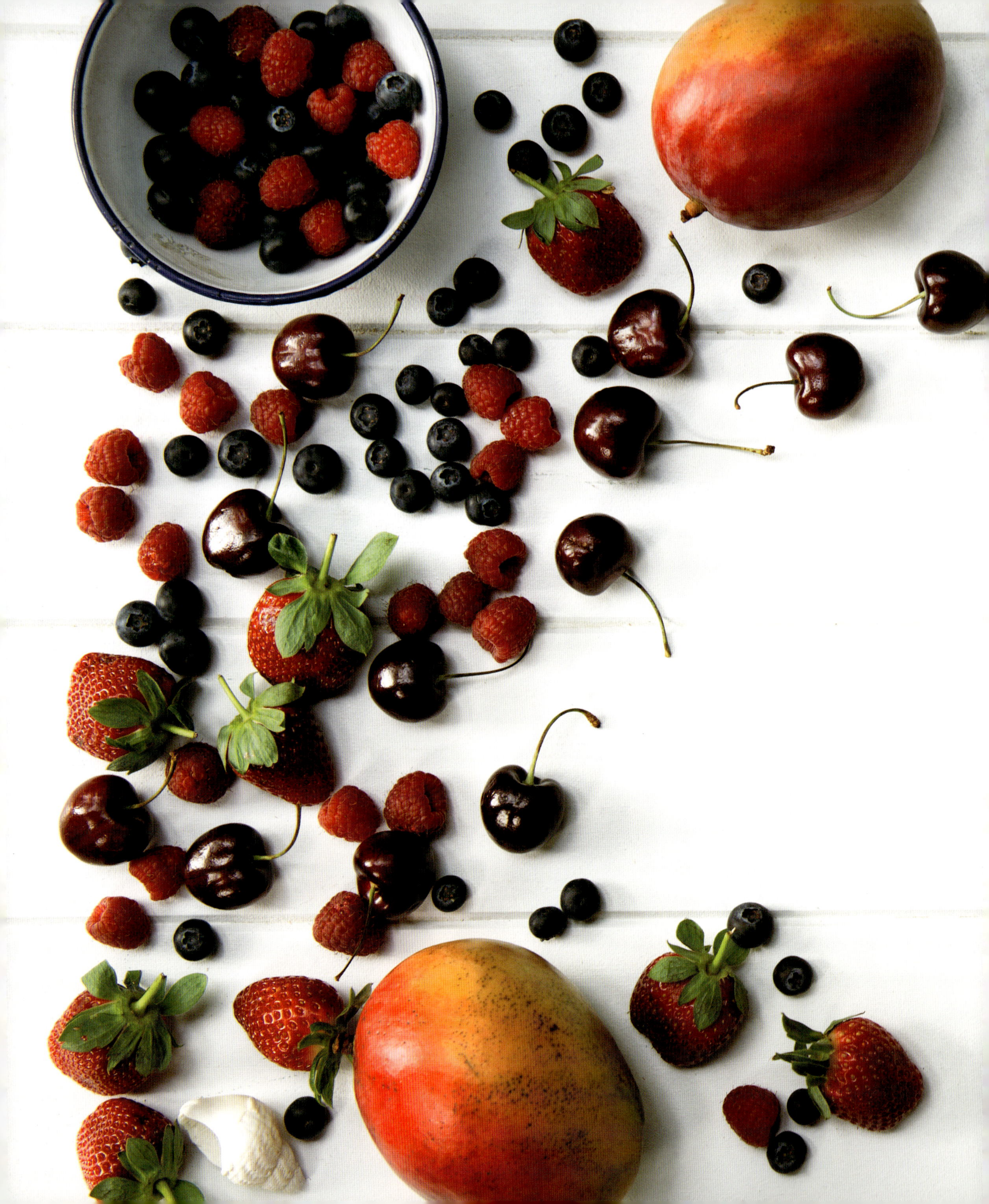

Just like any great main meal, an amazing dessert finds a balance of flavours. Most people expect desserts to deliver sweet, sweet and more sweet. However, this is not the case. We understand that a dessert is not a dessert without some sweetness but we have learnt to balance this with a sour or acidic flavour. We always endeavour to reduce the amount of butter and sugar in a recipe. Experiment with coconut oil and honey as alternatives. You will be surprised with the outcome. These are some of the treats that our families love to eat. Treats don't have to be off-limits when attempting a healthy lifestyle, you just have to choose carefully and make them a 'sometimes' food.

Treats

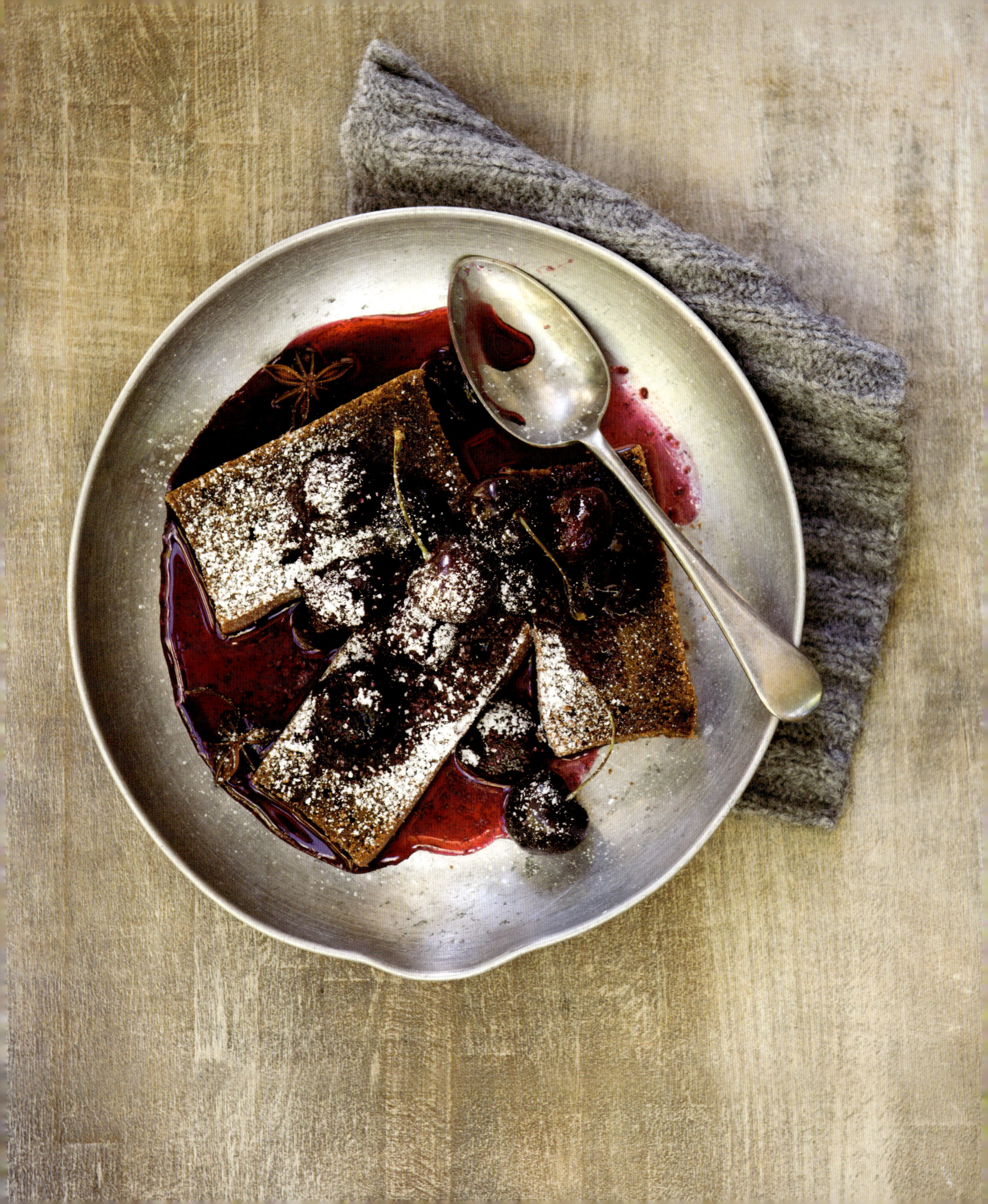

Chocolate and Beetroot Brownie with a Spiced Cherry Syrup

This is a twist on the classic brownie. Chocolate and beetroot are a match made in heaven. The combination at first glance seems a bit weird, but your tastebuds will tell a different story. We have learnt a thing or ten when it comes to desserts and one of those is that certain spices can accommodate sweetness. The spiced syrup with the brownie leaves the tongue with a slight zing from the chilli and peppercorns. Don't be scared to experiment with the quantities to suit your personal taste.

Ingredients

BROWNIE
- 10 eggs
- 200 g/7 oz caster (superfine) sugar
- 150 g/5 oz dark (bittersweet) chocolate, chopped
- 450 g/1 lb butter, diced
- 2 beetroots, peeled and grated
- 350 g/12 oz plain (all-purpose) wholemeal (whole wheat) flour, sifted

SPICED CHERRY SYRUP
- 500 ml (16 fl oz) water
- 100 g (3½ oz) caster (superfine) sugar
- 1 bird's eye chilli
- 1 star anise
- 6 peppercorns
- 10 cm/8 in strip orange peel
- 300 g/10½ oz cherries, pitted and halved

DECORATING
- crème fraîche
- icing (confectioners') sugar

Method

1. Preheat the oven to 150°C/300°F/Gas mark 2. Grease and line a baking tray approximately 40 x 30 cm/15¾ x 12 in.
2. For the brownie, beat the eggs and sugar until light and fluffy.
3. Place the dark chocolate and butter into a heatproof bowl and melt over a pan of simmering water. Remove from the heat.
4. Mix the beetroot into the melted chocolate mixture, stirring gently. Next, fold in the egg mixture until well combined. Add the flour gradually while stirring. The mixture should have a thick consistency.
5. Pour the batter into the prepared baking tray and leave 5 cm/2 in from the top of the tray for rising. Bake for 60 minutes, testing with a skewer after about 45 minutes. The brownie is cooked when an inserted skewer comes out clean. Remove from the oven and allow to rest for 10 minutes.
6. For the spiced cherry syrup, place all the ingredients except for the cherries into a pan. Heat with a low flame until the sugar has dissolved, then bring to the boil for 2 minutes. Next, add the cherries and reduce the heat to a simmer for 5 minutes. Remove from the heat to cool the mixture.
7. Remove the cherries, strain the mixture and bring back to the boil for about 5 minutes. Remove the syrup from the heat and allow to cool. Add the cherries to the cooled syrup.
8. To serve, slice the brownie and plate up. Drizzle with cherry syrup, sprinkle with icing sugar and serve with a dollop of crème fraîche.

Banana Nut Bread with Cinnamon Butter

We have always loved a tasty banana bread, especially toasted and served with a hot coffee straight after exercise outdoors on a chilly day. Our variation of the banana bread is sugar-free with the sweetness coming from the natural ingredients of banana, maple syrup and honey. The nuts provide a great textural element to the bread and add some protein value as well. Toast it up, spread with cinnamon butter and enjoy.

Ingredients

Wet Mix
3 bananas, chopped
2 tablespoons honey
1 tablespoon maple syrup
75 ml/2½ fl oz water
2 eggs
125 ml/4 fl oz milk
1 teaspoon vanilla bean paste

Dry Mix
225 g/8 oz wholemeal (whole wheat) flour
60 g/2 oz almond meal (ground almonds)
½ teaspoon bicarbonate of soda (baking soda)
1 teaspoon baking powder
1 teaspoon ground cinnamon
½ teaspoon ground nutmeg
¼ teaspoon of salt
3 tablespoons desiccated (dry, unsweetened, shredded) coconut
60 g/2 oz nuts, including chopped walnuts, slivered almonds, sunflower kernels or pepita (pumpkin seeds)

Cinnamon Butter
100 g/3½ oz butter, softened
½ teaspoon ground cinnamon

Method

1. Preheat the oven to 170°C/340°F/Gas mark 3½. Grease and line a loaf tin (pan).
2. From the wet mix, place the bananas, honey, maple syrup and water into a pan and place over a medium heat for 5 minutes. Stir occasionally to get a mashed consistency. Tip into a bowl and allow to cool.
3. Combine the dry ingredients and nuts in a bowl.
4. To the wet mix banana mixture add the eggs, milk and vanilla bean paste and stir to combine. Add the wet ingredients to the dry and mix until well combined. Use a mix master at this stage if you have one.
5. Pour the batter into a lined loaf tin and bake for approximately 50 minutes or until an inserted skewer comes out clean.
6. Stand in the tin for 10 minutes before turning out.
7. For the cinnamon butter, whip the butter using an electric beater until pale. Then, beat in the cinnamon.

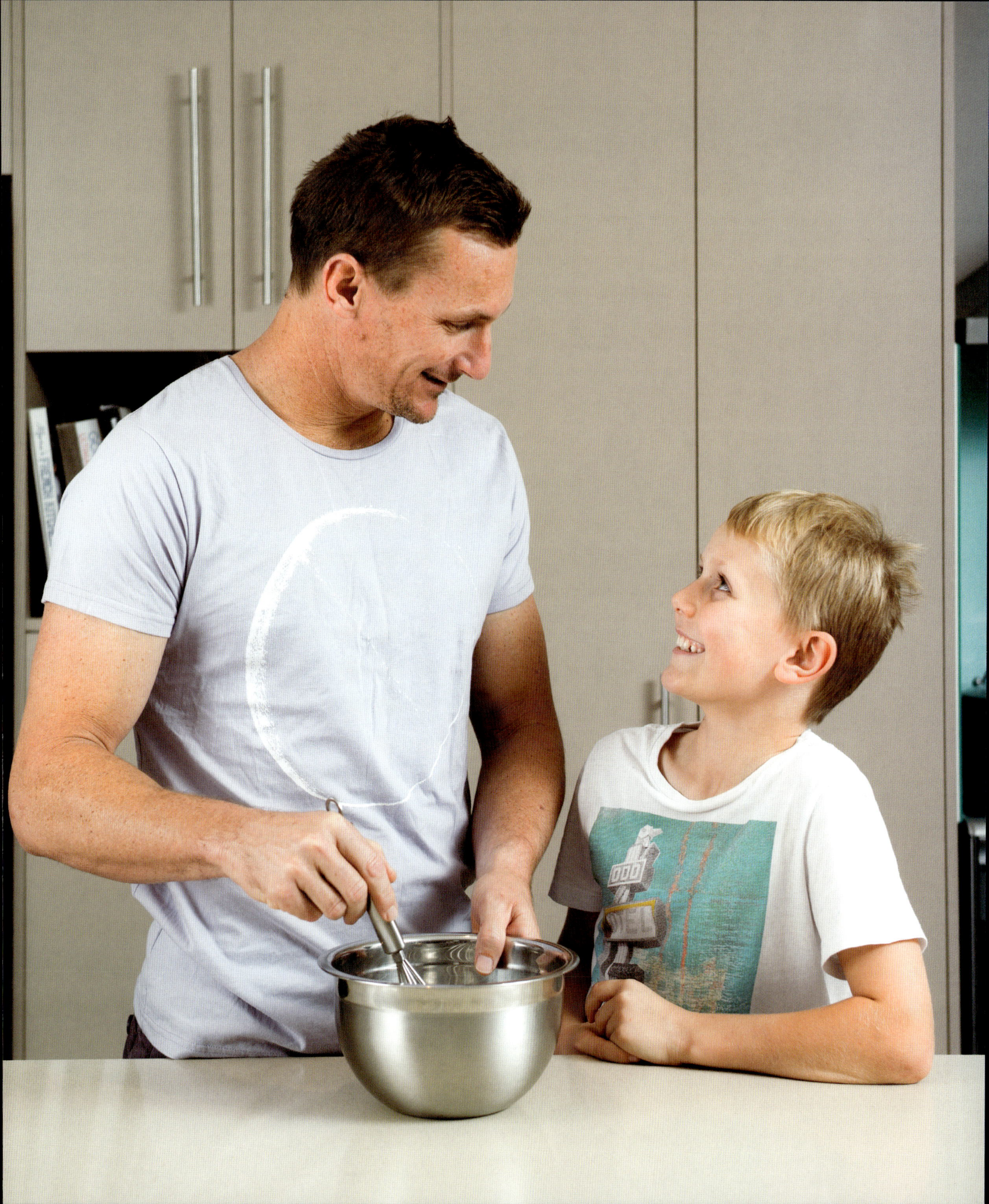

Jaime's Medjool Date and Ginger Muffins with Caramel Sauce

A major concern for us applying for MKR was the fact that we rarely cook or eat desserts. This was one of the recipes we took to the final audition and we believe it was paramount in engaging the producers to our ethos of healthy, nutritious and delicious food.

Ingredients

Muffin
150 g/5 oz Medjool dates, pitted and chopped
1 medium banana, sliced
250 ml/8 fl oz boiling water
2 tablespoons coconut oil
1 tablespoon ginger, grated
1 teaspoon bicarbonate of soda (baking soda)
175 g (6 oz) self-raising (self-rising) flour

Caramel Sauce
90 g/3 oz Medjool dates
60 ml/2 fl oz maple syrup
125 ml/4 fl oz coconut cream

Method

1. Preheat the oven to 180°C/350°F/Gas mark 4. Grease the cups of a muffin tray.
2. For the muffins, put all the ingredients, except for the flour in a pan and bring to the boil. Once boiling remove from the heat and allow to cool.
3. Gradually sift in the flour into the pan and stir to combine. If it thickens too much, add a tablespoon of water. Pour the batter into the muffin cups and bake for 20–30 minutes, or until an inserted skewer comes out clean. Remove and allow to sit for 5 minutes.
4. For the caramel sauce, purée the dates in a food processor. In a small pan, simmer the dates, maple syrup and coconut cream over a medium heat for 5 minutes. Remove the sauce and allow to cool.
5. Put a muffin on a plate and make a well in the top with a skewer. Fill with caramel sauce until it drizzles down the sides.

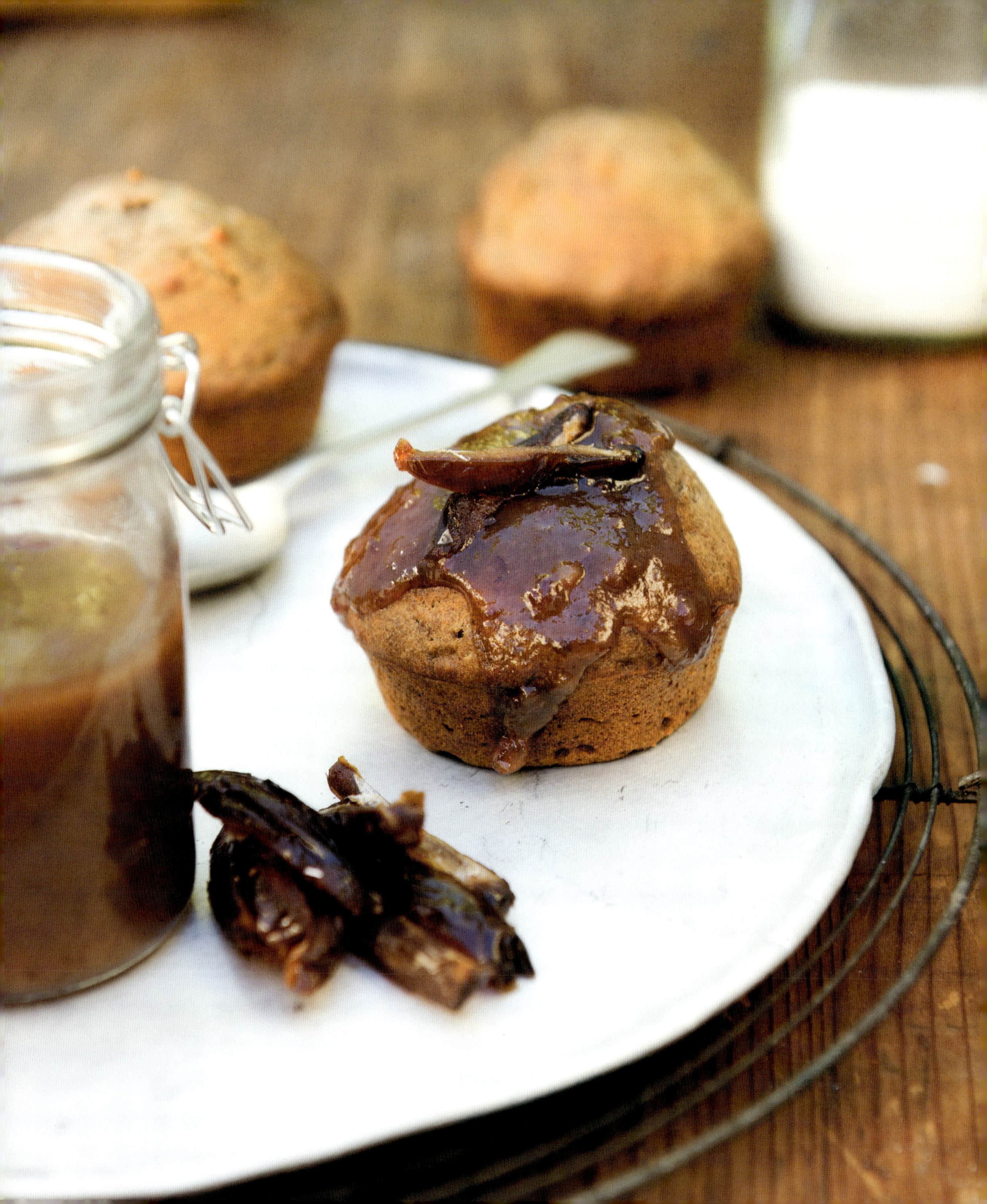

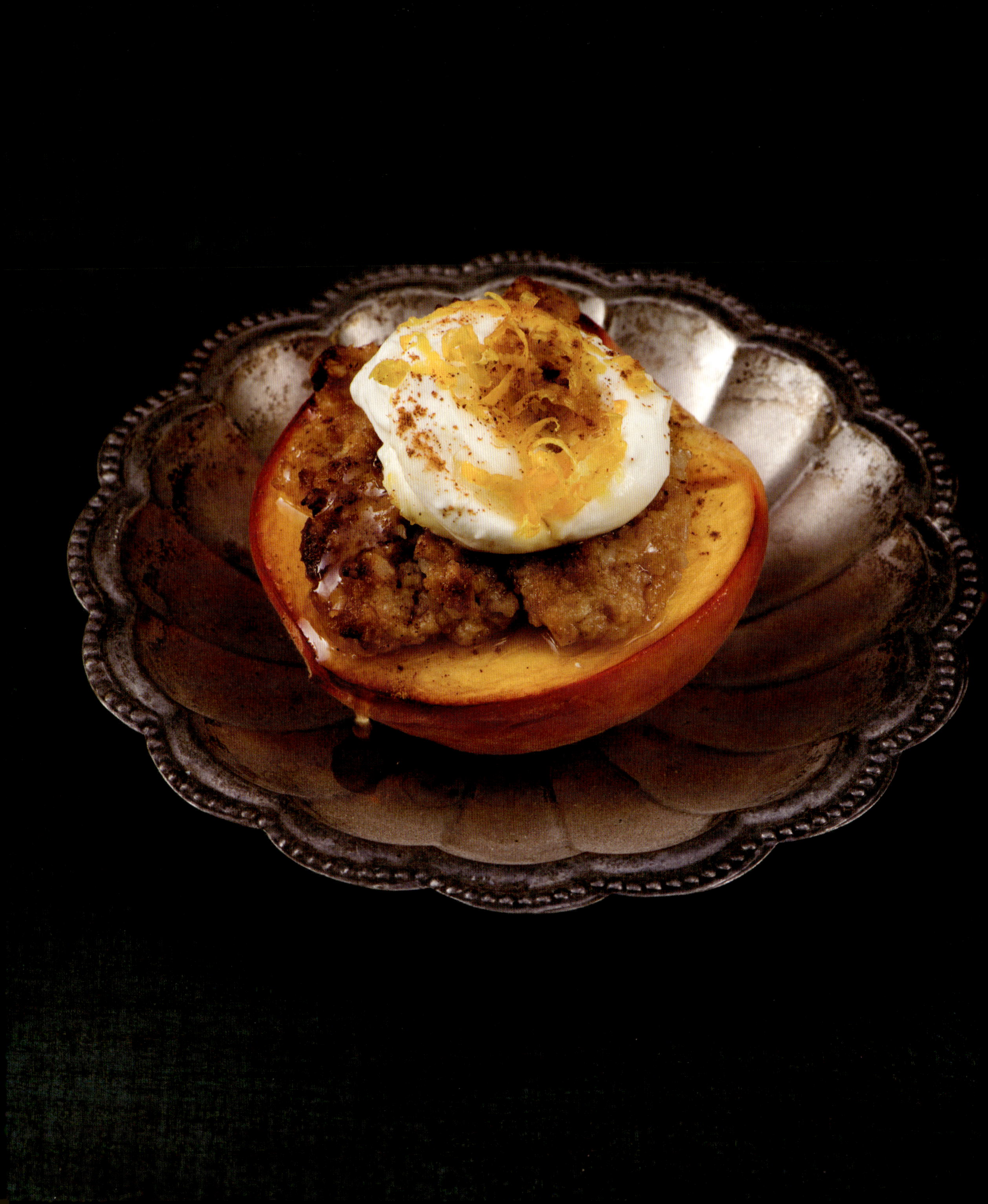

Stuffed Peaches with Lemon Crème Fraîche

Ingredients

4 ripe peaches, halved and pitted
zest and juice of 1 lemon
6–8 Scotch finger biscuits
50 g/1¾ oz slivered almonds, toasted
50 g/1¾ oz macadamia nuts, crushed and toasted
3 tablespoons brown sugar
1 teaspoon ground cinnamon, plus extra for decoration
50 g/1¾ oz butter, softened
1 egg yolk
2 tablespoons honey
crème fraîche, to serve
lemon zest, to serve

Method

1. Preheat the oven to 180°C/350°F/Gas mark 4.
2. Take a thin slice from the side of each peach so that lies sits flat. Dip the peach halves in lemon juice and arrange on a lined baking tray.
3. Lightly crush the biscuits in a large bowl and mix in the lemon zest, both nuts, sugar and cinnamon. Add the butter and work with your fingers until the mixture resembles breadcrumbs. Next, mix in the egg yolk until the mixture starts to come together.
4. Spoon the mixture onto the peach halves and compress lightly. Bake for 15 minutes, or until the peaches are tender.
5. Meanwhile, mix the crème fraîche with lemon zest to your taste.
6. Remove the peaches from the oven and plate two peach halves per serving. Drizzle with honey, top with crème fraîche and dust with extra ground cinnamon.

We love using fruit in a dessert. Fruit provide a natural sweetness that is second to none. Our boys leave nothing on the plate when this dish is served up. Come to think of it, there is no need for washing up as the plates are always licked clean. Hope you enjoy the dish just as much as they do.

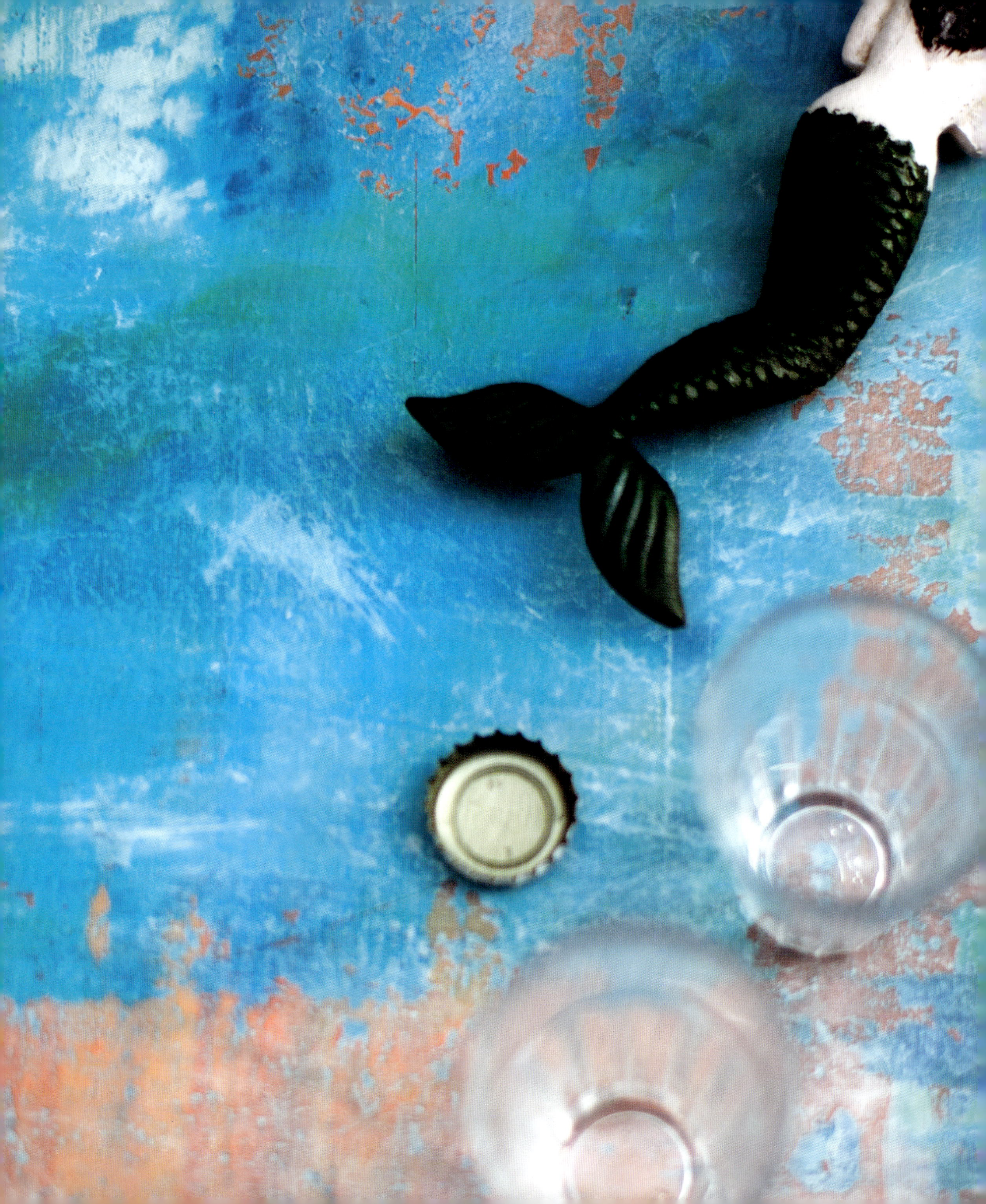

Berry Chocolate Fondants with Chocolate Dirt

Ingredients

Coconut oil, or melted butter, for greasing
4 tablespoons cream, for serving
200 g/7 oz raspberries, to serve

Fondant
125 g/4 oz caster (superfine) sugar
50 ml/1¾ fl oz water
200 g/7 oz raspberries
200 g/7 oz dark (bittersweet) chocolate, chopped
100 g/3½ oz unsalted butter, chopped
1 tablespoon unsweetened cocoa powder
1 tablespoon self-raising (self-rising) flour
3 eggs

Chocolate Dirt
50 g/1¾ oz plain (semi-sweet) chocolate biscuits
50 g/1¾ oz macadamia nuts

Method

1. Grease 4 x 250 ml/8 fl oz ramekins with coconut oil or melted butter.
2. For the fondant, heat 50 g/1¾ oz of the sugar, all of the water and the raspberries in a pan over low heat until the sugar dissolves and the raspberries soften. Remove from the heat and allow to cool.
3. In a small bowl, melt the chocolate and butter in a heatproof bowl set over a pan of simmering water, stirring occasionally with a metal spoon.
4. Sift the cocoa, flour and remaining sugar into a medium bowl. Whisk in the eggs, raspberry mixture and melted chocolate mixture.
5. Fill each ramekin, between half and three-quarters full, cover with foil and place in the freezer for at least 3 hours or overnight.
6. Preheat the oven to 200°C/400°F/Gas mark 6.
7. For the chocolate dirt, blend the chocolate biscuits and macadamia nuts until small crumbs form in a food processor.
8. Bake the frozen fondants for 7–9 minutes together in a baking tray. Turn the tray, and bake for another 7–9 minutes. Time may vary depending on ramekin size. Loosen the edges with a knife and gently ease the dessert out of each ramekin. Serve immediately. Decorate with chocolate dirt, a dollop of cream and raspberries.

This is one of the first desserts we experimented with when stepping into the world of sweets. Even back then, without knowing it, we tried to balance the sweetness with something refreshing. In this case it was the inclusion of raspberries. Dark chocolate and raspberries are a great combination. This is a good dessert to have in the freezer, especially on a cold night.

Raw Cashew, Lemon and Raspberry Slice

In this delicious dessert the sweetness from the cashews, coconut milk and honey is balanced beautifully by the lemon juice and zest. Tinker with the quantities until you get the right combination for your taste. This is a refreshing dessert that will surprise many.

Ingredients

Base
300 g/10½ oz plain biscuits such as Scotch fingers or arrowroot
10 Medjool dates, pitted
175 g/6 oz macadamia nuts
4 tablespoons coconut oil
2 tablespoons honey
2 tablespoons desiccated (dry, unsweetened, shredded) coconut

Cashew Filling
350 g/12 oz raw cashew nuts
175 ml/6 fl oz lemon juice
175 ml/6 fl oz coconut milk
1 tablespoon coconut oil
2 teaspoons vanilla extract
zest of 3 lemons
115 g/4 oz honey

Raspberry Topping
115 g/4 oz caster (superfine) sugar
100 ml/3½ fl oz water
450 g/1 lb raspberries
1 tablespoon boiling water
½ teaspoon gelatine

Method

1. Grease and line a 22 cm/8½ in springform cake tin (pan). Be sure to line the sides.
2. For the base, place all the ingredients into the bowl of a food processor and process until finely crushed and the mixture sticks together. Add a tablespoon of water if necessary.
3. Transfer the mixture to the prepared tin and use a straight-edged glass to press the mixture firmly on the base. The base should be about 0.5 cm/¼ in thick. Freezer while preparing the filling.
4. To make the cashew filling, combine all the ingredients in the bowl of a food processor until smooth. Pour on top of the base and return to the freezer for approximately 1 hour.
5. For the raspberry topping, heat the sugar and larger quantity of water in a pan over medium heat until the sugar dissolves. Add the raspberries to the pan and simmer for 5 minutes, or until the raspberries fall apart. Remove from the heat and allow to cool.
6. Dissolve the gelatine in the tablespoon of boiling water in a bowl and stir into the cool raspberry syrup. Pour onto the cashew filling and return to the freezer for 30 minutes.
7. Remove from the freezer 5 minutes before cutting into slices. A knife dipped in boiling water, then dried quickly can assist with cutting.

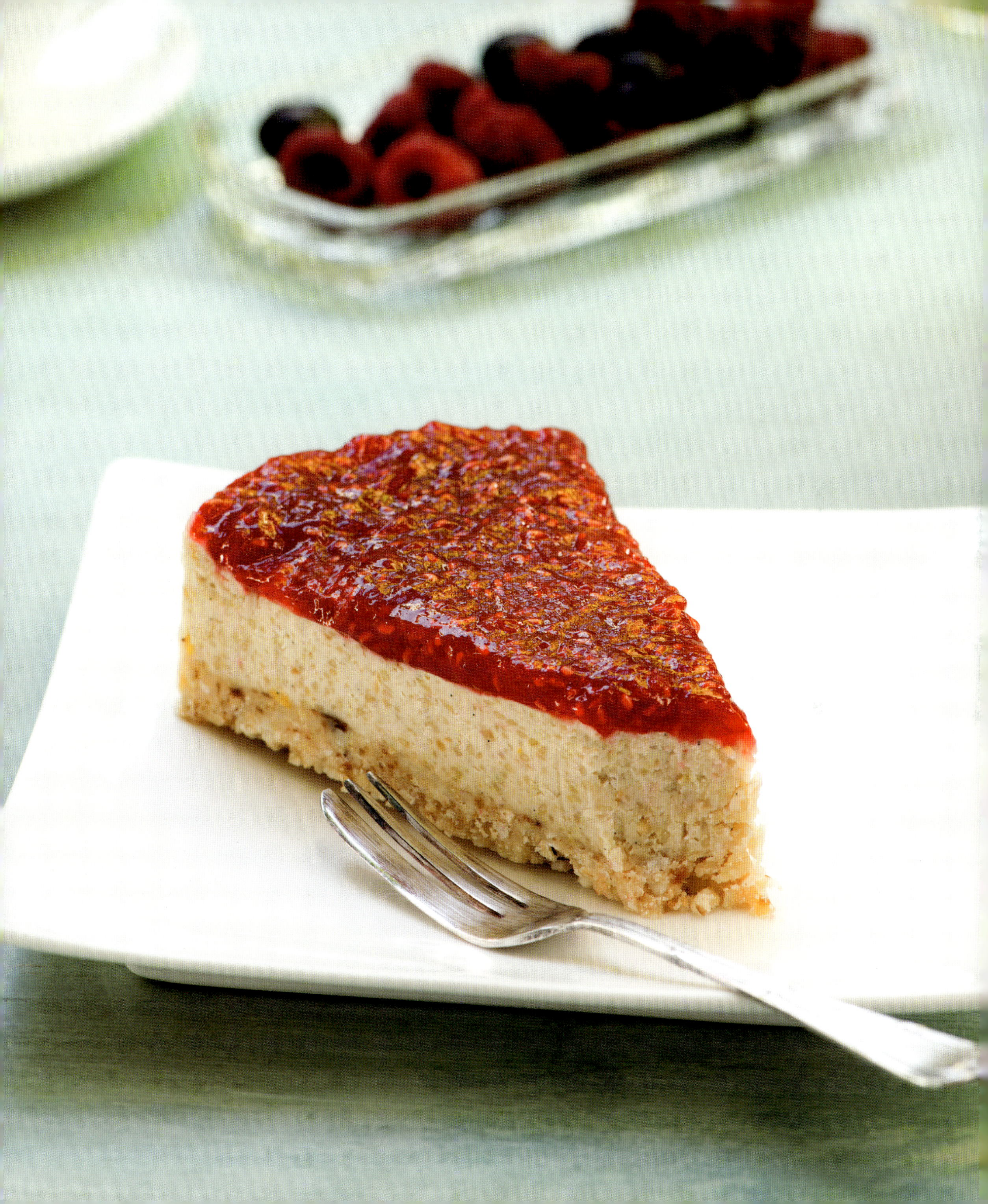

Spiced Date Loaf with Honeyed Natural Yogurt

A tasty loaf that, when sliced, goes great with a cup of tea or a brew of coffee. Fresh ginger is one of our favourite spices and we love using it in desserts. When the tastebuds are expecting some sweetness, the ginger provides a surprising zing.

Ingredients

Loaf
2 quantities Medjool Date and Ginger Muffins (see p. 130)
1 teaspoon cinnamon
½ teaspoon nutmeg
60 g/2 oz walnuts, chopped

Honeyed Natural Yogurt
125 ml/4 fl oz natural (plain) yogurt
1 tablespoon honey
zest of ½ lemon

Method

1. Preheat the oven to 180°C/350°F/Gas mark 4. Grease and line a loaf tin (pan).
2. For the loaf, follow the method given for Jamie's Medjool Date and Ginger Muffins adding the extra ingredients.
3. Pour the batter into the prepared loaf tin and bake for 30 minutes, or until an inserted skewer comes out clean. Rest for 10 minutes before turning out onto a wire rack.
4. For the honeyed natural yogurt, combine all the ingredients in a small bowl.
5. Slice the loaf and spread a slice with a teaspoon of yogurt.

Tip
If you have a sweet tooth, try the Caramel Sauce with the Medjool Date and Ginger Muffins recipe.

Baked Plums with Almond Crumble and Red Wine Syrup

When it's stone fruit season you are spoilt for choice. This recipe, like that for stuffed peaches, uses the natural sweetness of the fruit. However, this one is combined with the beautiful complexity of red wine to enhance the flavours. Don't let the leftover red wine go to waste!

Ingredients

- 9 blood plums, just ripe, halved and pitted
- 3 figs or 3 extra plums, halved
- 125 ml/4 fl oz Greek-style natural (plain) yogurt
- 1 teaspoon vanilla extract

Red Wine Syrup
- 250 ml/8 fl oz red wine
- 125 ml/4 fl oz honey

Almond Crumble
- 60 g/2 oz almond meal (ground almonds)
- 60 g/2 oz flaked almonds, toasted
- 60 g/2 oz brown sugar
- ¼ teaspoon ground cinnamon
- zest of 1 orange
- 30 g/1 oz unsalted butter, cold

Method

1. Preheat the oven to 200°C/400°F/Gas mark 6.
2. To make the red wine syrup, combine the wine and honey in a small pan. Bring to the boil, then simmer for 20 minutes, or until syrupy. Remove from the heat and allow to cool.
3. Meanwhile, to make the almond crumble, place all the ingredients except for the butter in a bowl. Using a box grater, coarsely grate (shred) the butter into the crumble. Using your fingertips, rub the butter into the nut mixture until it forms a crumble. Refrigerate until needed.
4. Line a large oven tray or baking dish with baking paper. Place the fruit, cut-side up, on the tray. Spoon the crumble over fruit, mounding slightly. Bake for 12 minutes, or until the crumble is golden.
5. Combine the yogurt and vanilla in a bowl. Divide the fruit among bowls and top with vanilla yogurt. Drizzle with red wine syrup to serve.

Tip
Syrups always thickens as it cools.

Chilli Mango Cakes with Coconut Ice Cream

The ingredients chilli, lime zest, kaffir lime leaves and coconut milk scream Asian main meal. However, this dessert balances the sweetness of coconut, the freshness of lime and the spicy kick of chilli for a fantastic finish to any evening.

Ingredients

Coconut oil or butter, for greasing
3 tablespoons desiccated (dry, shredded, unsweetened) coconut, toasted, to decorate
kaffir lime leaves, shredded, to decorate

Cake
450 g/1 lb honey
zest of 2 limes
2 long red chillies, seeded and finely chopped
2 mangoes, peeled, pitted and thinly sliced
450 g/1 lb unsalted butter, softened
430 g/15 oz caster (superfine) sugar
8 eggs
2 teaspoons vanilla extract
450 g/1 lb self-raising (self-rising) flour, sifted
4–8 tablespoons of milk

Ice Cream
100 g/3½ oz caster (superfine) sugar
¼ teaspoon vanilla extract
125 ml/4 fl oz sweetened condensed milk
500 ml/17 fl oz coconut milk
150 ml/5 fl oz double (heavy) cream

Method

1. For the ice cream, blend the sugar, vanilla extract and condensed milk together in a bowl and then stir in the coconut milk.
2. In another bowl, beat the cream until soft peaks form and fold into the coconut mixture. Tip into the bowl of an ice cream machine and switch on.
3. Preheat the oven to 170°C/340°F/Gas mark 3½. Grease the cups of a muffin tin (pan).
4. Make a syrup by the heating the honey, lime zest and chillies in a pan set over gentle heat. Place 1 tablespoon of syrup in each muffin cup. Place some thinly sliced mango on top.
5. In a mixing bowl, beat the butter and sugar until thick and pale and then add the eggs, one at a time, beating well after each addition. Add the vanilla extract and then fold in the flour. Stir in enough milk for a soft dropping consistency. Place the batter in the muffin cups, filling about three-quarters full. Bake for 20 minutes, or until a skewer inserted in the centre comes out clean.
6. When cool, invert using a baking tray. Place individually on a plate and serve with extra syrup and a scoop of coconut ice cream. Decorate cake with shredded kaffir lime leaves and toasted coconut.

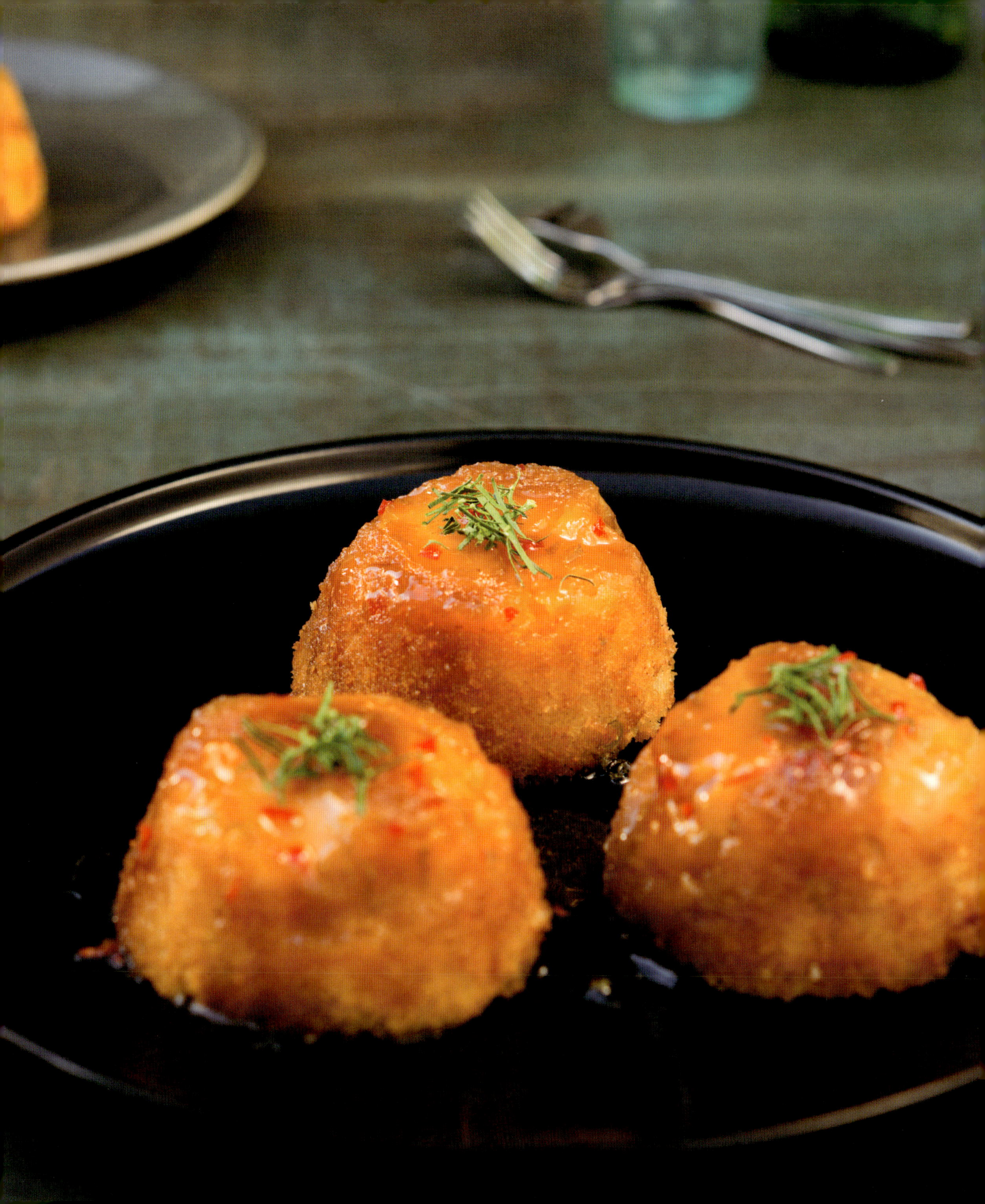

Chilli Chocolate Cheesecake with Macerated Strawberries

The chilli and chocolate combination goes way back! In fact it can be traced back to the ancient Aztecs–something that has lasted that long must be good. The spiciness in this dish comes from the cayenne pepper. Be careful when measuring because it packs a punch. This dessert is definitely a sometimes meal but after tasting it you'll wish that sometimes came around more often.

Ingredients

Base
150 g/5 oz chocolate biscuits, chopped
70 g/2½ oz walnuts
70 g/2½ oz macadamia nuts
8 Medjool dates, pitted and chopped
2 tablespoons desiccated (dry, unsweetened, shredded) coconut
2 tablespoons honey
4 tablespoons coconut oil
zest of 1 orange

Filling
400 g/14 oz dark (bittersweet) chocolate
¼ teaspoon cayenne pepper
450 g/1 lb cream cheese, softened
70 g/2½ oz caster (superfine) sugar
300 ml/10½ fl oz thickened cream
juice of ½ orange
1 teaspoon gelatine, dissolved in 1 tablespoon boiling water
150 g/5 oz frozen mixed berries

Macerated Strawberries
juice of 1 orange
50 g/1¾ oz caster (superfine) sugar
250 g/9 oz strawberries, washed and sliced

Method

1. Grease and line a springform tin (pan) that is approximately 23 cm/9 in in diameter. Line both base and sides.
2. For the macerated strawberries, combine the juice and sugar in a bowl and stir until the sugar is dissolved. Add the strawberries, cover and refrigerate for at least 1 hour.
3. Place all the base ingredients into the bowl of a food processor and process until combined and the mixture sticks together. Use extra coconut oil if the mixture is dry. Transfer to a prepared tray and use a straight-edged glass to press the mixture firmly. The base should be about 0.5 cm/¼ in high. For variety, you can press some of the base up the sides. Freeze until the filling is ready.
4. To make the filling, place dark chocolate and cayenne pepper in a heatproof bowl set over a pan of simmering water and stir with a metal spoon until it melts. Remove from the heat.
5. Beat the cream cheese and sugar, in a bowl, using an electric mixer, until smooth. Add the cream and beat until smooth.
6. Combine the cream cheese, dark chocolate and orange juice and stir until smooth. Add the gelatine and frozen berries and stir through. Pour over the base, smoothing with a spoon and freeze for 20 minutes before transferring to the refrigerator.
7. To serve, slice the cake and top with macerated strawberries and syrup.

Tips
The cayenne pepper leaves a very mild tingle at the back of the throat. Change the amount to suit your personal taste. Also, try different strengths of dark chocolate.

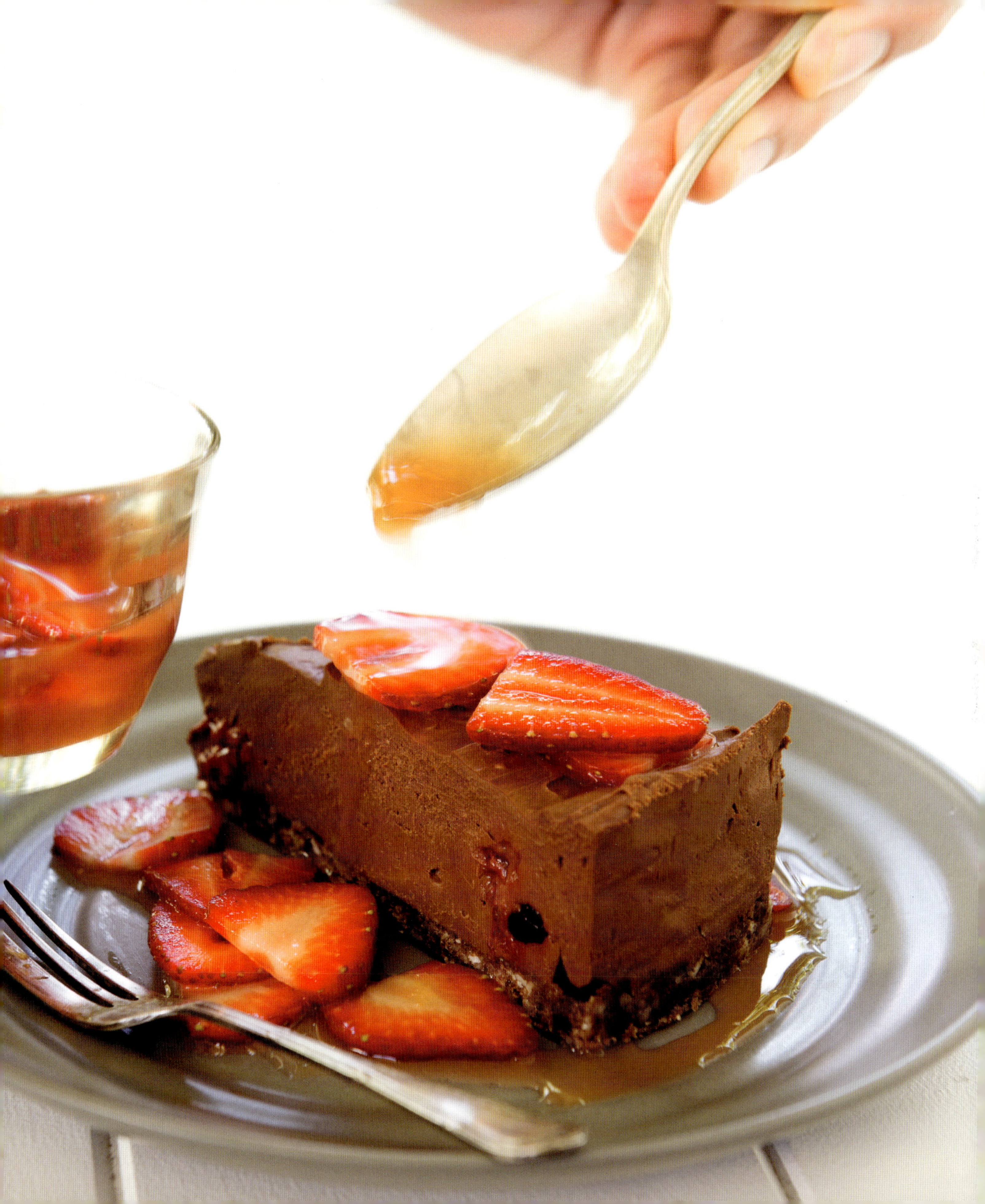

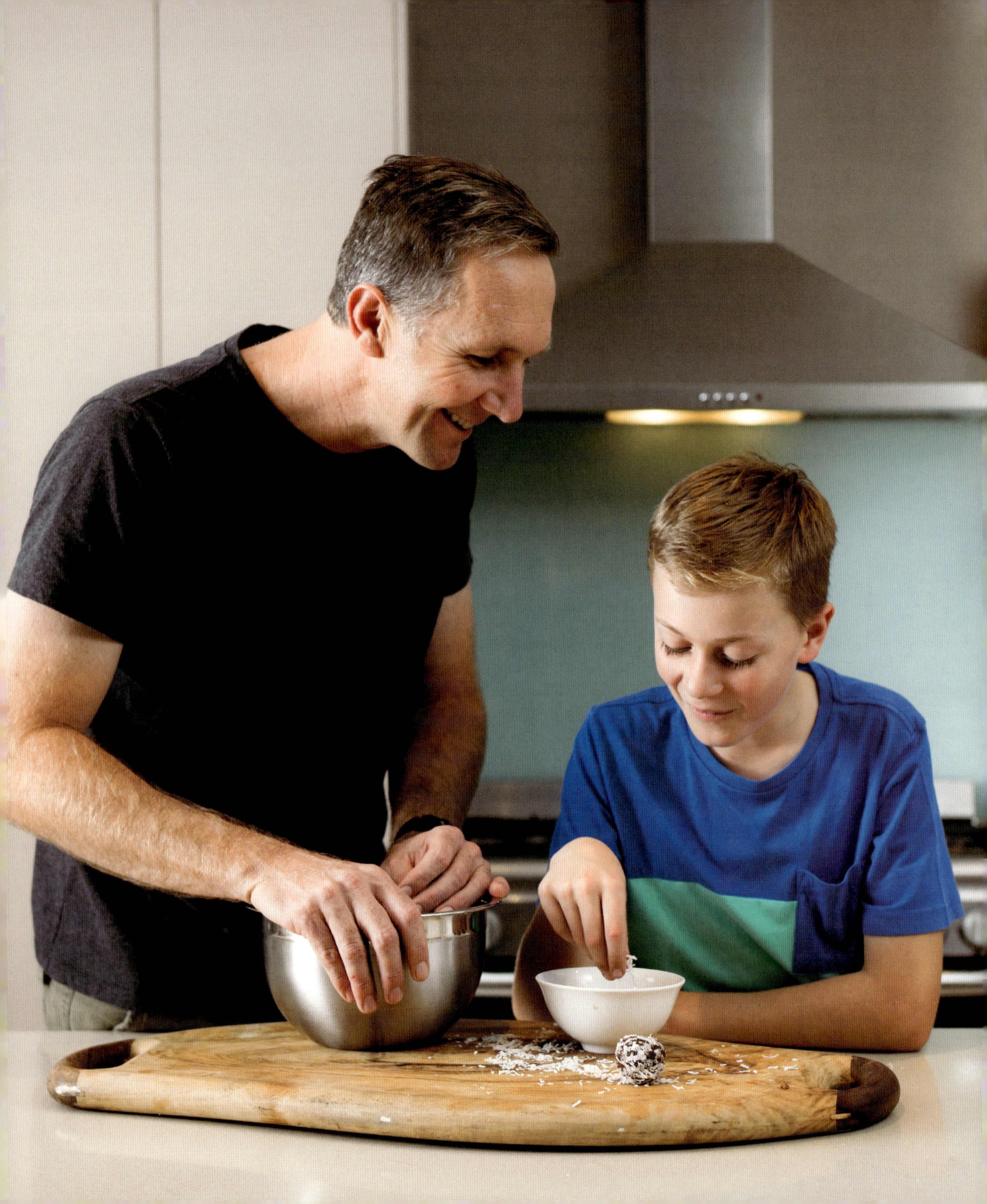

Amazeballs

The best thing about these little gems is the kids won't know how good they are for them—they are packed with protein and natural energy. They can be frozen or refrigerated and used for kid's lunches, a pre-training snack or as a treat at night before bed. They are definitely very trendy at the moment and getting a push courtesy of the health conscious, exercise-happy generation. This makes between 15-20 amazeballs.

Ingredients
- 100 g/3½ oz walnuts, chopped
- 100 g/3½ oz slivered almonds
- 2 tablespoons pumpkin seeds (pepitas)
- 200 g/7 oz Medjool dates, pitted and chopped
- 70 g/2½ oz soft dried apricots, chopped
- 70 g/2½ oz prunes, pitted and chopped
- 2 tablespoons unsweetened cocoa powder
- 2 tablespoons goji berries
- 1 tablespoon peanut butter
- 2 tablespoons honey
- 1 tablespoon ground cinnamon
- ¼ teaspoon nutmeg
- zest and juice of 1 lemon

Coating Options
- desiccated (dry, unsweetened, shredded) coconut
- sesame seeds
- unsweetened cocoa powder

Method
1. Lightly toast the walnuts and almonds in a small frying pan over medium heat. Combine the nuts and pumpkin seeds in the bowl of a food processor and pulse until finely chopped. Add the dates, apricots and prunes and process until smooth.
2. Add the remaining ingredients and process until the mixture starts to form a ball. Remove from the processor and divide into golf ball-sized portions, rolling each between your palms.
3. Coat using one of the options provided by rolling each ball in the ingredient and store refrigerated in an airtight container for up to 2 weeks.

Tip
Swap any of the ingredients like for like in this recipe. You can come up with some funky amazeballs of your own.

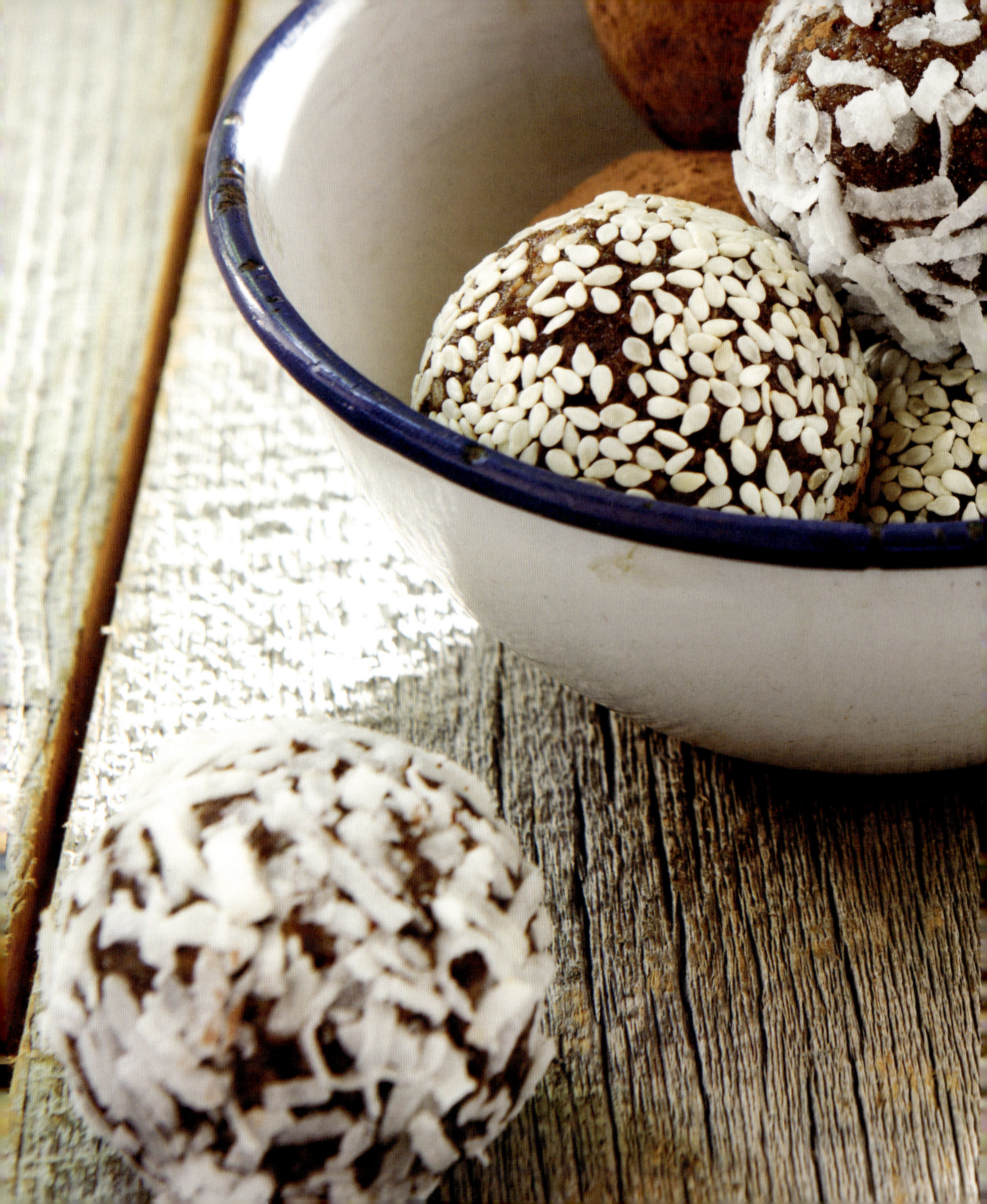

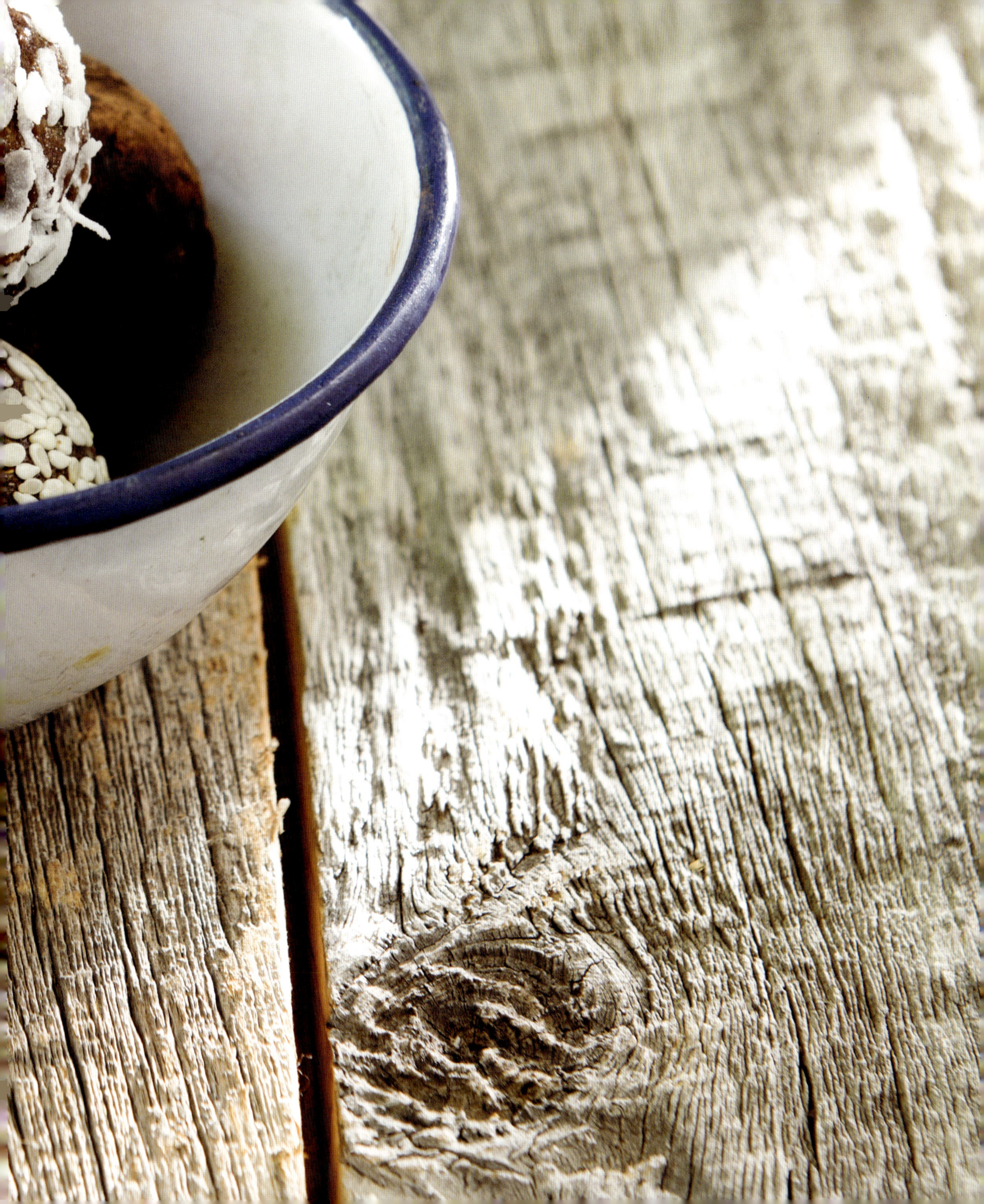

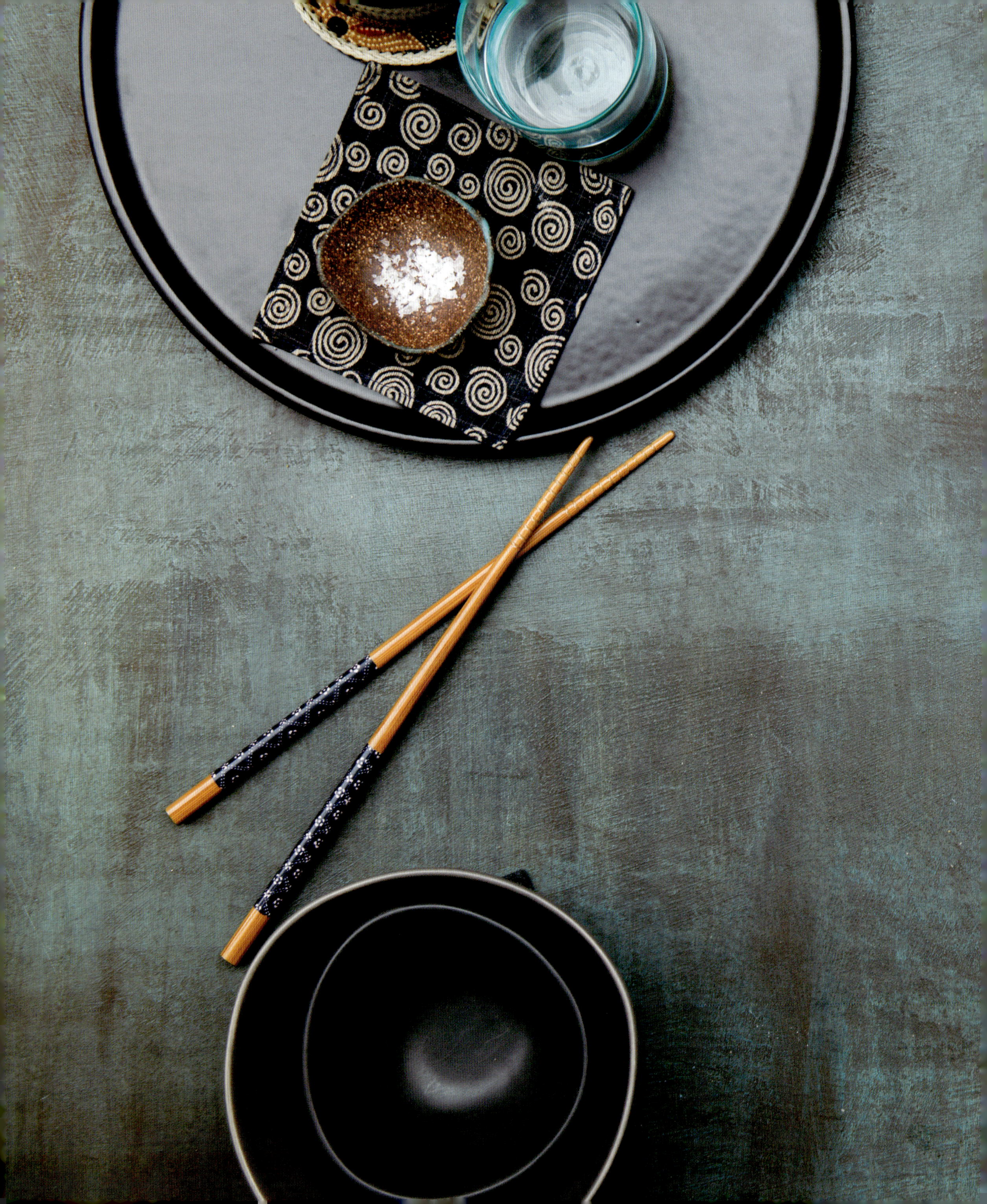

Dining In

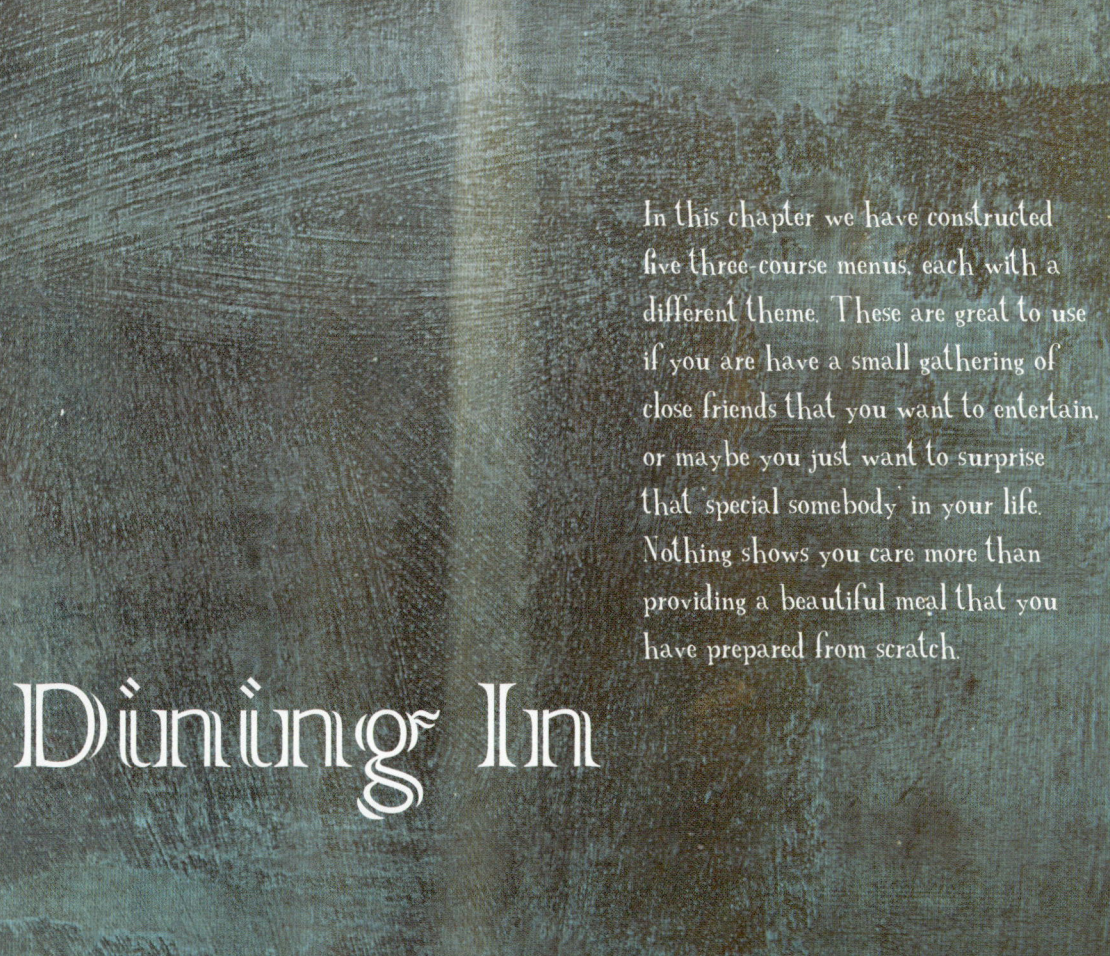

In this chapter we have constructed five three-course menus, each with a different theme. These are great to use if you are have a small gathering of close friends that you want to entertain, or maybe you just want to surprise that special somebody in your life. Nothing shows you care more than providing a beautiful meal that you have prepared from scratch.

Menu 1
Mediterranean

This menu has a distinctly Italian feel but draws on other areas of the Mediterranean region. With the complexity of the beef ragu, the fresh fish and yogurt flat bread to the beautiful coffee hints in the dessert, there is something here for everyone.

Poached Salmon Rillettes
on Yogurt Flatbread

...

Fettuccine with a Beef Ragu
and Mozzarella

...

Espresso Tower

ENTRÉE
Poached Salmon Rillettes on Yogurt Flat Bread

Ingredients

RILLETTES
1 litre/1¾ pints vegetable stock
2.5 cm/1 in piece fresh root ginger, peeled and sliced
2 bird's eye chillies, seeded and sliced
8 peppercorns
2 salmon fillets, skinned
2 tablespoons crème fraîche
1 tablespoon chives, finely chopped
1 tablespoon dill, chopped
zest of ½ lemon, finely grated (shredded)
1 tablespoon capers, rinsed and chopped
¼ teaspoon horseradish cream
salt and pepper, to taste
Watercress, to garnish

YOGURT FLAT BREAD
225 g/8 oz self-raising (self-rising) flour, plus extra, as needed
500 ml/16 fl oz natural (plain) yogurt
1 tablespoon salt
1 tablespoon baking powder
2 tablespoons dill

Method

1. In a medium pan, bring the vegetable stock to the boil with the ginger, chillies and peppercorns, then reduce the heat and simmer for 5 minutes. Remove from the heat.
2. Place the salmon fillets in a heatproof dish and pour in the stock, making sure that the fillets are covered. Cover with cling film (plastic wrap) and let stand for 15 minutes, or until the salmon is cooked through.
3. Place the remaining rillette ingredients in a bowl and combine. Remove the salmon from the poaching liquid, pat dry with paper towel and flake using a fork. Add the salmon to the bowl and stir to combine. Adjust the seasoning to taste.
4. For the flat bread, place all the ingredients into a food processor and pulse until a dough forms. If your dough is still wet, sprinkle with more flour. Knead the dough on a lightly floured surface for a couple of minutes. Divide the dough into sizes of your choice and roll flat using a floured rolling pin. Stack between layers of baking paper.
5. To cook the flat bread, heat a frying pan over a high heat. Fry for 1–2 minutes on each side, or until slightly fluffy and lightly charred.
6. Place a spoonful of salmon rillettes on the bread. Garnishing with watercress.

DESSERT
Espresso Tower

Ingredients

BASE
125 g/4 oz walnuts
2 tablespoons desiccated (dry, unsweetened, shredded) coconut
50 g/1¾ oz coconut oil
1 tablespoon honey
50 g/1¾ oz pistachios, crushed, to decorate

GANACHE
200 g/7 oz dark (bittersweet) chocolate, roughly chopped
100 ml/3½ fl oz single (light) cream

MOUSSE
300 g/10½ oz dark (bittersweet) chocolate, roughly chopped
3 tablespoons espresso coffee, cooled
ground coffee, to taste
3 eggs
60 g/2 oz caster (superfine) sugar
300 ml/10½ fl oz whipping cream

Method

1. Line 4 x 7.5 cm/3 in food presentation rings with baking paper and place on a dish lined with baking paper.
2. For the base, place all the ingredients, except for the decoration, into the bowl of a food processor and blend until combined. Divide evenly between the food rings and press firmly to pack down with a straight-edged glass. Each bases should be less than 1 cm/½ in deep. Refrigerate the bases for 10 minutes to set.
3. Meanwhile, for the ganache, combine the chocolate and cream in a heatproof bowl over a pan of simmering water and stir with a metal spoon until smooth. Remove the bowl from the heat and allow to cool, stirring occasionally. When cooled, divide the ganache between the food rings. The ganache should be about 1 cm/½ in deep. Return to the refrigerator.
4. For the mousse, place the chocolate in a heatproof bowl over a pan of simmering water. Stir with a metal spoon until melted. Remove the bowl from the heat and set aside to cool. Add the espresso coffee and ground coffee and mix to combine.
5. Place the eggs and sugar in a large bowl and beat with an electric beater until thick, pale and doubled in size. Fold in the cooled chocolate until combined.
6. In a separate bowl, whip the cream until thickened and fold into the chocolate mixture. Try to keep the mixture as light as possible. Divide between the food rings, then refrigerate for 1 hour.
7. Remove from the refrigerator 15 minutes before serving. Gently remove the food rings and baking paper and serve with a sprinkle of crushed pistachios.

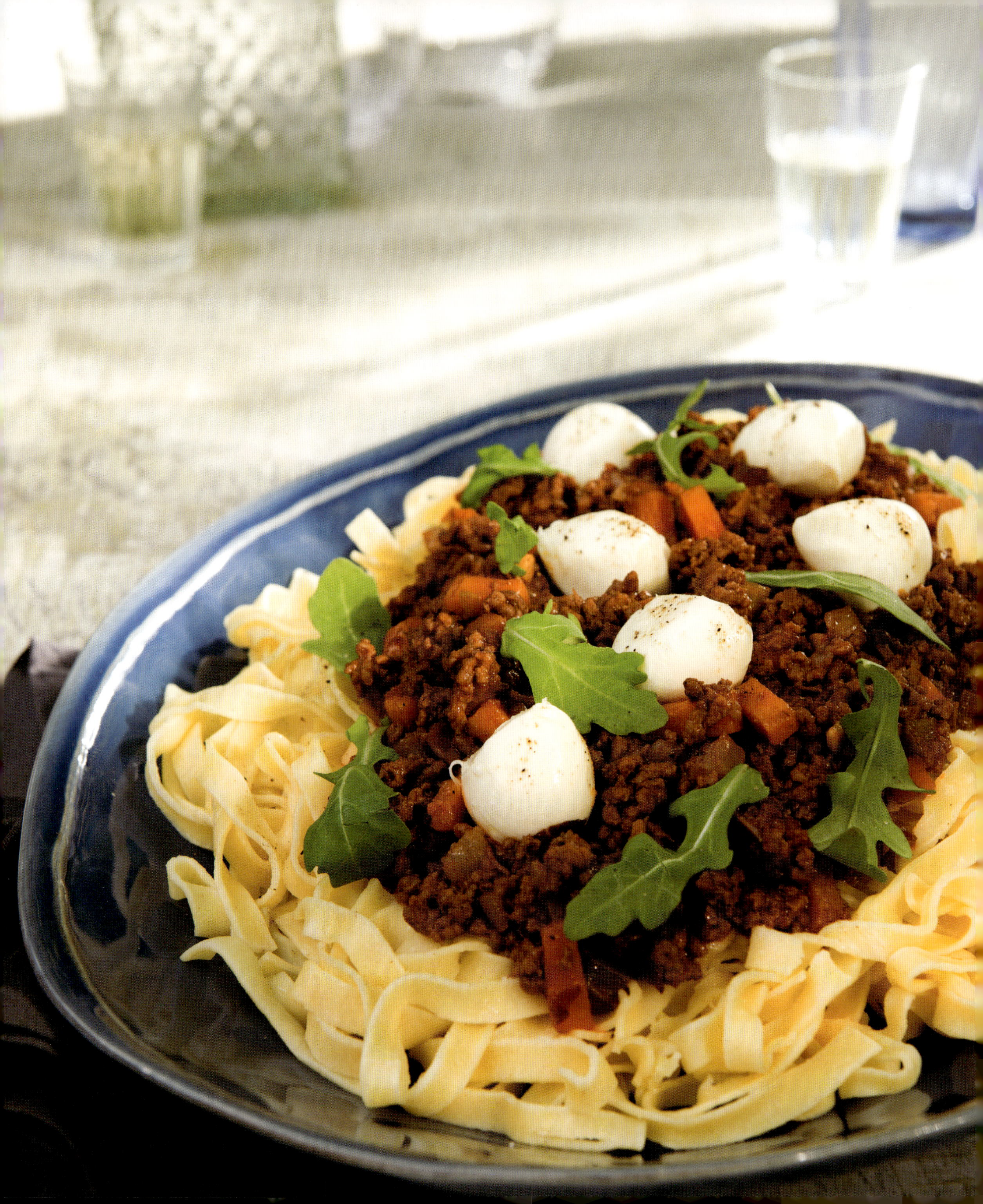

MAIN
Fettuccine with a Beef Ragu and Mozzarella

Ingredients

1 quantity homemade fettuccine (see recipe marinara p. 53) or 250 g/9 oz fettuccine

80 g/2½ oz buffalo or bocconcini mozzarella, to serve

50 g/1¾ oz rocket (arugula), to serve

Ragu
2 tablespoons olive oil
1 onion, diced
1 garlic clove, finely chopped
1 carrot, diced
1 celery stalk, diced
200 g/7 oz lean minced (ground) beef
30 g/1 oz prosciutto, chopped
100 g/3½ oz tomato paste
200 ml/7 fl oz red wine
500 ml/17 fl oz chicken stock

Method

1. For the ragu, heat the olive oil in a frying pan over a medium heat. Sauté the onion and garlic. Add the carrot and celery and cook until soft. Add the beef and prosciutto and cook until the mince has browned. Add the tomato paste and cook for 2 minutes. Add the wine and cook for 2–3 minutes. Add the chicken stock and simmer for at least 30 minutes, or until the ragu reduces to a thick consistency.
2. Cook the fettuccine in a pan of bolling water until *al dente*.
3. To plate up, place the ragu on a serve of fettuccine and top with mozzarella and rocket.

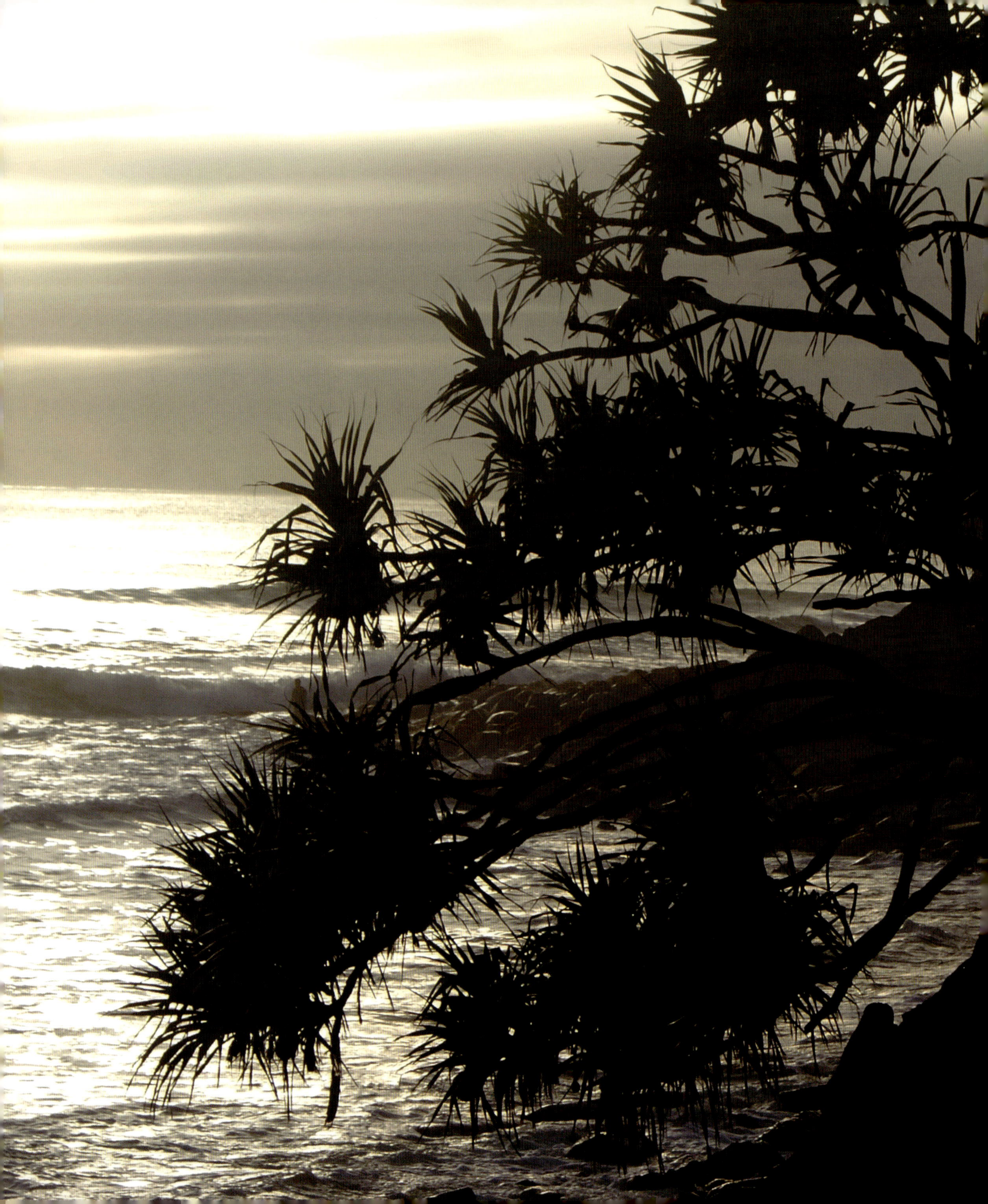

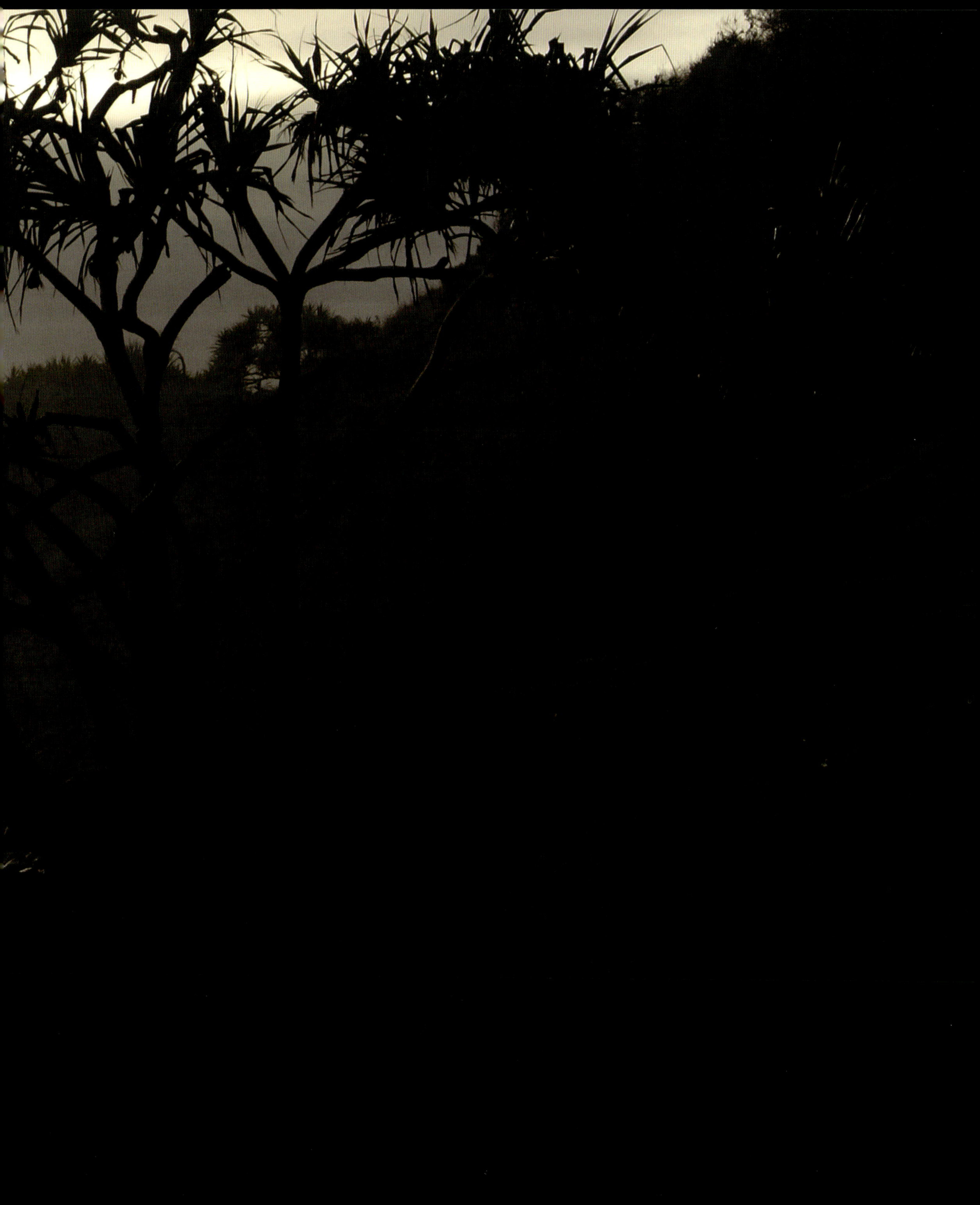

Menu 2
Asian

This menu is influenced by Japan, China and even Indonesia. Each course is different but still manages to flow together. We love Asian-inspired food and we think you will too after this three-course meal. We have included steps on how to make your own gyoza wrappings, though can buy these from the refrigerated section of your local supermarket.

Seafood Gyoza with
Asian Dipping Sauce

...

Twice-cooked Chicken, Seared Scallops
with a Pickled Salad

...

Spiced Cake and Syrup

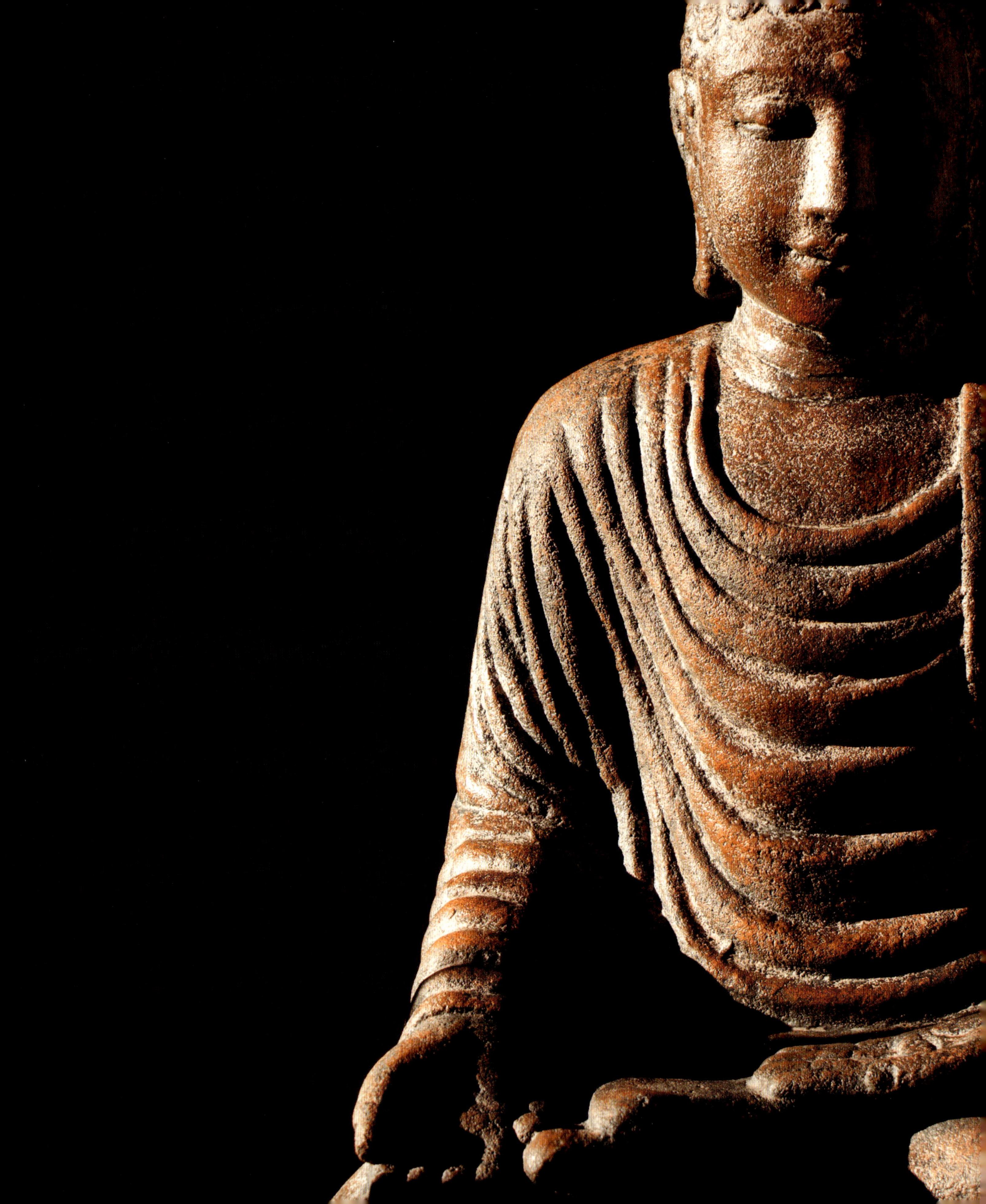

ENTRÉE Seafood Gyoza with Asian Dipping Sauce

Ingredients

Gyoza Wrappers
175 ml/6 fl oz water
200 g/7 oz plain (all-purpose) flour

Gyoza Filling
150 g/5 oz white fish, chopped
6 uncooked shrimp (prawns)
1 cm/½ in peeled ginger, finely chopped
2 garlic cloves, crushed
¼ red onion, finely diced
2 tablespoons soy sauce
1 teaspoon fish sauce
1 teaspoon sesame oil
1 egg, beaten
1 tablespoon olive oil
250–500 ml/8–16 fl oz chicken stock

Dipping Sauce
60 ml/2 oz soy sauce
60 ml/2 oz rice wine vinegar
1 tablespoon honey
1 tablespoon ginger, finely grated
1 garlic clove, minced
1 teaspoon sesame oil

Method

1. For the gyoza wrappers, make the dough by mixing the water with the flour in a medium bowl. Knead the dough until it is no longer sticky but is still soft. Cover with a dampened tea towel and stand for 30 minutes. Cut the dough into approximately 32 pieces and roll through a pasta machine. Continue rolling through to the smallest setting. Using a 10 cm/4 in cookie cutter to cut circular wrappers.
2. For the filling, put the fish, shrimp, ginger, garlic, onion, soy sauce, fish sauce and sesame oil into the bowl of a food processor and pulse until combined.
3. Brush the edge of each gyoza wrapper with beaten egg and place a spoonful of filling in the centre. Fold the wrappers in half, to make semi-circles, then crimp the edges with a fork to prevent the filling escaping during cooking.
4. Heat the oil in a large frying pan over a medium heat and sear each gyoza, several at a time, until browned on each side. Add enough stock to just cover the parcels and reduce the liquid over a high heat until it is all evaporated, about 8 minutes.
5. To make the dipping sauce, mix all the ingredients together and serve on the side.

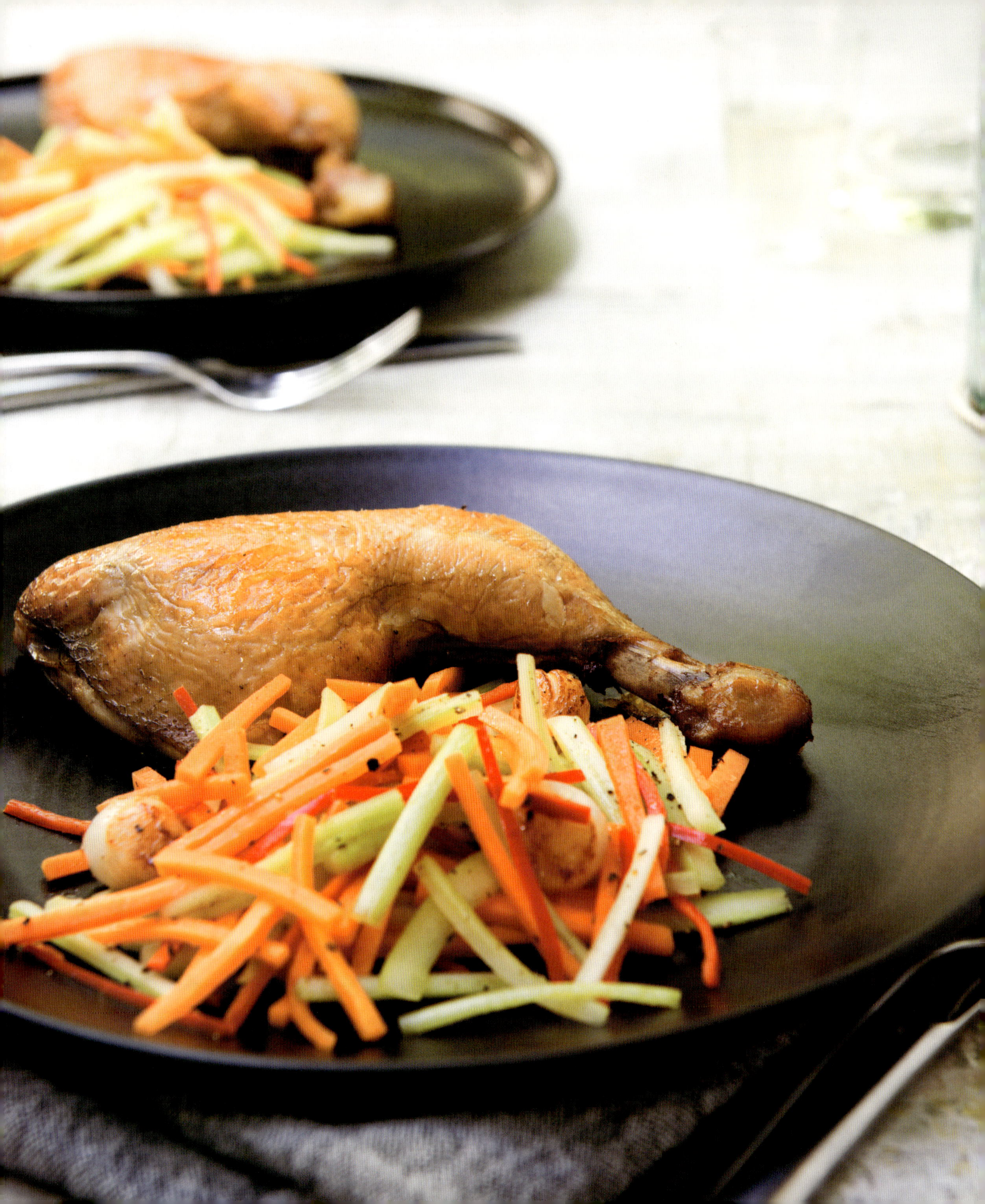

MAIN
Twice-cooked Chicken, Seared Scallops with a Pickled Salad

Ingredients
4 chicken Maryland (legs and thighs, skin on)
3 tablespoons oil
1 tablespoon cornflour (corn starch)
16 scallops

Stock
1.5 litres/2¾ pints water
250 ml/8 fl oz light soy sauce
250 ml/8 fl oz shaoxing rice wine
150 g/5 oz brown sugar
2 pieces dried mandarins or orange peel
2 cinnamon quills
4 star anise
1 large piece of fresh root ginger, peeled and sliced
3 garlic cloves, chopped
2 continental cucumbers, sliced thinly

Pickled Salad
250 ml/8 fl oz water
125 ml/4 fl oz rice vinegar
1 teaspoon salt
2 tablespoons caster (superfine) sugar
1 celery stalk, julienned
1 large cucumber, peeled, seeded and julienned
1 carrot, julienned
2 long red chillies, seeded and julienned

Method
1. For the pickled salad, stir the water, rice vinegar, salt and sugar in a large bowl until the salt and sugar dissolve. Add the celery, cucumber, carrot and chillies, then cover and refrigerate for at least 30 minutes. About 10 minutes before serving, drain the pickled vegetables using a colander.
2. In a pan that is just large enough to hold the chicken, bring all the stock ingredients to a boil. Reduce the heat and simmer for 20 minutes. Submerge the chicken in the stock and bring back to a boil. Lower the heat and cook at a strong simmer for 20 minutes. Turn the chicken and let it to simmer for another 3 minutes. Cover and remove the pan from the heat. Let the chicken cool in the stock.
3. Once the stock has cooled, remove the chicken. Strain the stock and set aside.
4. Heat 2 tablespoons of the oil in a large pan set over medium heat and fry the chicken pieces, skin side down, until they are lightly browned and heated through.
5. Combine 2 tablespoons of the strained stock with the cornflour to make a paste. Heat 250 ml/8 fl oz of strained stock in a pan and bring to the boil. Add the paste and reduce the heat until the sauce thickens.
6. Heat the remaining oil in a frying pan over a high heat and sear the scallops for 1 minute on each sides, or until they start to caramelise.
7. Serve the chicken resting on a portion of pickled salad, with scallops and a drizzle of sauce.

DESSERT
Spiced Cake and Syrup

Ingredients
50 g/1¾ oz walnuts, chopped and roasted, to serve
4 tablespoons crème fraîche, each formed into a quenelle, to serve
zest of 1 lime

Syrup
200 g/7 oz caster (superfine) sugar
300 ml/10½ fl oz water
1 tablespoons fresh root ginger, grated (shredded)
1 star anise
1 cinnamon quill
2 cardamom pods
1 bird's eye chilli, seeded and halved
1 teaspoon ground allspice

Method
1. Preheat the oven to 160°C/320°F/Gas mark 3. Grease and line a large loaf tin (pan).
2. For the syrup, place the sugar and water in a pan set over a low heat. Stir occasionally until all the sugar has dissolved. Add the ginger, star anise, cinnamon, cardamom, chilli and allspice and bring to the boil. Once boiling, reduce the heat and simmer for 15 minutes. Strain the syrup and return the liquid to the heat and continue to simmer until thickened. The syrup will thicken slightly on cooling.

Cake

175 g/6 oz self-raising (self-rising) flour
½ teaspoon baking powder
1 teaspoon ground ginger
1 teaspoon ground cinnamon
1 teaspoon ground nutmeg
1 teaspoon ground cardamom
2 eggs
125 ml (4 fl oz) milk
2 tablespoons crème fraîche
1 tablespoons fresh root ginger, grated (shredded)
100 g/3½ oz butter, plus extra for greasing
75 ml/2½ fl oz golden (lightcorn) syrup
125 g/4 oz brown sugar

Lime Crème Fraîche

75 g/2½ oz crème fraîche
zest of 1 lime

3. Meanwhile, for the cake, sift the flour, baking powder, ground ginger, cinnamon, nutmeg and cardamom into a bowl.
4. In another large bowl, beat together the eggs, milk, crème fraîche and ginger.
5. In a small pan, set over gentle heat, melt the butter, golden syrup and brown sugar. Stir the melted butter mixture into the egg mixture. Add the spiced flour mixture and beat until well combined.
6. Pour the cake batter into the prepared tin. Bake for 20 minutes, or until a skewer inserted into the centre comes out clean. Remove from the oven and allow to set for 5 minutes before turning out onto a wire rack.
7. For the lime crème fraîche, beat the crème fraîche and lime zest together in a small bowl until soft peaks form.
8. To serve, place a slice of cake on a serving plate and drizzle with syrup. Sprinkle with walnuts and finish with a quenelle of crème fraîche and a sprinkling of lime zest.

Menu 3
Asian 2

Once again this menu will take you on a ride across many countries in Asia. The secret to any menu is flow. This starts with a Japanese-inspired seafood dish, moves to the lovely depth of flavour provided by duck and finishes with a visually pleasing and tasty vanilla cake topped with a coconut sauce.

Seafood Nori Roll with
Wild Rice Salad and
Wasabi Dressing

...

Tea-soaked Duck with a
Mandarin Sauce

...

Pandan Cake and
Coconut Sauce

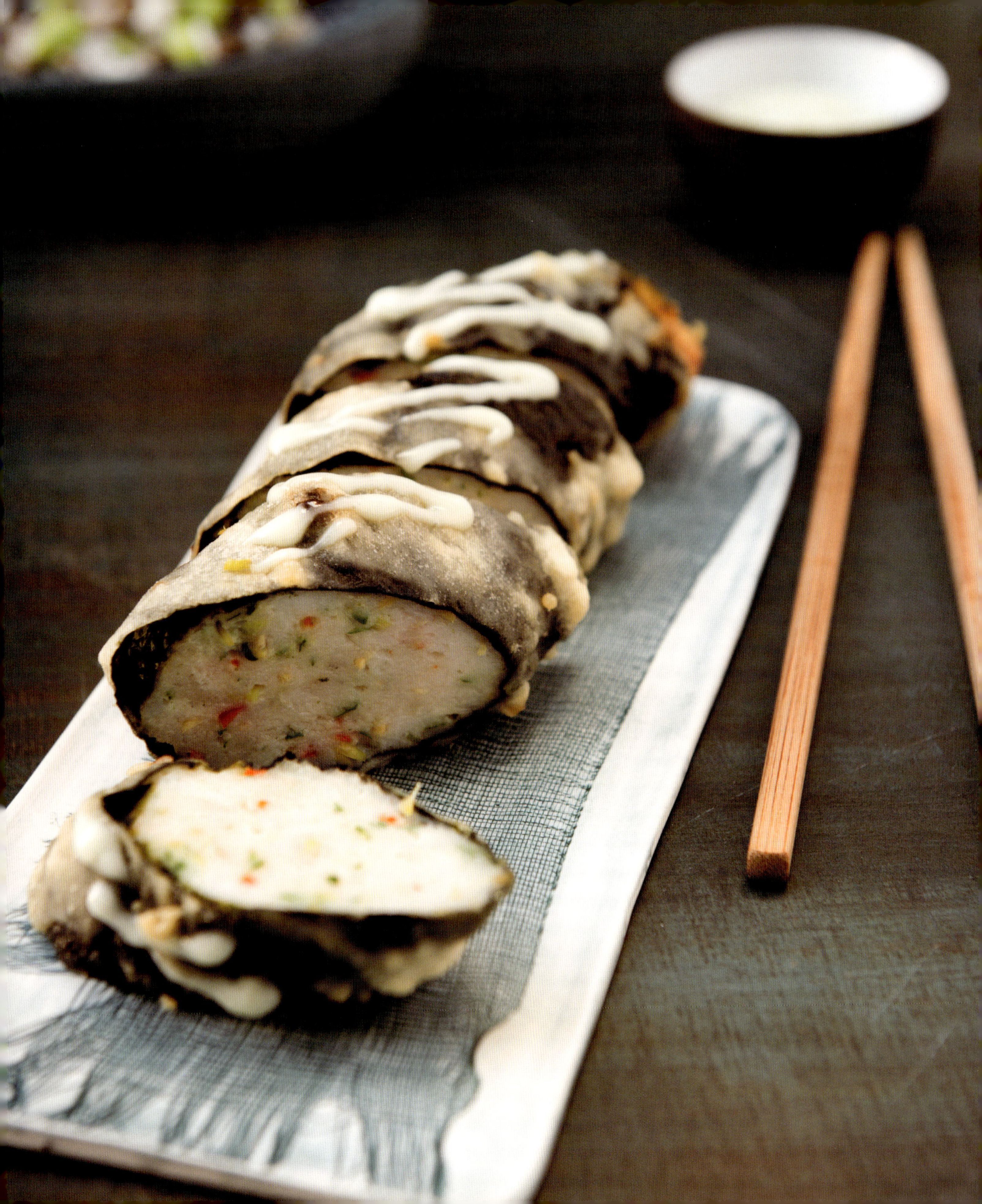

Ingredients

RICE SALAD

½ cup edamame beans (available at Asian supermarkets)
100 g/3½ oz wild rice
100 g/3½ oz jasmine rice

WASABI DRESSING

200 g/7 oz silken tofu
1 tablespoon white miso paste
1 tablespoon mirin
2 teaspoons rice wine vinegar
1 teaspoon wasabi paste
salt and pepper, to taste

NORI ROLLS

800 g/1¾ lb flathead or whiting, or other white-fleshed fish
200 g/7 oz uncooked shrimp (prawns), peeled and deveined
1 tablespoon ginger, chopped
3 tablespoons fish sauce
2 large red chillies, chopped
1 lemongrass stalk, white part only, thinly chopped
3 tablespoons palm sugar
1 tablespoon coriander (cilantro) leaves, chopped
80 ml/2½ fl oz coconut cream
6 nori sheets

BATTER

140 g/5 oz plain (all-purpose) flour, plus extra for dusting
250 ml/9 fl oz ice cold water
200 g/9 oz crushed ice
pinch of salt

Method

1. For the rice salad, bring a pan of water to the boil and cook the edamame beans for about 2 minutes. Set aside.
2. Rinse the wild rice in cold water, then tip into a large pan with 600 ml/1 pint of water. Cover and bring to a boil, then simmer for 45 minutes until the grains swell and curl. Drain, then fluff lightly with a fork.
3. Cook the jasmine rice, according to the packet instructions. When cooled, mix both types of rice in a large bowl with the edamame beans.
4. Meanwhile, for the wasabi dressing, place all the ingredients in the bowl of a blender and purée until smooth. Season to taste.
5. For the nori rolls, put the fish, shrimp, ginger, fish sauce, chillies, lemongrass and sugar into the bowl of a food processor and process until combined. Tip into a bowl with the coriander and slowly mix in the coconut cream.
6. Set the deep-fryer to 180°C/350°F.
7. To form nori rolls, put a layer of fish paste on each nori sheet allowing a 2.5 cm/1 in gap at each end of the sheet. Smooth the paste with the back of a spoon. Use a bamboo sushi mat to firmly roll the nori sheets. Lightly wet the uncovered portion of the nori sheet before rolling so that the sheet seals to itself when rolled. Cover in cling film (plastic wrap) and refrigerate.
8. For the batter, in a large bowl gently stir the flour, water and ice together until a thin batter forms with some small lumps remaining. Do not over-mix the batter and prepare just before using.
9. Remove the rolls from refrigerator and lightly coat with flour. Dip the rolls into the batter and fry for 2–3 minutes, or until cooked through.
10. To serve, cut the rolls to the desired length. Place a small amount of rice salad in the centre of the plate and surround with sliced rolls. Drizzle with wasabi dressing.

ENTRÉE
Seafood Nori Roll with Wild Rice Salad and Wasabi Dressing

MAIN
Tea-smoked Duck with a Mandarin Sauce

Ingredients
4 duck breasts
1 tablespoon oil, plus extra for greasing
8 scallops
3 bunches of bok choy

Curing Mix
100 g/3½ oz salt
100 g/3½ oz caster (superfine) sugar

Smoking Mixture
5 tablespoons oolong tea leaves
5 tablespoons jasmine tea leaves
4 pieces dried orange peel
200 g/7 oz jasmine rice
5 star anise
1 tablespoon Sichuan peppercorns
5 pieces cassia bark

Mandarin Sauce
60 g/2 oz caster (superfine) sugar
3 tablespoons red wine vinegar
500 ml/17 fl oz mandarin juice
250 ml/9 fl oz chicken stock
zest of ½ mandarin
50 g/1¾ oz butter, diced
salt and pepper, to taste

Method
1. For the curing mix, stir the ingredients together in a bowl. Put the duck breast on a plate, dust with curing mix, cover and refrigerate for at least 15 minutes. When ready to cook, remove from the refrigerator, wash off the curing mix and pat dry.
2. Line a wok with aluminium foil and place all the ingredients for the smoking mixture on the top. Heat the wok over a medium heat. Place a metal rack over the smoking mixture. When the mixture starts smoking, place the duck breast, skin side down, on the rack and cover with a lid. Cook for 5 minutes and remove from heat. The duck breast will still be rare.
3. For the mandarin sauce, place the sugar and red wine vinegar in a pan and simmer until the sugar dissolves. Add the mandarin juice and cook until reduced by half. Add the chicken stock and continue to cook until reduced by half. Add the mandarin zest, butter and some seasoning and continue to simmer until a sauce-like consistency.
4. Heat 1 tablespoon of oil in a frying pan over a medium heat. Cook the duck breasts, skin side down, until the fat has rendered and the skin is crispy. Turn and cook for 1 more minute. Transfer to a plate and set aside. Retain the fat.
5. Lightly oil a frying pan and set over high heat. Fry the scallops in the pan for about 1 minute on each side. Remove and set aside.
6. Blanch the bok choy quickly in the duck fat and season with salt and pepper.
7. Serve by placing duck breasts on the bok choy. Arrange the scallops next to the duck breast and drizzle over mandarin sauce.

DESSERT
Pandan Cake with Coconut Sauce

Ingredients

5 eggs, separated
2 tablespoons honey
100 ml/3½ fl oz coconut milk
¼ teaspoon pandan flavouring (available at Asian supermarkets)
100 g/3½ fl oz self-raising (self-rising) flour
3 tablespoons olive oil
½ teaspoon cream of tartar
60 g/2 oz caster (superfine) sugar
50 g/1¾ oz pistachio nuts, roasted and crushed, to serve
50 g/1¾ oz desiccated (dry, unsweetened, shredded) coconut, toasted, to serve

Coconut Sauce
250 ml/9 fl oz coconut cream
2 tablespoons honey
1 teaspoon salt

Method

1. Preheat the oven to 150°C/300°F/Gas mark 2. Grease and line a loaf tin (pan).
2. Beat the egg yolks with the honey, in a mixing bowl, for 3 minutes, or until it begins to pale. Add the coconut milk, pandan and combine. Sift the flour slowly into the egg mixture, stirring continuously. Add the oil and beat well.
3. In a separate bowl, beat the egg whites using an electric beater until they turn white, frothy and triple in size. Mix in the cream of tartar. Slowly add the sugar, beating continuously until soft peaks form.
4. Fold the egg whites gently into the egg yolk mixture with a spatula until just combined.
5. Pour the cake batter into the prepared tin. Bake for 35 minutes, or until a skewer inserted into the cake comes out clean. Remove from the oven and allow to set for 5 minutes before turning out onto a wire rack to cool.
6. For the coconut sauce, heat all the ingredients in a pan over medium heat until the honey and salt dissolve. Serve hot or cold.
7. To serve, slice the cake and place in a dish. Drizzle with coconut sauce and sprinkle with pistachio nuts and coconut.

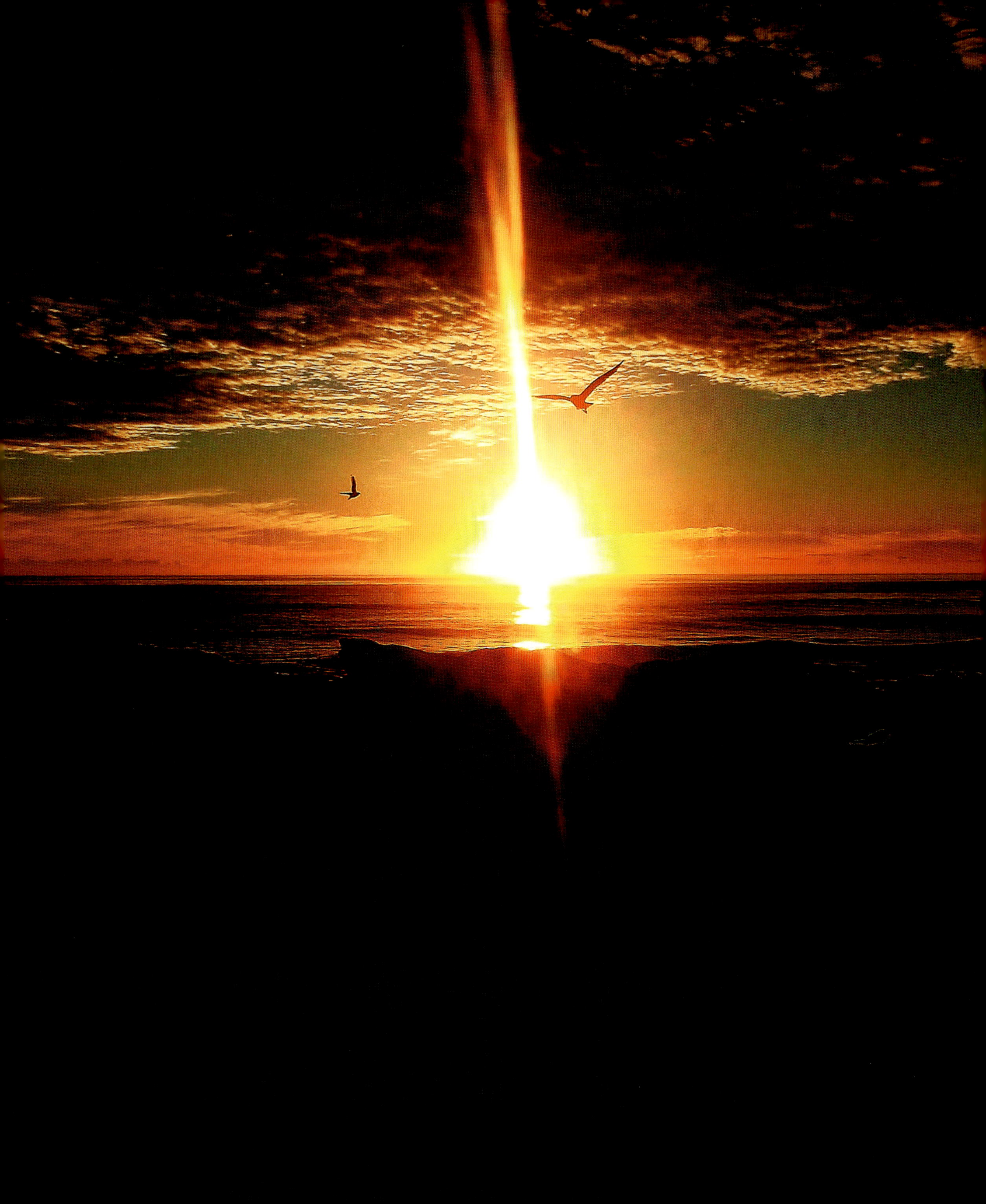

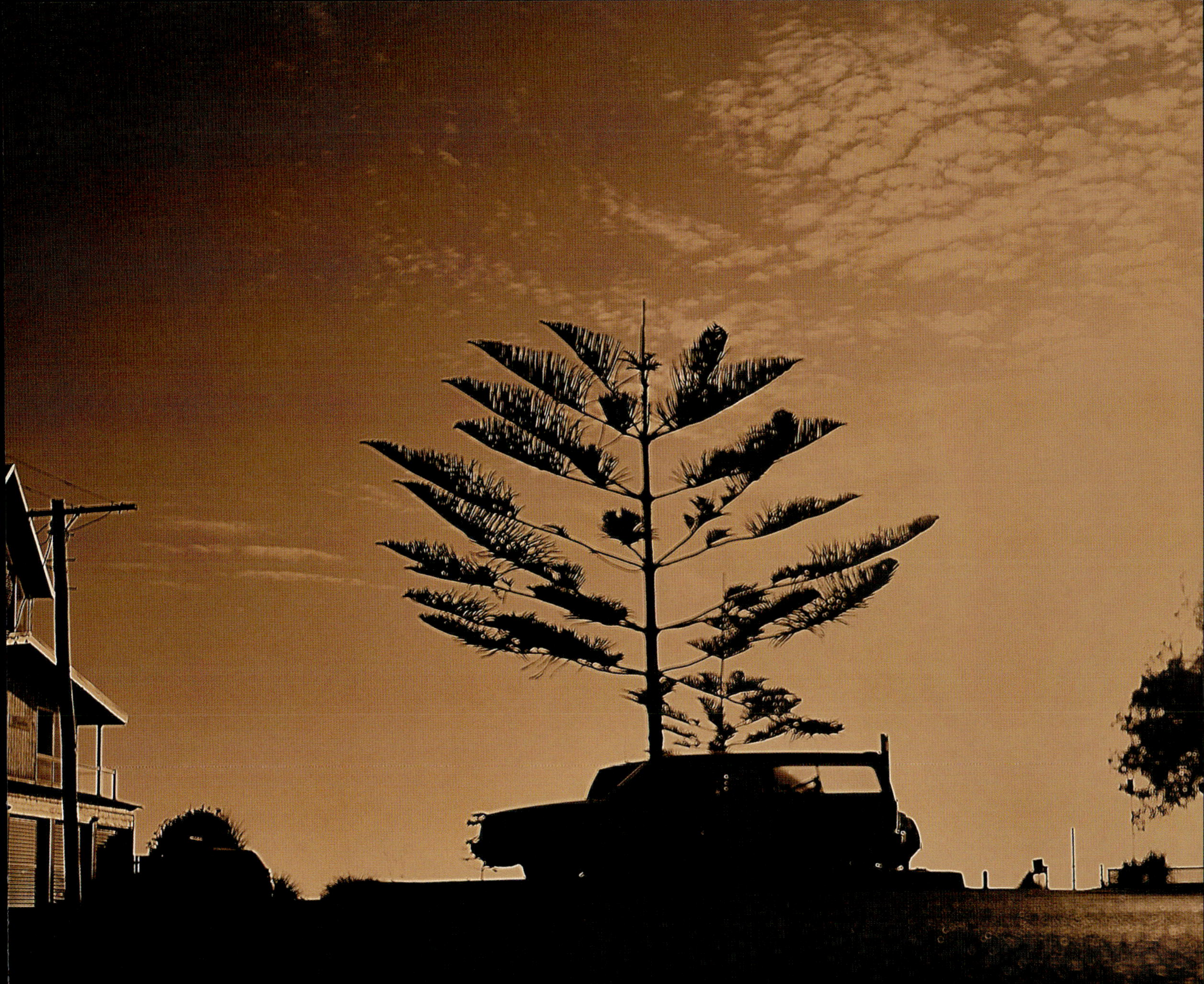

Menu 4
Mexican

There aren't too many people who don't love good Mexican food. In this menu, we serve dishes that we just adore. From the stuffed chillies, our good friend Martin's Mole and the absolute crowd pleaser, churros, this is sure to be a menu you will use many times over.

Cheese-stuffed Jalapeños
with Chorizo Dust

...

Martin's Chicken Mole

...

Churros with Orange
Chocolate Dipping Sauce

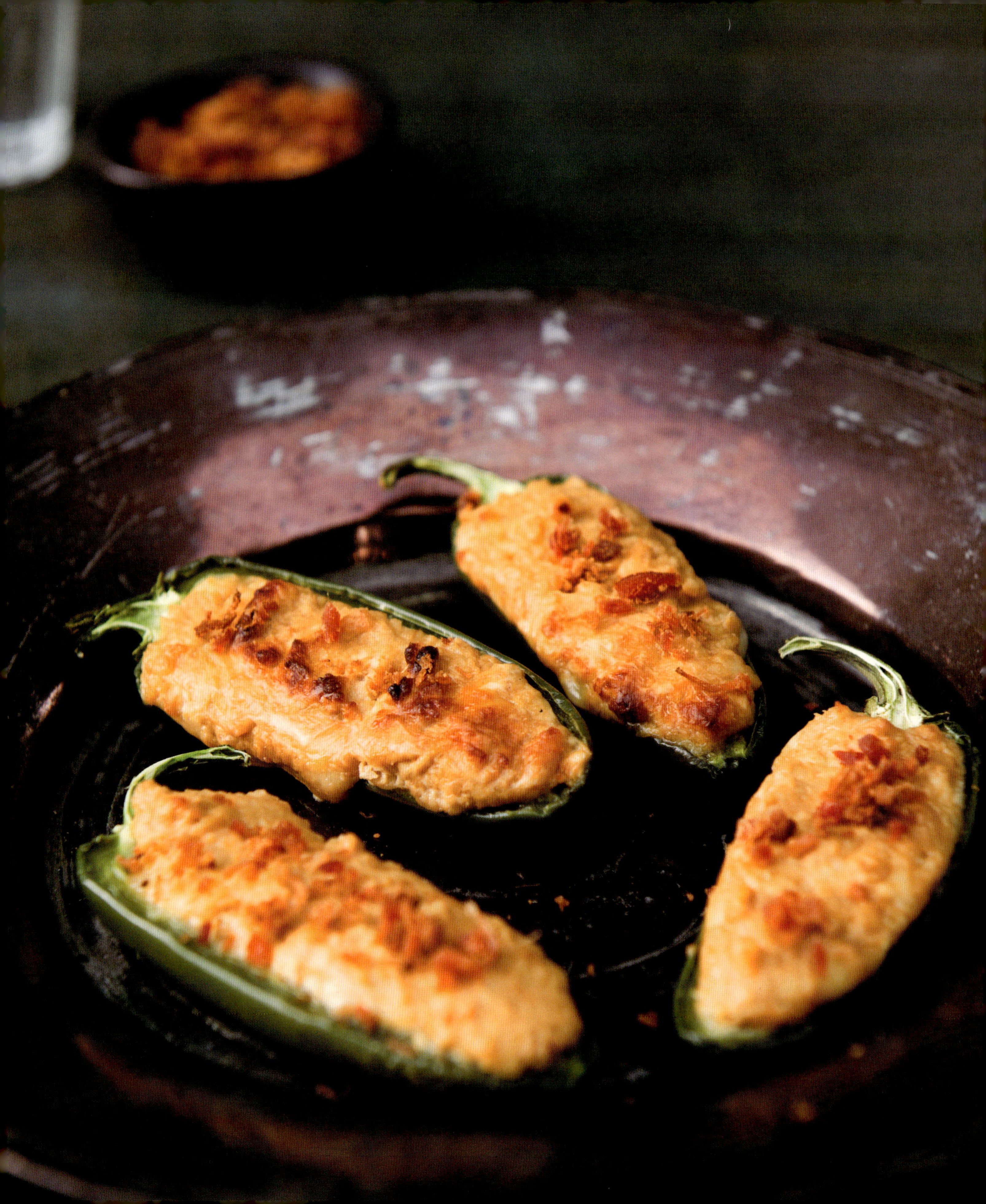

ENTRÉE
Cheese-stuffed Jalapeños with Chorizo Dust

Ingredients
10 jalapeños, halved and seeded
½ chorizo, thinly sliced
100 g/3½ oz cream cheese, softened
100 g/3½ oz Cheddar cheese, finely grated (shredded)
50 g/1¾ oz Parmesan cheese, finely grated (shredded)
1 teaspoon Worcestershire sauce
¼ teaspoon Tabasco sauce, more if you like it hot

Method
1. Preheat the oven to 180°C/350°F/Gas mark 4.
2. Bring a large pan of water to the boil over medium heat. Add the jalapeños and boil for 5 minutes. The longer the jalapeños are boiled, the milder they become. Drain, rinse in cold water and set aside.
3. Place the chorizo slices on a lined baking tray and bake for 10 minutes, or until crispy. Remove and place on paper towel to dry out and cool completely. When cold, pulse the chorizo in the bowl of a food processor until a coarse grain-like consistency is reached.
4. In a small bowl, blend the cheeses and Worcestershire and Tabasco sauces together until smooth. Spoon the mixture into the jalapeño halves and bake in a lined baking tray for 5 minutes, or until the cheese begins to brown. Serve warm and sprinkled with chorizo dust.

MAIN
Martin's Chicken Molé

Ingredients
- 4 tomatoes or 1 x 400 g/14 oz can chopped tomatoes
- 4 tablespoons olive oil
- 4 chicken Maryland (thighs and legs)
- 1 large brown onion, quartered and separated
- 3 teaspoons salt
- 60 g/2 oz plain (all-purpose) flour
- 3 tablespoons chilli powder
- 6 garlic cloves, chopped
- 2 tablespoons fresh oregano, chopped
- 3 tablespoons ground cumin
- 30 g/1 oz unsalted peanuts, crushed
- 100 g/3½ fl oz dark (bittersweet) chocolate, chopped

Method
1. If you are using fresh tomatoes, preheat the oven to 220°C/420°F/Gas mark 7. Using a knife, cut a shallow X in the base of each tomato just through the skin. Place the tomatoes in a roasting pan, cut side up, drizzle with 2 tablespoons of the olive oil and roast the tomatoes until the skin begins to peel away, about 15–20 minutes. Remove from the oven and allow to cool. Peel and discard the skin and crush the tomato flesh in a bowl.
2. Cut each of the chicken Maryland into a leg and a thigh and place in a large pan with the onion and salt. Add enough water to just cover the chicken, then set the pan over a medium heat.
3. Meanwhile, in a frying pan, heat the remaining olive oil over a medium heat, then add the flour and chilli powder, stirring continuously until brown. Remove from the heat and add to the chicken.
4. Bring the liquid in the pan to a boil and then add the rest of the ingredients, stirring constantly to incorporate them all into the sauce. Once incorporated, reduce the heat and simmer for 30–45 minutes, or until the chicken is almost cooked through. Remove the chicken pieces and set aside on a plate, covered, with aluminium foil. Bring the sauce back to a low boil and cook until reduced, about 25 minutes, or until the sauce begins to thicken.
5. Return the chicken pieces to the sauce and simmer for 5–10 minutes to reheat and finish cooking. Skim any oil that collects on the surface as you simmer.
6. Serve over mashed potatoes or with tortillas.

DESSERT
Churros with Orange Chocolate Dipping Sauce

Ingredients

Churros

125 g/4½ oz butter, chopped
250 ml/8 fl oz water
115 g/4 oz plain/all-purpose flour, sifted
¼ teaspoon salt
3 eggs, lightly whisked
oil, for frying
75 g/2½ oz caster (superfine) sugar
1 teaspoon ground cinnamon

Chocolate Orange Dipping Sauce

300 ml/10½ fl oz double (heavy) cream
zest of 2 oranges
150 g/5 oz dark (bittersweet) chocolate, roughly chopped

Method

1. Preheat the deep-fryer to 180°C/350°F.
2. For the churros, place the butter and water in a medium pan over a low heat. Stir until the butter melts and the water just comes to the boil. Remove from the heat, sift in the flour and stir until a smooth dough forms. Allow to cool.
3. Transfer the dough to the bowl of an electric mixer. Add the salt and eggs slowly while beating until the mixture is smooth. Use to part fill a piping bag fitted with a large star nozzle.
4. If using a frying pan to deep-fry the churros, fill the frying pan with oil, 5 cm/2 in deep. To test if the oil is hot enough, toss in a cube of bread and if it browns in about 15 seconds the oil is ready.
5. Working in batches, pipe 10 cm/4 in lengths of dough into the oil, using a knife to cut the lengths. Cook for about 1½ minutes on each side, or until golden brown, then remove and place on a paper towel.
6. Meanwhile, mix the caster sugar and cinnamon in shallow dish. Quickly toss the churros gently in the sugar mixture to coat. Repeat with the remaining dough.
7. For the chocolate orange dipping sauce, bring the cream and orange zest to a boil in a medium pan. Reduce the heat and simmer for 10 minutes. Remove from the heat and sieve the mixture into a heatproof bowl. Add the chocolate pieces, stirring until the chocolate has melted.
8. Serve the churros with a bowl of sauce.

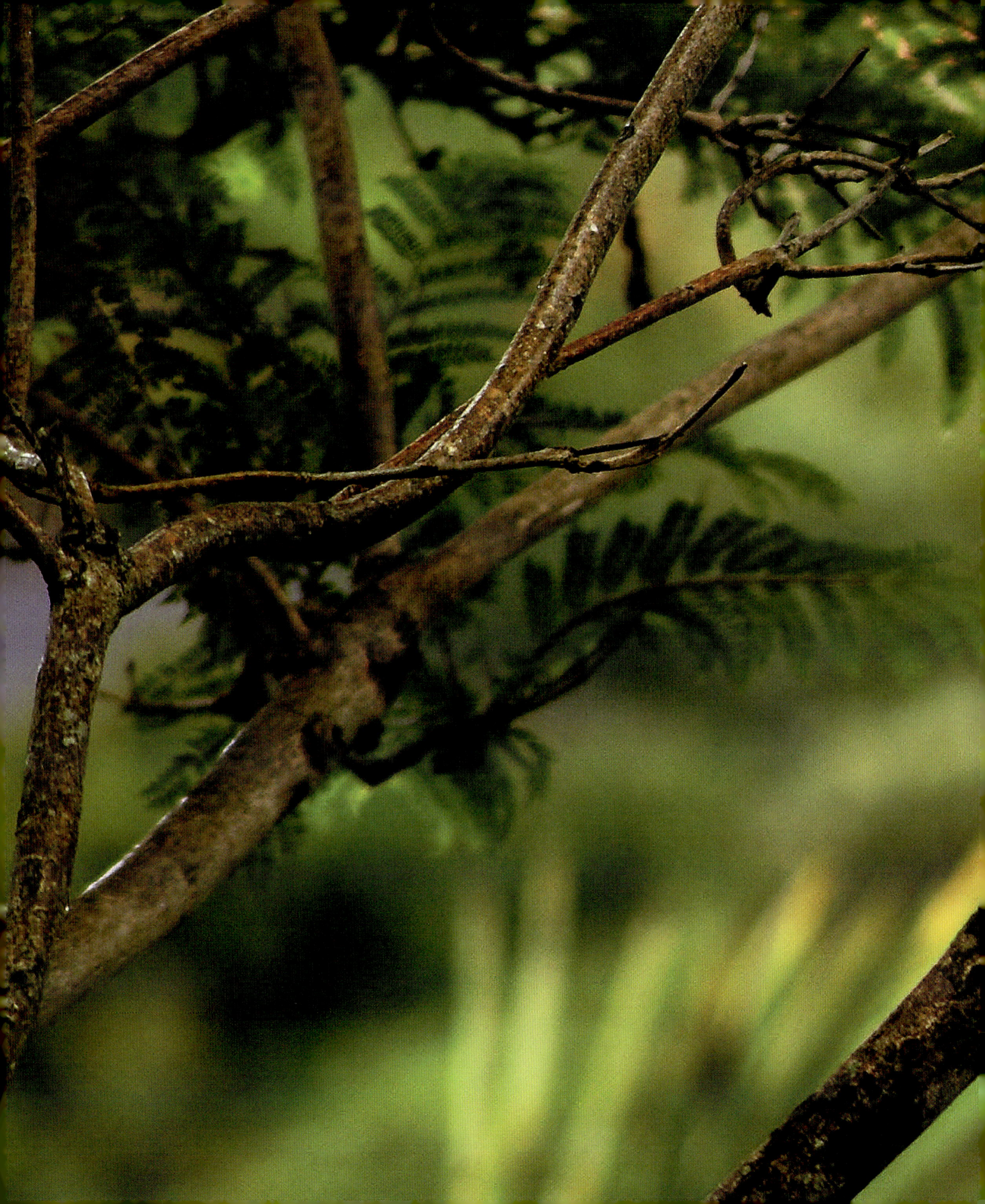

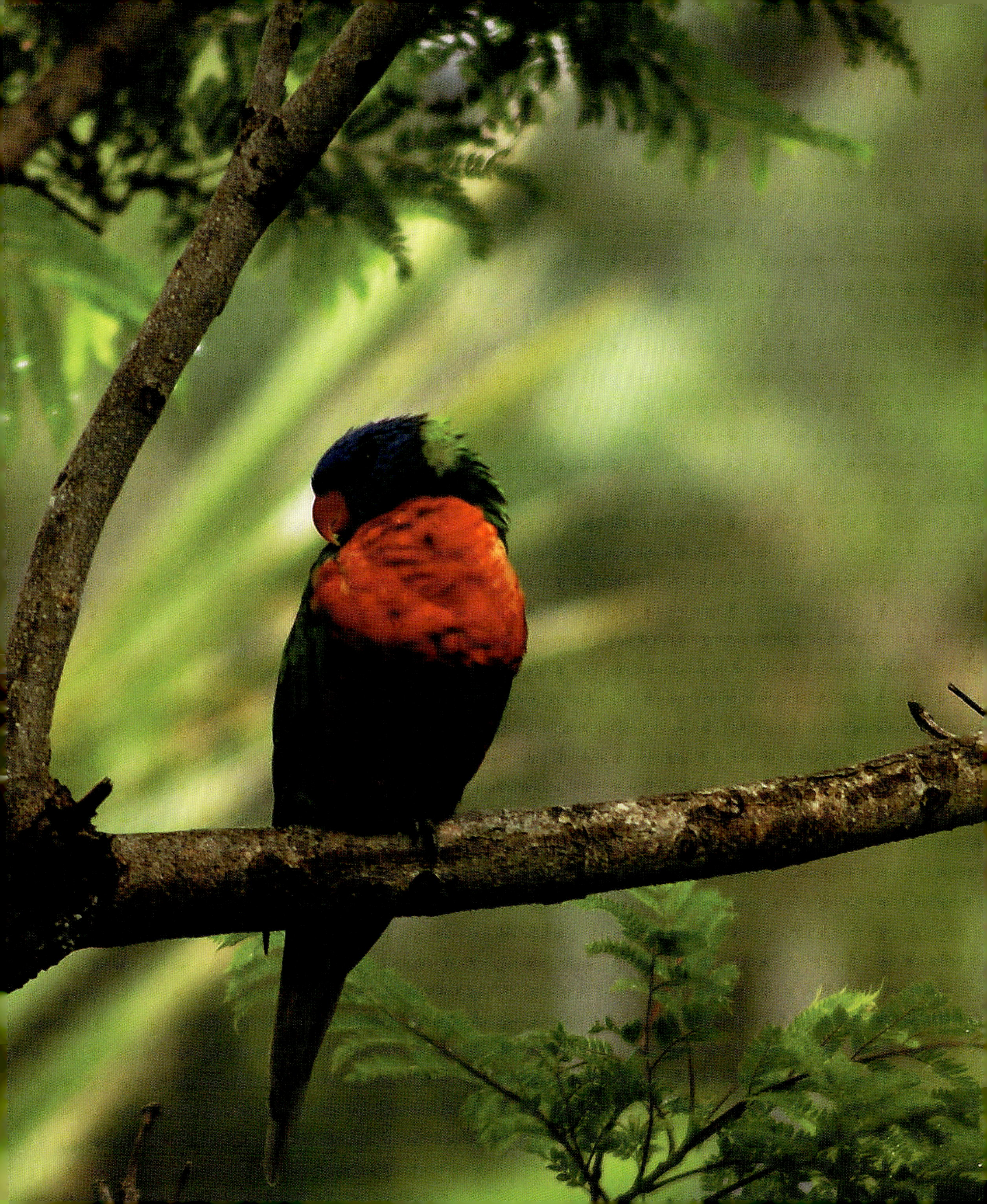

Menu 5
Greek

Greek food is about good simple meals with heaps of flavour. We tasted many a flavoursome Greek dish made by our favourite twins on MKR during the show. That was our introduction to Greek food. Apparently you have to leave a messy kitchen when cooking Greek food. Isn't that right girls? We hope the menu here honours the beautiful flavours traditional to Greek-style cooking.

Battered Zucchini Chips with
Roasted Garlic Aioli

...

Slow-roasted Leg of Lamb

...

Orange and Almond Cake
with Zest Syrup

ENTRÉE
Battered Zucchini Chips with Roasted Garlic Aioli

Ingredients

3 medium zucchini (courgettes), sliced on the diagonal

Batter
175 g/6 oz plain (all-purpose) flour
1 teaspoon salt
¼ teaspoon ground pepper
2 egg yolks
1 tablespoon oil
250 ml/8 fl oz beer
oil, for deep-frying

Aioli
500 ml/17 fl oz olive or vegetable oil
20 garlic cloves
2 eggs
1 teaspoon Dijon mustard
juice of 1 lemon
salt and pepper, to taste

Method

1. Heat the oven to 180°C/350°F/Gas mark 4.
2. For the aioli, place the garlic cloves on a baking sheet, drizzle with some of the oil and roast for 15 minutes. Set aside to cool. Peel the garlic cloves and crush in a mortar and pestle to form a paste. Put the garlic paste, eggs, mustard, lemon juice and salt and pepper into the bowl of a food processor and pulse until combined.
3. Slowly add the remaining oil at a drizzle while pulsing the food processor until the mixture thickens. Season with salt and pepper to taste.
4. Transfer to a container with a lid and store in the refrigerator until ready to use.
5. For the batter, combine the flour, salt and pepper in a large bowl. In a separate small bowl, whisk together the egg yolks and vegetable oil. Tip the egg mixture onto the flour and mix with a fork to form a dough-like consistency. Slowly add the beer, whisking constantly until a smooth batter forms. Cover and refrigerate for up to 1 hour.
6. Preheat the deep fryer to 180°C/350°F. If using a frying pan to deep-fry the zucchini, fill the pan with oil to 5 cm/2 in deep. To test if the oil is hot enough, toss in a cube of bread and if it browns in about 15 seconds the oil is ready.
7. Remove the batter from the refrigerator and stir. Coat a small batch of zucchini chips with batter and gently add them to the oil and fry until golden brown, about 4 minutes. Remove from the oil and drain on a plate lined with paper towel. Sprinkle with salt, if desired. Repeat with the remaining chips.
8. Serve the zucchini chips with a large dollop of aioli or have a central bowl to use as a dip.

MAIN
Slow-roasted Leg of Lamb

Ingredients

1 head of garlic
1 leg of lamb (bone in)
125 ml/4 fl oz extra-virgin olive oil
fine sea salt
fresh ground pepper
2 teaspoons garlic powder
2 teaspoons sweet paprika
2 medium onions, peeled and quartered
250 ml/8 fl oz dry white wine
10 sprigs of fresh thyme
2–3 bay leaves
2–3 sprigs of fresh rosemary
2–3 teaspoons dried oregano
juice of 2 lemons
hot water
salt and pepper, to taste
450 g/1 lb potatoes, peeled and quartered

Method

1. Break open the garlic bulb and peel the individual garlic cloves. Slice the cloves into slivers. Using a paring knife slit a hole in the surface of the lamb, then slip in a sliver of garlic. Repeat all over the lamb, inserting as many slivers of garlic as you can.
2. Preheat the oven to 220°C/420°F/Gas mark 7 and place the rack in the centre. Place the lamb in a roasting pan, drizzle with olive oil and season with salt, pepper, garlic powder and paprika. Roast in the oven uncovered for 10–15 minutes, or until browned. Turn the leg and roast for another 10–15 minutes.
3. Remove the lamb from the oven and reduce the heat to 180°C/350°F/Gas mark 4. Place the quartered onions around the lamb, add any leftover garlic, the thyme, bay, rosemary, oregano lemon juice and wine. Add the olive oil.
4. Place the lamb back in the roasting pan. Add enough hot water to cover one-third of the way up the lamb, then return to the oven for 2 hours (add more hot water if needed). Baste the lamb once every hour.
5. After two hours, place the potatoes in a separate baking tray. Drizzle them with pan juices and place in the oven. Cook until they are browned and soft on the inside.
6. Flip the lamb again and season with salt and pepper, if needed.
7. Remove the lamb and the potatoes from the oven after another 1 hour and allow the lamb to rest. Baste with pan juices to keep it moist. The total cooking time for the lamb should be about three hours. It should be browned on the outside and still moist on the inside. The lamb will be well done and should not be pink on the inside.
8. To serve, break chunks of lamb away from the bone and add to the baked potatoes. Drizzle with pan juices.

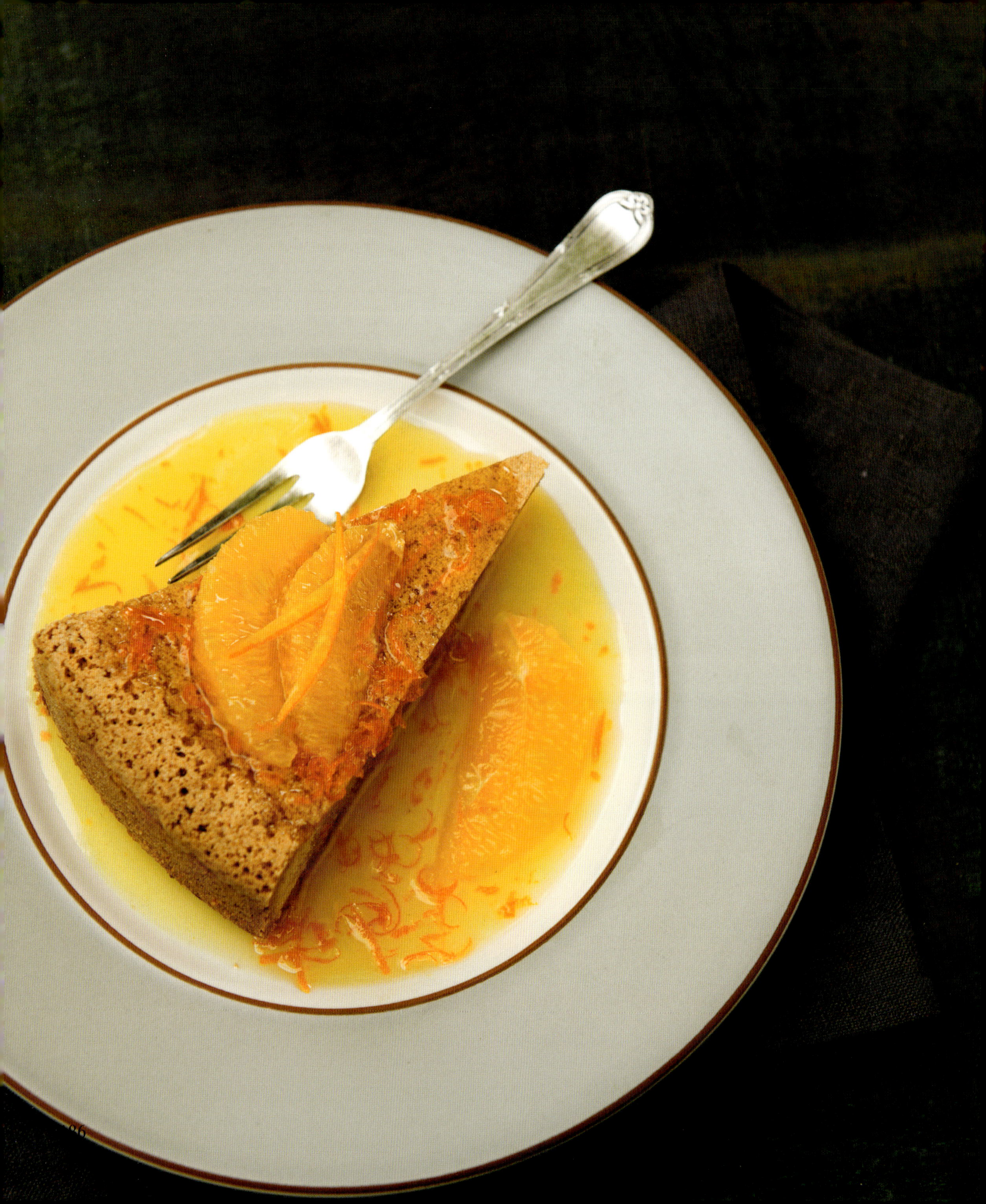

DESSERT
Orange and Almond Cake with Zest Syrup

Ingredients

2 oranges, peeled, chopped and pips removed
2 tablespoons honey
4 eggs
300 g/10½ oz caster (superfine) sugar
150 g/5 oz almond meal (ground almonds)
150 g/5 oz self-raising (self-rising) flour
1 teaspoon ground cinnamon
½ teaspoon nutmeg
mascarpone, to serve
ground cinnamon, to serve

Zest Syrup
Zest and juice of 1 orange
100 g/3½ oz caster (superfine) sugar
60 ml/2 fl oz water

Method

1. Preheat the oven to 150°C/300°F/Gas mark 2. Grease and line the base of a 20 cm/8 in round springform tin (pan).
2. For the cake, put the chopped oranges and honey in a small pan with 3 tablespoons of water and set the pan over medium heat. Bring to a simmer and simmer for 15 minutes, or until the orange breaks down. Discard the liquid and process the orange in a blender until smooth. Strain again, reserving the liquid.
3. Use an electric mixer to whisk the eggs and sugar until it is thick and pale. Add the processed orange, almonds, flour, cinnamon and nutmeg, and fold gently until combined. Pour the batter into the prepared tin and bake for 1 hour, or until an inserted skewer comes out clean. Remove from the oven, leave to set for a few minutes then turn out onto a wire rack to go cold.
4. For the zest syrup, put the juice, sugar and water in a small pan over a low heat, and cook until the sugar dissolves and the syrup begins to thicken. Remove from the heat, stir in the zest and allow to cool completely.
5. In a bowl, mix the ground cinnamon with the mascarpone.
6. Pour the syrup over the cooled cake and allow it to soak in or pour onto individual slices. Slice the cake into portions and serve with spiced mascarpone.

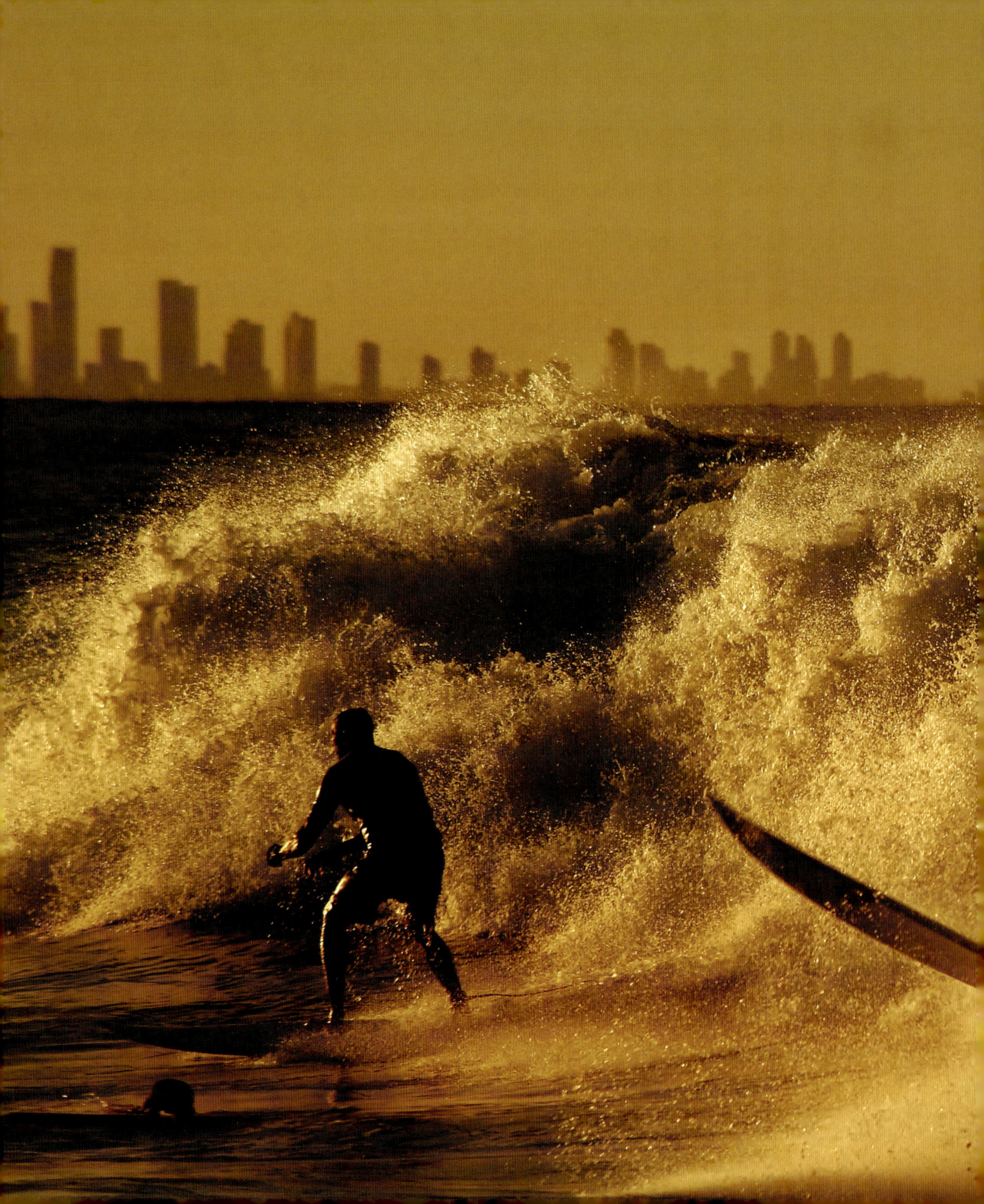

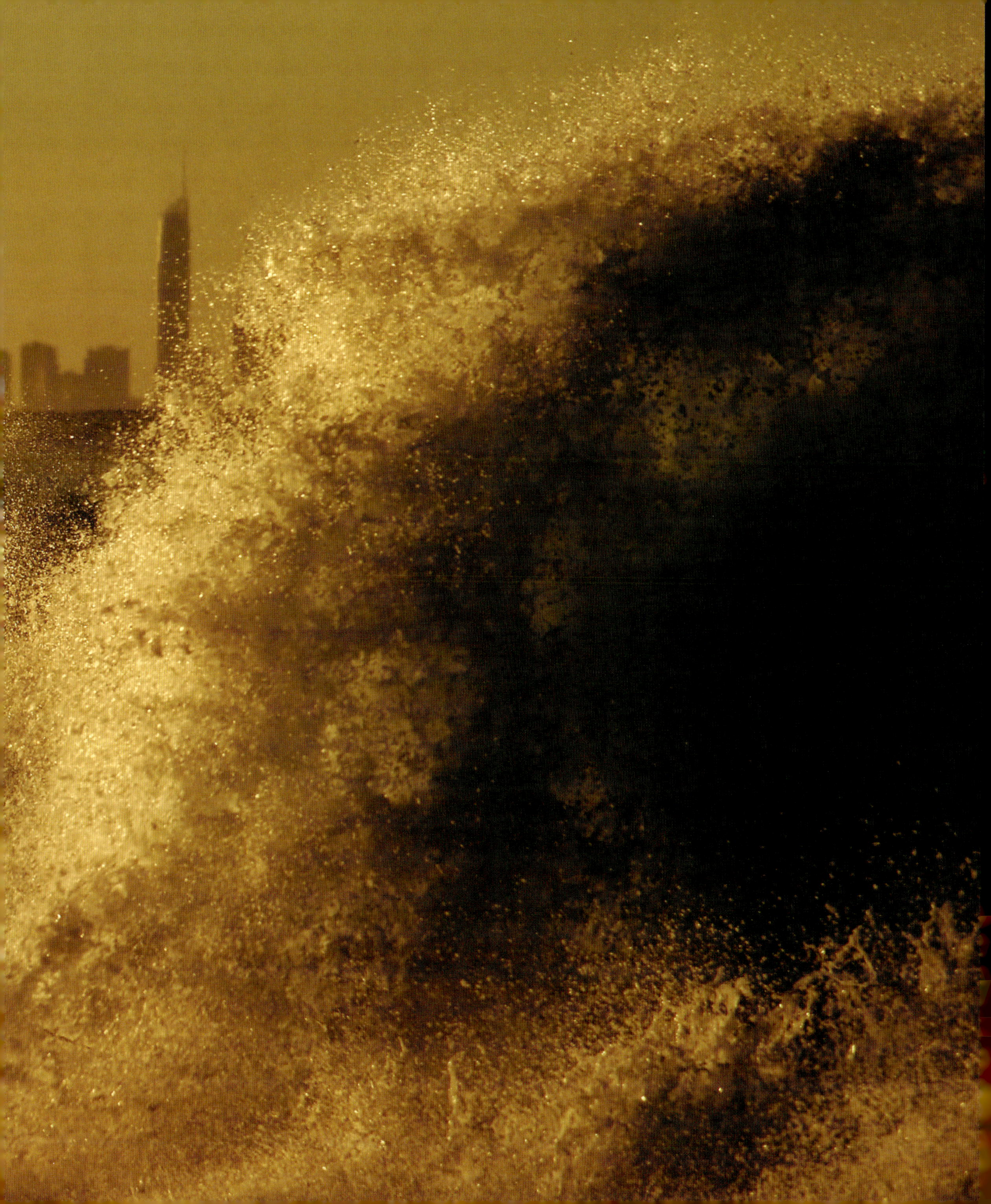

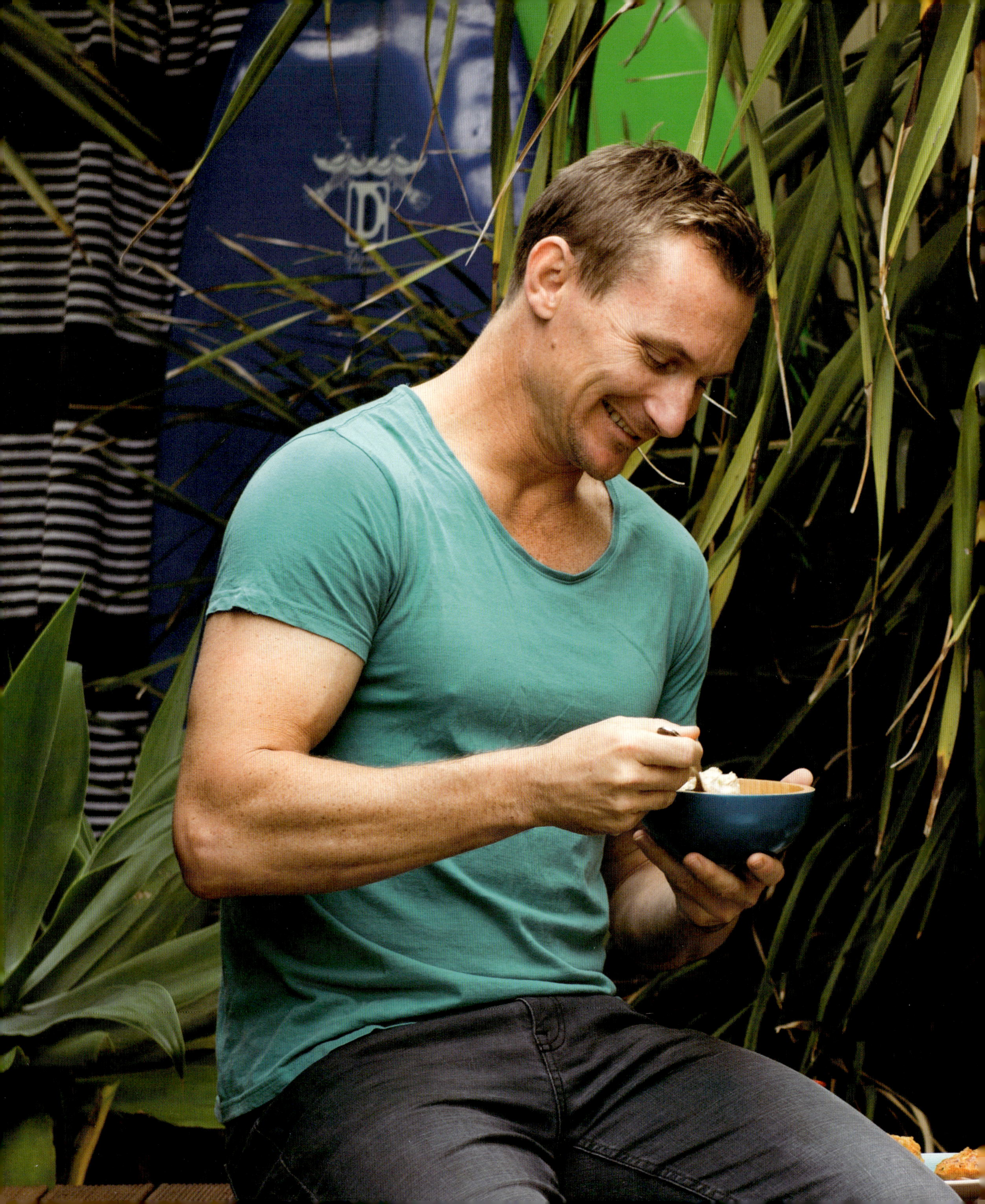

Index

8-hour Slow-Cooked Beef Brisket	56
Amazeballs	145
Annie's Zucchini Slice	40
Baked Beans, Chorizo and Eggs	18
Baked Eggs with Cauliflower and Gorgonzola	23
Baked Plums with Almond Crumble and Red Wine Syrup	139
Baked Tomatoes with Pesto and Bacon Dust	26
Banana Nut Bread with Cinnamon Butter	128
Battered Zucchini Chips with Roasted Garlic Aioli	184
Beef Rendang and Spicy Eggplant	44
Berry Chocolate Fondants with Chocolate Dirt	135
Bircher Muesli	21
Caramel Pork	50
Caramelised Pineapple with Spiced Mascarpone and Lemon Syrup	123
Cheese-stuffed Jalapeños with Chorizo Dust	177
Chilli Chocolate Cheesecake with Macerated Strawberries	142
Chilli Mango Cakes with Coconut Ice Cream	140
Chocolate and Beetroot Brownie with a Spiced Cherry Syrup	127
Churros with Orange Chocolate Dipping Sauce	179
Coconut and Shrimp Soup	38
Creamy Balinese Chicken	101
Crispy Skin Salmon with Asian Salad and Tomato Nahm Jim	49
Crunchy Fish	78
Duck with Scallops and Sichuan Pickled Cucumber	65
Dukkah-crusted Chicken on Red Quinoa Salad	82
Espresso Tower	153
Fettuccine with a Beef Ragu and Mozzarella	155
Fettunccine Marinara with Creamy White Wine and Tarragon Sauce	53
French Toast 2 Ways	24
Green Chicken Korma	58
Hot and Spicy Pizza	98
Indonesian Chicken Drumsticks	104
Jaime's Medjool Date and Ginger Muffins with Caramel Sauce	130
Jamaican Jerk Pork Chops with Mango Salsa	115
Kare Ayam (Balinese Chicken Curry)	62
Lamb Tagine with Dates	70
Marinated Steak on Asparagus Slaw	85
Martin's Chicken Molé	178
Mediterranean Burger	86
Middle Eastern Fish Fillets, Tabbouleh and Yoghurt Sauce	61
Mushroom and Leek Freekeh Risotto	81
Nasi Goreng	16
Open Salmon Burger	88
Orange and Almond Cake with Zest Syrup	187
Pan-fried Fish with Fennel and Beetroot Remoulade	73
Pancake Toppers	31
Pancakes	29
Pandan Cake with Coconut Sauce	171
Pear, Bacon and Blue Cheese Pizza	94
Peppercorn, Beef Fillet, Grilled Sweet Potato and Field Mushrooms	113
Pizza Dough	93
Pizza Time	93
Poached Chicken with a Cranberry and Pistachio Quinoa Salad	46
Poached Salmon Rillettes on Yogurt Flat Bread	152
Pork Belly with Caramelised Apple	43
Pork Fillet with Sweet Chilli Sauce	114
Pulled Pork Burger	89
Raw Cashew, Lemon and Raspberry Slice	136
Roasted Vegetables with Goat's Cheese and Caramelised Onion Pizza	96
Satay Sticks	110
Scallop, Chorizo and Fennel Salad	77
Seafood Gyoza with Asian Dipping Sauce	161
Seafood Nori Roll with Wild Rice Salad and Wasabi Dressing	169
Seared Tuna with a Roasted Capsicum Salad	57
Sesame Seared Tuna and Apple Salad with Miso Dressing	99
Sichuan Salt and Pepper Tofu	37
Slow-roasted Leg of Lamb	185
Snapper and Warm Mushroom Salad with Corn Purée	69
Spiced Cake and Syrup	164
Spiced Chicken, Chickpea Salad and Minted Yogurt Dressing	76
Spiced Date Loaf with Honeyed Natural Yogurt	138
Spiced Lamb and Pearl Couscous	116
Spicy Fish Stack with Coconut Dressing	75
Stuffed Peaches with Lemon Crème Fraîche	133
Tea-smoked Duck with a Mandarin Sauce	170
Thai Chicken with Fragrant Rice	109
The Breakfast Burrito	32
The Kickstarter	15
The Perfect Steak with Chimichurri Sauce	120
Twice-cooked Chicken, Seared Scallops with a Pickled Salad	163
Vegetarian Pizza	95
Veggie Stack Burger	91
Warm Seafood Salad with Citrus Dressing	106
Yogurt Flat Bread Pizza Base	93